AF608159

# China's Encounter with Global Hollywood

# CHINA'S ENCOUNTER WITH GLOBAL HOLLYWOOD

## Cultural Policy and the Film Industry, 1994–2013

WENDY SU

Scholarly publisher for the Commonwealth,
serving Bellarmine University, Berea College, Centre College of Kentucky, Eastern Kentucky University, The Filson Historical Society, Georgetown College, Kentucky Historical Society, Kentucky State University, Morehead State University, Murray State University, Northern Kentucky University, Transylvania University, University of Kentucky, University of Louisville, and Western Kentucky University.


*Editorial and Sales Offices:* The University Press of Kentucky
663 South Limestone Street, Lexington, Kentucky 40508-4008
www.kentuckypress.com

Figures by Richard A. Gilbreath, University of Kentucky Cartography Lab

Library of Congress Cataloging-in-Publication Data

Names: Su, Wendy.
Title: China's encounter with global Hollywood : cultural policy and the film industry, 1994–2013 / Wendy Su.
Description: Lexington : University Press of Kentucky, 2016. | Series: Asia in the new millennium | Includes bibliographical references and index.
Identifiers: LCCN 2016000229| ISBN 9780813167060 (hardcover : alk. paper) | ISBN 9780813167084 (pdf) | ISBN 9780813167091 (epub)
Subjects: LCSH: Motion picture industry—China—History—21st century. | Motion pictures—Political aspects—China—History and criticism. | Motion pictures industry—United States—History—21st century.
Classification: LCC PN1993.5.C4 S887 2016 | DDC 791.430951—dc23
LC record available at http://lccn.loc.gov/2016000229

This book is printed on acid-free paper meeting the requirements of the American National Standard for Permanence in Paper for Printed Library Materials.

Manufactured in the United States of America.

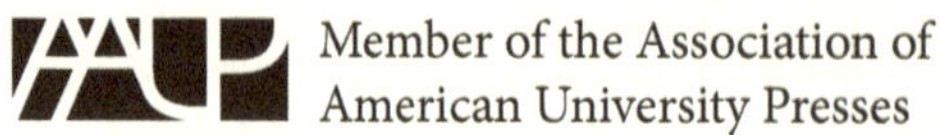

For my parents
For Jerry and Susan

# Contents

# Introduction

Mainland China's engagement with Hollywood is an interesting and complicated story. Hollywood marched into China and occupied more than 75 percent of the Chinese film market by the 1930s and 1940s. However, the establishment of the People's Republic of China (PRC) by the Communist Party in 1949 marked the decline of the influence of Hollywood films, and with the outbreak of the Korean War, American movies were forbidden. Starting on November 15, 1950, American films were completely prohibited in mainland China. On January 3, 1951, the Chinese Communist Party's mouthpiece, the *People's Daily,* ran an article declaring that China had almost "swept out American movies that poison the Chinese people."[1] During the thirty years from 1951 to 1981, only one American movie, *Salt of the Earth,* was allowed to be shown publicly in mainland China. Ironically, this film had been banned by the US government because it was written, directed, and produced in 1954 by members of the original Hollywood Ten, who were blacklisted for refusing to answer congressional inquiries into their alleged communist affiliations. Based on a true story, the film depicts a strike in New Mexico protesting discrimination against Mexican American workers. Therefore, it was considered "progressive" by the Chinese government.

When China opened the door to the outside world and launched economic reforms in the early 1980s, US films that could pass the strict state censorship rules began to reenter China. Imported American movies were also exhibited on China's satellite TV channels. However, the importation of American films was temporarily interrupted from 1990 to 1992 due to the Tiananmen Square incident in 1989.

Starting in 1994, mainland China adopted the internationally common practice of revenue sharing to import about ten foreign blockbusters per year (the number rose to twenty after China joined the World Trade Organization [WTO] in 2001, and an additional fourteen 3D and IMAX movies were added beginning in 2012); most of these were American movies. This practice, whereby foreign and domestic film distributors share the box office revenue generated by these films, was considered a termination of the PRC's forty-year convention of purchasing outdated foreign films at a flat fee, as well as a remedy for China's debt-ridden state-owned studios. These foreign megaproductions caused an unprecedented stir in China; they seriously challenged and fundamentally transformed China's domestic film industry and triggered a long-lasting debate on the validity of the government's cultural policy. Thus, the period from 1994 to the present offers the best opportunity to observe the impact of global Hollywood and transnational media capital on the reshaping of the local cultural landscape.

This book explores the global-local interplay by studying China's encounter with global Hollywood, transnational media conglomerates, and American culture from 1994 to 2013. Because the cultural dimension of globalization has become an increasingly popular research theme for international communication and international cultural studies, a critical approach often centers on the "global-local dialectic"[2] by exploring "the vital relationships between that international landscape and a local society's internal struggle."[3] This book is, therefore, fundamentally about global-local dynamics as they unfolded between global media capital and local agency. It is the first systematic investigation of the contemporary encounter between mainland China and global Hollywood, as well as the impact of this encounter on China's project to modernize its film industry.

The Chinese government's Hollywood import policy met with complicated responses from various groups. Liberal film critics and distributors-exhibitors cheered market revitalization, economic gains resulting from these Hollywood hits, and the audience's "freedom of choice." Ordinary moviegoers embraced Hollywood blockbusters and welcomed competition from Hollywood. The majority of China's filmmakers and left-wing intellectuals, in contrast, strongly opposed imports from Hollywood and advocated protection of the indigenous film industry. Some called for efforts to "resist Hollywood," while others predicted that "the wolf is coming" and the entire Chinese film industry would be destroyed by Hollywood. Yet the Chinese government pressed forward with its strategy of "going to sea by borrowing a boat"—namely, taking advantage of Hollywood resources to transform the Chinese film industry. As one official from the state film bureau asserted, "We should use the language of Hollywood to portray our own 'Moments in Peking.'"[4] Twenty years later, China had become the world's third largest film producer, trailing only India and the United States. In 2012 China's total output had skyrocketed to 745 films, with gross box office revenue of 17 billion yuan,[5] compared with 91 films and 960 million yuan in 2000. China is the only market in the world with an annual box office growth of more than 30 percent.[6] Meanwhile, China's domestic films outperformed foreign imports in terms of box office receipts for eight consecutive years from 2004 to 2011. Some people have even optimistically declared that "China is the only giant film-production country that is not knocked down by American blockbusters."[7] However, the overwhelming triumph of *Avatar* in the Chinese film market conflicts with this optimistic view: *Avatar* garnered 1.32 billion yuan (roughly US$194 million) at the box office between January 4 and the end of March 2010, making China the film's top overseas moneymaker and enabling 20th Century–Fox to net US$34 million in China.[8] In 2011 seventeen Hollywood imports, including *Transformers 3: Dark of the Moon, Kung Fu Panda 2, Pirates of the Caribbean 4: On Stranger Tides*, and *Harry Potter and the Deathly Hallows: Part 2,* each earned more than 100 million yuan on the Chinese domestic market, indicating that China is gradually replacing Japan as Hollywood's number-one overseas box office contributor.[9] Furthermore, as a direct consequence of lifting the quota on imports in 2012, only 231 of China's 745 domestically produced films (31 percent) actually made it into cinemas, making it even harder for domestic movies to compete with Hollywood imports.[10] As such, how do we evaluate the current status of China's domestic film sector and its complex relationship with Hollywood? Can China avoid becoming part of the "New International Division of Cultural Labor (NICL)"?[11] What is the role of the Chinese government in this global-local battle? How has this battle shaped global and local cultural landscapes, and how will it continue to do so? These are the questions that drive this book.

Three major conflicts exist in China's encounter with Hollywood and in the Chinese film industry's existence in the shadow of global Hollywood: the conflict among the Chinese state, Chinese film professionals, and Hollywood-represented global capital in their battle for the Chinese market; the conflict between the Chinese state's censorship and artists' freedom of expression, which is essential for the prosperity of China's film industry; and the conflict between market (audience) demand and filmmakers' artistic pursuits. In examining these three conflicts, this book explores the intertwined relationship among the Chinese state, global capital, and local dynamics. Ultimately, my aim is to answer two questions: Who wins in the China-Hollywood battle? And how does this global-local interplay define and shape China's path toward modernity in the postsocialist era?

To answer these questions, *China's Encounter with Global Hollywood* gives much weight to local strategies and practices. It focuses on China's state cultural policy and its direct influence on the transformation of the domestic film industry. Cultural policy becomes a site of contestation and negotiation of power in the global-local battle, and it represents the state's strategy for countering Hollywood hegemony. This book tracks real-world developments while engaging in theoretical debates on the relationship among global capital, state and local agency, and the current stage of postsocialist China. These complex and evolving relations have brought research on the global-local dialectic to a crucial point in the last decade.

## The Changing Chinese State in the Era of Globalization

The changing nature of the nation-state is central to globalization theories. The old assumption of the 1990s—that nation-states are gradually being dismantled by various economic, military, and cultural globalization forces—has become increasingly untenable. As media scholars Silvio Waisbord and Nancy Morris succinctly summarized, there are essentially two positions with regard to the relationship between nation-states and media globalization: (1) media globalization is a beneficial force for democracy, with the potential to "bypass government control," and (2) media globalization equates with the untrammeled power of capitalism and with media conglomerates that hinder state projects for self-determination and self-protection. However, media globalization theory has not sufficiently considered the possibility of a third position: that the state and media globalization are not two opposing forces but two forces that are both mutually beneficial and competing, as in the case of China. Furthermore, states are "largely absent" from current media and communications studies.[12] A few researchers have defined the state as protectionist or as a "regulator of communication processes that shape hybridity,"[13] and they see "self-conscious state interventions" and policy as essential for commercial operations and market forces.[14] However, how the state intervenes, and under what conditions, remains unexplored.

In accordance with the Western liberal perspective, one popular view is that China's WTO membership and the expansion of foreign media corporations in China will inevitably undermine the Communist Party's authoritarian control and facilitate freedom of the press. For example, News Corporation chief Rupert Murdoch predicted that the international media penetration of China (e.g., his company's satellite television capabilities) will undermine authoritarian governments everywhere, although he later admitted that transnational corporations have a limited capacity to check the Chinese government's power. Media scholar Zhao Yuezhi refutes this "liberal democratization framework" and argues that it "underestimates the ability of the Chinese state to negotiate with transnational capital over the terms of entry while maintaining its regime of power in the media." She analyzes how the party-state has reconfigured its power to control communication in China and stresses the "convergence" of capitalists and communists and a "market state."[15] Meanwhile, Anthony Fung poses this question: "State and global: enemies or partners?" Fung argues that the government's strategy is "to subsume the market into state control so as to ensure the continued existence of hegemony." He concludes that the PRC's strategy with regard to global capital has changed "from resistance to collaboration." As a result, "the state and the market transform each other, and ultimately push China to a higher geopolitical stage," becoming "one of the globalizing powers."[16] Fung's argument resonates with Eric Ma's 2000 observation that the Chinese state and the market are "transforming each other to become new sociopolitical powers."[17] Chinese media experts Michael Keane, Stephanie Hemelryk Donald, and others further conceptualize this state-market relationship and the hybrid model of governmentality as "authoritarian liberalism," a term that differs significantly from "neoliberalism with Chinese characteristics," which Zhao Yuezhi, David Harvey, and others prefer.[18]

In summary, scholars have acknowledged the transformative and modernizing capabilities of the Chinese state, in contrast with the popular Western belief that "the Chinese government is still the unchanging evil authoritarian state of 1989."[19] Furthermore, they have stressed the Chinese state's alliances with capital and the market while maintaining its power. It is not my intention to provide a definitive conceptualization of the current reconfiguration of the Chinese state, market, and global capital or of the state's mode of governmentality, as all types of conceptualization are debatable and contextual. Rather, my purpose here is to focus on the complicated interplay of the state, market, and global capital and the direct consequences of such interplay.

Several things differentiate this book from the other positions mentioned above. First, while acknowledging the two alliances of state-capital and state-market to some extent, I investigate the specific ways and conditions under which the two alliances are possible and under which the two alliances are broken and the Chinese state governs everything. Put another way, conflict and competition between the state and global Hollywood always exist, as do tensions between the state and the market. The two alliances are always conditional and sometimes temporary. The Chinese state determines its own policy about when, where, and how to open up to global capital and market forces, as well as when, where, and how to maintain state domination through state-owned media groups.[20] Second, this book traces the changing role of the Chinese state and its refinement of statecraft during the global-local interplay. Global and market forces have pushed the state to transform itself from an ossified, omnipresent communist ruler to a manager, negotiator, and regulator. The state has also changed its way of governing by introducing the market mechanism into the cultural arena and by combining more business management methods with mandatory administrative means. Third, this book explores the material impact of changing state policy on the formation of the Chinese film industry. By charting the creation of the Chinese film industry, this book examines the material and empirical consequences of state policies, thereby adding another dimension of policy study and avoiding unsubstantiated speculation about the effect of state policies and the outcome of the China-Hollywood encounter.

China experts commonly agree that the Chinese Communist Party and the party-state have reclaimed their legitimacy based on the economic achievements of China's "socialist market economy" after the 1980s. Since the 1990s, when global capital began to flow into China at an unprecedented rate, the Chinese government has treated global capital as another source of its enrichment and power. In addition, the Chinese state has changed its strategy of cultural governance: it has transformed its cultural sector from one that emphasizes public service and ideological control to one that focuses on profit-seeking cultural industries that cater to market demands. I argue, therefore, that the Chinese state weaves both global capital and market forces into the state mechanism and maneuvers these two forces to empower the Chinese state. Through complex interactions with Hollywood, the state alters the course and power relationship of international communication.

Further, the book investigates the role of Hollywood cinema in China's cultural modernization project and how Hollywood's technology, capital, and experience with genre filmmaking fit the Chinese government's agenda of transforming the domestic film industry and enhancing China's "soft power." My central argument is that the Chinese government has effectively consolidated its authoritarian power through both an alliance and a tug-of-war with global capital and through the advancement of film-inclusive cultural industries. This book also explores the possibility and connotations of "new transnational third cultures" through the hybridization of Hollywood models and local cultures. Ultimately, I strive to shed some light on the issue of cultural modernity and alternative modernities.

## Conceptualizing the Current State of Postsocialist China

What does China's global routing mean to its social transformation? What will emerge from this global-local encounter? And how do we conceptualize the current stage of China's societal and cultural configuration? These are the questions I hope to answer. Therefore, this book is, finally, about a particular brand of Chinese modernity.

Japanese philosopher Takeuchi Yoshimi maintains, "It must first be recognized that Oriental modernity is the result of European coercion, or is something derived from that result." He states: "Regardless of how Europe has interpreted it, Oriental resistance has continued, and it is through this resistance that the Orient has modernized itself. This history of resistance is the history of modernization, and there is no modernization that does not pass through resistance."[21]

Lawrence Grossberg concludes that "modernity happens in encounters." He suggests locating "contemporary struggles over and around the nation-state within the broader conjuncture of struggles over modernity." He further proposes that modernity be understood "as an on-going contestation, as something to be won, not merely in a struggle over interpretations, but in material struggles over power and the very becoming of reality."[22]

Echoing both Yoshimi and Grossberg, I hope to demonstrate, through China's case, the agency of the oppressed and their capability to reverse "unequal relations of power."[23] As Professor Liu Kang has noted, "Deng's developmentalist strategy was to integrate China into the capitalist world-system only in the economic and technological sectors. In political, social and cultural spheres there was never a clearly articulated acceptance of the norms and values of global capitalism. Integration into globalization, therefore, was never conceived as a total submission to capitalism in a strategic sense."[24] This developmentalist model indicates new spaces for new social beings and alternatives. A particular brand of modernity with Chinese characteristics may be created from this model and China's encounter with global capital.

Many China experts, including Arif Dirlik, Zhang Xudong, Sheldon Lu, Paul Pickowicz, Chris Berry, and Zhang Yingjin, have used the term "postsocialism" as the analytical framework to define contemporary China. This term helps make sense of ambiguities, contradictions, and uncertain trajectories in China's development since the initiation of reform and the open-door policy in the late 1970s and early 1980s. Postsocialism also refers to the state's drastic shift to a market economy and integration with the global capitalist system in the 1990s. Dirlik was the first to employ the term:

> Postsocialism is of necessity also postcapitalist, not in the classical sense of socialism as a phase in historical development that is anterior to capitalism, but in the sense of a socialism that represents a response to the experience of capitalism and an attempt to overcome the deficiencies of capitalist development. Its own deficiencies and efforts to correct them by resorting to capitalist methods of development are conditioned by this awareness of the deficiencies of capitalism in history. Hence postsocialism seeks to avoid a return to capitalism, no matter how much it may draw upon the latter to improve the performance of "actually existing socialism." For this reason, and also to legitimize the structure of "actually existing socialism," it strives to keep alive a vague vision of future socialism as the common goal of humankind while denying to it any immanent role in the determination of present social policy.[25]

Sheldon Lu explains postsocialism as, first, "a cultural logic" with which "the residual socialist past and the emergent capitalist present" are negotiated. Second, it is "everyday life" in which "ordinary citizens struggle to make a transition." Third, it is "a place for the emergence of a new life-world" and the creation of "new socioeconomic practices." And fourth, postsocialism is "a battlefield of intellectual and ideological contention." He declares that "the aim of postsocialism is 'to use capitalism to develop socialism.'"[26]

According to Zhang Yingjin, the term "postsocialism" is based on Fredric Jameson's theory of postmodernism. Like "post New Era," it is used to describe the radical break between the 1980s and the rapid turn to a market economy and consumer culture in the 1990s.[27] As such, postsocialism is widely accepted as a valid analytical framework.

This book acknowledges the validity and usefulness of the postsocialist framework but further defines the components of postsocialist modernity by applying two dimensions: the tangible-material dimension, and the intangible-nonmaterial dimension. The former is related to economic, institutional, and industrial structure and facilities; the latter is related to ideas, principles, and ideals of humanity. Based on this definition, I argue that the current state of postsocialist Chinese modernity is an "unbalanced" or a struggling modernity. Because of this imbalance, the state struggles to navigate through capitalist surroundings by absorbing capitalist economic elements and integrating with the global economic system. In the meantime, it also tries to maintain control, uphold national interests, and reassert its national identity, which reinforces its suppressive nature. During this process, the infrastructure of the state's film industry has been modernized, integrating the American business model and Chinese cultural elements. However, ideological conflicts, discontent with state monopoly and censorship, and the fight for freedom of expression remain everyday struggles for Chinese filmmakers. This contradictory condition suggests an unbalanced modernity that is conducive to both the status quo and the possibility of new developments. Accordingly, I argue that this unbalanced modernity aids the party-state's soft power, and a new transnational "third culture" has yet to arrive.

## A Cultural Studies Approach to Global Communication

*China's Encounter with Global Hollywood* makes a unique contribution to scholarly debates by applying a cultural studies approach to the analysis of global communication. Although cultural studies research has contributed much to textual analysis and audience research, it has traditionally "undervalued political-economic-sociological-anthropological approaches." Thus, scholars have called for more research in cultural policies, global cultural labor, and the "distributional, promotional and exhibitionary protocols of the media."[28] Likewise, scholars have called for "internationalizing cultural studies" and "de-Eurocentricizing cultural studies" by stressing the interpretation of the local in the international landscape. As such, the conceptual framework for international cultural studies includes "the dilemmas of theoretical universalism vs. particularism; the architecture of local cultural institutions/industries as well as their powers and interplay with politics; and the relationships between North Atlantic and non–North Atlantic formations."[29] I fully agree with and echo this conceptual and methodological call, and this book integrates the analysis of both text and context in terms of film texts, intellectual debates, cultural policy, and a cultural industry.

This book can also be considered a "critical cultural policy" study.[30] In advanced Western countries, "cultural policy embraces that broad field of public processes involved in formulating, implementing, and contesting governmental intervention in, and support of, cultural activity."[31] In China, cultural policy refers mainly to governmental regulations produced and performed by the state apparatus. "'Culture' is inseparable from 'policy' because cultural production in post-socialist China is heavily bound to national cultural policies."[32] This critical, interdisciplinary study crosses the borders of Asia and China studies, cultural studies, global studies, and cinema and media studies, and it should appeal to a diverse audience in a number of fields.

## Scope, Method, and Structure of the Book

The book covers a twenty-year period from 1994 to 2013. It uses materials from a variety of sources, including government documents, books, newspapers, magazines, and professional and academic journals. Other sources come from the Academic Search Premier Database and China National Knowledge Infrastructure Databases. In addition, a number of intensive interviews were conducted between the summer of 2010 and 2012. Thus, the project combines both primary and secondary data.

Chapter 1 historically situates the Chinese government's policy of importing foreign blockbusters within the larger context of the domestic film industry's marketization reform. It examines how the importation of Hollywood blockbusters and the government's counterhegemonic strategies coexisted, and it conceptualizes cultural policy as a site of negotiation. First, I argue that China's evolving Hollywood policy parallels the state's pursuit of a so-called socialist market economy, its WTO bid, and its film sector's marketization and industrialization process. Second, I demonstrate how China's Hollywood policy has changed from containment to "competitive cooperation." Hollywood, which has always been a figure on the Chinese government's chessboard, is used to fulfill the state's agenda of transforming cultural industries to advance China's soft power. The state never loses its control of the film sector through policy protection, quotas, and shareholding control. Third, I contend that it has long been a central concern of the Chinese government to strengthen national culture and national identity and to maintain its ruling legitimacy during its complicated engagement with global Hollywood. The Chinese state is not only a key player in global communication but also an authoritarian power, weaving both market forces and global capital into the state mechanism through its policies.

Chapter 2 examines how the debate over the validity of the government's Hollywood import policy and the symbolic meaning of Hollywood movies played out from 1994 to 2013. It investigates the discourses and arguments advanced by the three main interpretive communities and discusses how the debate speaks to theoretical arguments about cultural homogenization and heterogeneity. The chapter teases out China's unique yet ambivalent perspective on globalization, contributing new insights into the role of the postsocialist state in the global-local interplay. My contention is that the debate over Hollywood cinema actually serves as a reference for the Chinese people to make sense of their own modernization process and national identity. The entire debate is, in fact, part of China's quest for a new, modern national identity, and it illustrates how the Chinese can draw on the American experience to build a modern China.

Chapter 3 traces the birth of mainland China's film industry—from production to distribution to exhibition. I argue that the formation of China's film industry has been a government-sponsored, top-down process combining both market forces and significant governmental interventions. This process is another counterhegemonic strategy adopted by the Chinese government in its confrontation with global Hollywood, and it involves a negotiation of operating space for the domestic film sector. I suggest that all these strategies have been purposefully employed by the Chinese government in an attempt to use global capital to revitalize the domestic film industry under the rubric of party-state control. As a result, a strong market-oriented film industry is being formed from production to distribution, and box office revenue has become the sole measure of a film's success. Transnational, transregional coproductions have become the major contributors to domestic film revenue and the backbone of the domestic film industry.

Chapter 4 analyzes the intertwined relationship among the state, Hollywood capital, and Chinese film producers. Citing case studies of sixth-generation filmmakers such as Jia Zhangke, Zhang Yuan, Wang Xiaoshuai, Wang Quan'an, and Gu Changwei, as well as younger-generation filmmakers Lu Chuan, Guanhu, Yang Shupeng, Ning Hao, and others, the chapter discusses film professionals' strategies against state repression, their subtle relations with global capital, and their unfailing efforts to pursue art while struggling for market survival. I argue that their movies reflect fractured national identities and a moral collapse, indicating a strong sense of dislocation and a "no way out" dilemma. Trapped by the state censorship system, box office pressure, and the unswerving power of global Hollywood, Chinese film modernity has yet to arrive.

Chapter 5 integrates the analysis of text and context to position the new Chinese martial arts cinema during the first decades of the twenty-first century as a collective cultural phenomenon arising from the larger context of the Chinese government's full embrace of the concept of "soft power" in an attempt to battle the global dominance of US popular culture in general and Hollywood films in particular. I argue that the new Chinese martial arts cinema is, first of all, a direct outcome of China's changing cultural policy and a survival strategy adopted by mainland Chinese and Hong Kong filmmakers under the dual pressures of film marketization and state censorship. Second, this genre has reemerged in a seemingly hybrid mode that conforms to the aesthetics of the Hollywood spectacle but reinforces nationalism, patriotism, and orthodox Confucian values that are especially conducive to state rule. Last, this genre is a deliberate construction and promotion of Chinese history, culture, and philosophy that is especially encouraged by the government to advance Chinese soft power. Contrary to the rebellious implications of martial arts cinema during times of social upheaval and identity crises, the new Chinese martial arts cinema represents both escape from and conformity to the established social order. This genre, consequently, advances both governmental power and cultural power.

The conclusion analyzes the consequences of the China-Hollywood encounter and argues that this encounter has resulted in a struggling modernity. The rebirth and renaissance of China's film industry and cultural modernization are eagerly expected.

# 1

# Cultural Policy as Negotiation of Power

## *The Chinese State's Role and Strategies in Its Tug-of-War with Global Hollywood*

China's Hollywood policy actually parallels its film sector's marketization and industrialization process and its bid to join the World Trade Organization (WTO) in the context of its expedited pursuit of a "socialist market economy" after 1992. To borrow a phrase from the *New York Times,* a "One Party Market Economy" may be the best description of China's experiment with "socialism with Chinese characteristics" during the last two decades of the twentieth century.[1] After a temporary stagnation following the 1989 incident at Tiananmen Square, Chinese helmsman Deng Xiaoping embarked on a South China tour to push a new round of economic reform. During the Fourteenth National Congress in 1992, the Chinese Communist Party (CCP) decided that the ultimate goal for national development was to establish a socialist market economy. At the same time, the CCP promulgated a resolution to speed up the development of the tertiary sector, including film, TV, and broadcasting, which paved the way for reform of China's film sector.[2]

Following the Soviet model of state ownership and a planned economy, the Chinese film industry was nationalized in 1953, and not-for-profit public institutions were established for film production, distribution, and exhibition. A total of sixteen state-owned film studios were created to produce 120 to 150 feature films each year, according to the state plan. The state allocated operating funds based on the studios' budgets for production costs, facilities expenses, and staff salaries. After studios completed their production quotas, the China Film Export and Import Corporation

(CFEIC; also called the China Film Distribution and Exhibition Company), the only distribution agent franchised by the state, would purchase the films at 110 percent of production costs and issue prints to local distribution companies. With intensified economic reform in the 1980s, the Chinese film industry underwent a series of institutional restructurings. In 1984 the state urged the film sector to employ entrepreneurial management.[3] Film studios became responsible for their own economic efficiency and received only limited governmental subsidies. By the end of the 1980s, the average shortfall between rapidly rising production costs and state subsidies had reached 10 million yuan per studio. In addition, profits from film distribution went largely to the distribution companies, with smaller shares for the studios. Despite many attempts to redistribute profits and revitalize studios, before 1993, reform in the film sector was merely a modification within the framework of the planned economy. The production sector remained untouched under the regime of state control and ideological censorship, the distribution system was fundamentally unchanged, and the nationwide film market remained split and separate.[4] In addition, competition from commercial television programs, the rampant underground market for pirated DVDs and videotapes and the theaters that showed them, and the newly imported, very popular entertainment of karaoke drew audiences away and led to "audience/market fragmentation."[5]

Since the mid-1980s, China's domestic film audience had declined by 5 million tickets per year, resulting in a sharp decrease in national box office receipts. Surveys also showed that of the more than 100 Chinese-made films shown in Beijing each year, "70 percent [failed] to recover even their copyright and printing costs, 15 percent [broke] even, and only 15 percent [recovered] their costs and made a profit." The Beijing Horizon Survey Corporation questioned 1,500 residents in five Chinese cities and found that while 46.9 percent of interviewees cited going to the cinema as their favorite pastime, less than 10 percent regularly watched Chinese-made films.[6] In 1989 more than one-third of studios, more than 900 of 2,300 distribution companies, and about 1,000 of 3,100 urban theaters were debt ridden. Between 1979 and 1991, the national film audience decreased from 27 billion to 14.39 billion. The decline was even more precipitous in 1992: annual box office sales dropped from 2.36 billion yuan in 1991 to 1.99 billion yuan in 1992, and attendance dropped by 3.84 billion.[7] In the first half of 1992 alone, the financial losses of state-owned film studios reached 70 million yuan, and 6,000 film-related enterprises either closed or converted to other businesses.[8] In 1993 CFEIC earned 35 million yuan from its traditional method of buying out foreign films, far less than the 87 million yuan required to subsidize domestic film production. This situation placed a heavy burden on national finances and posed a severe challenge to the domestic film industry.

## Film Reform and the Hollywood Import Policy

Reform in the film sector turned a new page in 1993. The Ministry of Radio, Film, and Television promulgated "Suggestions on the Deepening of Institutional Reform of the Chinese Film Sector," commonly known as Document 3, to end the forty-year model of vertical distribution. Studios now had the right to bypass CFEIC and issue prints of their films directly to local distribution companies and share the profits with them, but they still faced strong regional constraints. The difficulty of selling low-cost prints, the serious shortage of production capital, and high payroll costs gradually brought studios to the brink of bankruptcy.[9]

Under such circumstances, the most feasible solution seemed to be to come up with a new way to make profits from foreign imports.[10] Between 1993 and 1994, CFEIC tried to introduce an internationally acceptable system of revenue sharing to import big foreign hits. In September 1993 CFEIC organized the general managers of distribution companies nationwide to lobby the central government in Beijing. In December the newly appointed general manager of CFEIC, Wu Mengchen, submitted a report to the Film Bureau (part of the Ministry of Radio, Film, and Television) on the revenue-sharing system. At a national conference of general managers of film distribution companies held on January 13, 1994, Wu said that the most effective way to revitalize the weak domestic film market was to import foreign blockbusters that had already achieved good box office records overseas. Revenue from these imported films would "enable 500,000 employees of film distribution companies to make a living."[11] In early 1994 the Film Bureau finally approved the revenue-sharing plan to import ten foreign blockbusters annually, a move that ended "the 40-year-old tradition of buying outdated and low-grade but cheap foreign movies."[12] From the 1950s to the 1980s, China had primarily purchased outdated foreign films at an average flat fee of US$20,000. Many film exhibitors in China thus believed the Chinese were "second-class citizens" in terms of their access to world cinema.[13] In fact, as early as 1980, the United States had attempted to negotiate with the Chinese about the method of distributing American movies. In 1980 a delegation from CFEIC visited the United States and met with Jack Valenti, president of the Motion Picture Association of America (MPAA). Valenti proposed a revenue-sharing distribution system, but the Chinese insisted on the traditional flat fee. The two sides failed to reach an agreement, partly due to China's old economic system and the limit on foreign currency at the time.[14] By 1994, the time was finally right for the introduction of a revenue-sharing system.

The criteria for imports were loosely defined by the Film Bureau: they should reflect "the excellent fruits of world civilization and represent contemporary cinematic achievement," without detailed explanations. Revenue sharing was considered a plan to rescue the market and the economy, rather than a well-defined ideological and cultural policy. Policy makers expected imported megaproductions to fill the gap between production and consumption that most China-made films failed to achieve, revive China's film market, and raise funds.

With the approval of the government, CFEIC approached Golden Harvest Entertainment, a major Hong Kong company that had set up an office in Shanghai to target the mainland market. The two companies eventually reached a tentative agreement to distribute Golden Harvest films on the mainland on a revenue-sharing basis.[15] Hearing of this unprecedented move on the Chinese side, Warner Bros. and other major Hollywood studios quickly reached similar agreements with CFEIC. After the importation of the first blockbuster, *The Fugitive,* in November 1994, Hollywood hits such as *True Lies, Forrest Gump, The Lion King,* and *Speed* flowed into China. According to the revenue-sharing system, foreign distributors and CFEIC received 46 percent of the total box office earnings, domestic film distributors got 8 to 10 percent, and the remaining 44 to 46 percent went to the theaters. Foreign distributors were responsible for publicity costs and customs tariffs.[16]

From the beginning, Hollywood's return to China was intertwined with reform in the distribution-exhibition sector, and it was sometimes used as leverage to negotiate among different regional and district interest groups. Cold War ideology and old ways of thinking often came into play to complicate this "go global" mentality. A typical example was the distribution process for the first of the Hollywood hits, *The Fugitive.*

Various accounts have described the fate of this first Hollywood import to China between late 1994 and early 1995.[17] What happened was basically a conflict between CFEIC and the Beijing Municipal Film Distribution Company. The latter was opposed to the former's strategy of importing Hollywood blockbusters, and as early as April 17, 1994, the company had written to a minister of the central government, accusing CFEIC of being a "newly born comprador." From March to July 1994, CFEIC attempted to negotiate the distribution of Hollywood imports in Beijing, but the Beijing Municipal Film Distribution Company refused to cooperate. "We Chinese drove eight American film studios out of China forty years ago," said the company. "These American studios have always been thinking of returning to China, not just out of economic benefit, but out of an attempt to cultivate the third and fourth Chinese generations. How can we invite American movies to conquer the Chinese market, and feed foreign studios by exploiting China's box office sales?"[18] In September, after CFEIC signed the contract with Warner Bros. to release *The Fugitive* in China, it had no choice but to bypass the Beijing Municipal Film Distribution Company and sign a distribution contract with the Haidian District Film Distribution Company, which was within the jurisdiction of the Beijing municipality.

Fourteen years later, Han Maorui, general manager of the Haidian District Film Distribution Company in 1994, recalled that when CFEIC contacted him about distributing *The Fugitive* in the Beijing area, he hesitated at first because of the financial risk associated with revenue sharing. He asked for two days to consider the offer. Han then approached the managers of thirteen urban theaters in the Beijing municipality to solicit their opinions. To his surprise, they all expressed a strong interest in Hollywood imports, given the tremendous box office potential, and they offered Han their full support. Backed by the theaters, the Haidian District Film Distribution Company signed the contract with CFEIC to screen *The Fugitive.* However, this move escalated tensions, and the Beijing Municipal Film Distribution Company filed a complaint. As a result, the Beijing Cultural Administration, the highest authority governing cultural affairs in the area, ordered Han on October 20 to terminate the contract. But this order came a bit too late: all thirteen theaters had already sold out tickets for the film's premiere.

On November 11, 1994, the eve of *The Fugitive*'s release in the Beijing area, prints of the film were transported to the Haidian District Film Distribution Company's storage facility, and Han went to bed early to get a good night's sleep before the big day. At 10:00 p.m. several officials from the Beijing Cultural Administration sent for Han and ordered the immediate cancellation of the next day's premiere of *The Fugitive.* Han refused because his company would have to pay a large fine if it reneged on the contract. Talks continued until midnight, when the officials suddenly requested to see the prints. Han worried that the prints would be confiscated, so he lied and said they had not yet arrived. When the officials finally gave up, Han immediately removed the prints from the company's storage facility and drove his car around Beijing's streets until morning. "I am like an underground agent protecting secret materials," he said. At 7:00 a.m. on November 12, Han called the theater managers and had them meet him at the Jimen Bridge, where he had parked the car, to pick up the prints. *The Fugitive* was finally released in the Beijing area, and box office sales reached 800,000 yuan in the first seven days.[19]

However, the conflict between the two distribution companies led to an unpredicted disturbance in the release of Hollywood hits: only seven days into the screening of *The Fugitive,* the Beijing Cultural Administration banned the film, claiming that Haidian had violated some relevant regulation. Although the film was shown in other cities, it was banned in Beijing for two months, which forced CFEIC to file a lawsuit. At last, after the intervention of the Film Bureau, the Beijing Municipal Film Distribution Company agreed to redistribute *The Fugitive* and reconciled with CFEIC and Haidian, at least partly due to the 25 million yuan in box office sales in other cities.[20] On January 20, 1995, *The Fugitive* returned to Beijing theaters and was shown for one week. As a consequence of the delay, box office receipts in Beijing were less than one-sixth those in Shanghai.[21]

The conflict seemed to be centered on the political and ideological front, and the importation of *The Fugitive* was condemned as a case of "using socialist money to fatten the capitalist pig."[22] CFEIC was accused of being a "comprador," selling out China's national interest to foreigners. But the conflict was actually among different interest groups. As the revenue-sharing system started to operate, foreign distributors and CFEIC began to supervise box office receipts, and distribution companies at various administrative levels could no longer hide this revenue and keep some of it for themselves. These distribution companies therefore strongly opposed the introduction of revenue sharing for foreign imports, resorting to Cold War ideology and socialist rhetoric. Tension existed among different interest groups and among various kinds of regional protectionism in the name of the national interest and socialist ideology. The contradiction between market interest and political ideology is adequately revealed in the *Fugitive* case.

Hollywood thus returned to China in the distribution and exhibition sectors, and it was used to fulfill the state's financial needs and reform agenda. Seventeen years later, Mao Yu, the current deputy director of the Film Bureau under the State Administration of Radio, Film, and Television (SARFT)—which replaced the Ministry of Radio, Film, and Television in March 1998—recalled that the Hollywood import decision had been based on audience demands, market requirements, and the need to combat the pirate market for Hollywood movies. He commented that the Hollywood import policy had exerted a very positive influence on China's film market and introduced commercial film marketing strategies into China. Hollywood imports completely changed Chinese filmmakers' mind-set about how to produce films, and the imports speeded up the establishment of Hollywood-style theater chains in China in the years that followed. He said that, because of China's censorship system, officials viewed Hollywood movies as a source of entertainment and did not worry too much about their ideological implications.[23]

Imported films stimulated the ailing Chinese film market and played the role of savior.[24] By 1994, Hollywood imports accounted for 60 percent of China's film revenue of 900 million yuan (about US$112 million). In 1995 *The Fugitive* set a record for domestic box office receipts; gross box office sales during the first half of 1995 jumped by 50 percent over the same period in 1994, and summer theater attendance in Beijing increased by 70 percent.[25] In 1996 and 1997 the gross sales of American blockbusters totaled approximately 404 million yuan (US$50.5 million) and 265 million yuan (US$33.13 million), respectively. In 1998 the eight American imports led to a 45 percent increase in box office sales, totaling 587 million yuan (US$73.38 million). *Titanic* alone accounted for one-fifth of that year's total market receipts of 1.45 billion yuan. In 1999, after NATO's bombing of the Chinese embassy in Yugoslavia and the ban on American films for six months, China's domestic box office receipts dropped to only 850 million yuan. By the turn of the twenty-first century, ten imported, revenue-sharing American megaproductions accounted for about 70 percent of China's film market, whereas approximately 100 domestic films had only a 30 percent market share.[26] Some critics concluded, "It was clear that imported films had become essential to the survival of the Chinese film industry."[27]

The unprecedented popularity of Hollywood movies in China triggered a long-lasting debate on the validity of the government's policy and the possible consequences to the domestic film industry. The Chinese state tried to cope with these concerns and calm down the debate.

## The Chinese Strategy: Use Money Earned from Hollywood to Promote "Main Melody" Films

The Chinese government adopted a contradictory attitude toward Hollywood movies. Because the decision to import Hollywood movies was considered an economic policy rather than a well-defined ideological and cultural policy, the government took a pragmatic stance to justify Hollywood imports: that is, they would bring huge profits. Yet the government still stressed the ideological function of domestically made movies to reinforce the legitimacy of its rule. It thus cooperated with both liberal film distributors-exhibitors and left-wing intellectuals.

The central policy of the Chinese government can be summarized by what Liu Jianzhong, director of the Film Bureau, said in March 1996: "Yi wo wei zhu" (China's national interest takes precedence).[28] After new reform initiatives were launched by the Ministry of Culture and SARFT in 2000, "Yi wo wei zhu, wei wo suo yong" (China's national interest takes precedence, and imports should serve China's agenda) became the guiding principle for the importation of foreign films.[29] Under that principle, all film imports must serve China's needs and national interests and should be used to achieve China's goals. The government hoped to use Hollywood movies to fill the gap between domestic film production and the huge market demand, making enough money to ease the heavy financial burden on the state stemming from inefficient studios. The government originally believed that, with its enormous administrative power and strict censorship, it could harness Hollywood movies and make the best of revenue sharing in order to compensate the domestic film industry. To achieve this goal, the government adopted a strategy of using "main melody" films to battle Hollywood movies and minimize Hollywood's influence.

The term "main melody" (*zhu xuan lü*) was first proposed in March 1987 by Teng Jinxian, director of the Film Bureau, at a national filmmaking conference. When Chinese president Jiang Zemin reiterated the main-melody idea on multiple occasions, Teng's proposal to "foreground main melody while encouraging diversity" became the motto for China's film industry. Jiang defined "main melody" as embodying patriotism, socialism, and collectivism; resolutely resisting money worship, hedonism, and excessive individualism; and unshakably opposing capitalism and all corrupt, exploitative trends.[30] This idea reflected official concern about both the rising trend of "bourgeois liberalism," which eventually led to the 1989 student democratic movement, and the popularity of commercial films such as kung fu and detective movies. The government attempted to tighten its ideological control on the cultural front. On July 4, 1987, the Central Committee of the CCP established a special committee to oversee the production of films with "significant revolutionary and historical themes." Ding Qiao, deputy director of the Ministry of Radio, Film, and Television, was named to head the committee.[31] However, not until 1989, after the events in Tiananmen Square, did the production of main-melody movies begin on a large scale. The government realized it was imperative to reinforce state ideological apparatuses, and the film industry was one of the most important.

The production of main-melody movies is considered an official, state-sponsored project. In terms of film production, the party-state, through the special committee composed of party bureaucrats, is directly involved in the whole process: screenplay writing and revising, filmmaking, and censoring. In terms of film investment, the government subsidizes most of the filmmaking costs. In terms of film function, these movies are responsible for conveying the official rhetoric of Marxism-Leninism-Maoism, as well as socialism, patriotism, and collectivism. In terms of film distribution and exhibition, there is little voluntary purchase of tickets; audiences receive mandatory orders (issued through their work units) to go to theaters and watch these movies.

Main-melody movies are thus a unique cultural product of postsocialist China. They consumed huge resources yet accounted for few market profits. Between 1995 and 2000, of the 80 to 100 movies produced each year, approximately 80 percent could be considered main-melody films. These movies usually have three narrative story lines, First, there is the "politically correct" narrative of the revolutionary history of the Communist Party and its civil war against the Nationalist Party from 1920 to 1949, when the communists took over and established the People's Republic of China; this includes glorified portraits of party leaders Mao Zedong, Zhou Enlai, Deng Xiaoping, and others. Second, there is the historical narrative of the anti-Japanese war and the anti-imperialist battles against Western invaders since the Opium War, which stresses the themes of nationalism and patriotism. The third story line is the positive portrayal of Communist Party cadres and their dedication to serving the people. Many of these movies were produced to commemorate the fiftieth anniversary of the founding of the People's Republic of China in 1999, the seventieth and eightieth anniversaries of the Chinese Communist Party in 1991 and 2001, and the fiftieth anniversary of victory in the antifascist war in 1995. These movies are usually called "dedication movies" (*xian li pian*) by the Chinese people and "propagandistic movies" by foreigners.

Collectively, these movies are one of the most important state ideological apparatuses, and they function to educate and instill the "politically correct" way of thinking into people's minds—a role unmatchable by political classes and historical textbooks. Main-melody films help convince people of the inevitability and validity of a socialist China, maintain the legitimacy of the ruling party, and contribute to the establishment of a national identity that serves the best interests of the ruling party—an identity that is red, socialist and communist, anti-imperialist and anticapitalist. The party-state hopes to use these movies to pass on the revolutionary legacy and to demonstrate to the world its socialist national identity with a distinct Chinese character.

To promote main-melody films and minimize the impact of Hollywood, the government took several specific measures. First, in the area of film production, the government employed a strategy of using earnings from Hollywood imports to pay for the production of domestic films. It launched the so-called 9550 Project at the 1996 Changsha Film Work Conference, which required the major state-owned film studios to produce fifty finely made main-melody movies during the ninth Five-Year Plan from 1996 to 2000, or ten films each year. The Film Bureau stipulated that when a domestic studio produced one such "significant film," it would be allowed to select one foreign film from ten blockbusters to distribute and keep the receipts itself.[32] Those studios that failed to meet the production quota would be criticized and deemed ineligible to distribute foreign films and receive state compensation. Further, the government required all theaters to contribute 5 percent of their annual box office receipts to a fund established for domestic film production. The state would also allot a certain amount of earnings from foreign imports and TV revenue for investment in domestic film production. Finally, the government exempted film prints sold by studios from the value-added tax.[33]

The year 1996 witnessed the largest state input into the production of "significant films," as well as the technological renovation of studios. The total investment reached 125 million yuan. Funds from TV amounted to 69 million yuan, and the state's special fund invested 34.15 million yuan in the production of thirty-one films.[34] CFEIC also invested 10 million yuan for the production of significant films and children's movies, as well as for the dubbing of movies for minorities and Tibetans. Between 1996 and 2000, state funding of the studios totaled more than 600 million yuan, including a direct state subsidy of 400 million, the special film fund of 130 million for the renovation of theaters and studios, and 80 million provided by CFEIC from its distribution of foreign imports. In addition, the domestic film industry received 4 million yuan in subsidies from the Ministry of Finance, as well as 500 million yuan (out of a total advertising revenue of 1.2 billion yuan) from China Central Television's film channel.[35]

Second, from 1995 to 1997, the state promulgated a series of regulations to break the monopoly of sixteen state-owned film production studios, and it allowed collectively owned companies, shareholding companies, private businesses, and even individuals to invest in film production, subject to the state approval. The goal was to encourage competition and bring in more investment. Reform measures are covered in more detail in chapter 3.

Third, in the area of film distribution and exhibition, the government stipulated that two-thirds of the screen time in theaters must be reserved for domestic films. On every major festival day—Labor Day (May 1), Children's Day (June 1), National Day (October 1), New Year's Day, and the Chinese Spring Festival—domestic movies must be shown.[36]

Fourth, learning from Hollywood's studio system and marketing strategy, China launched a series of reforms to organize Hollywood-style theater chains. In April 1995 Shanghai became the first city in China to have a national theater chain. Guangzhou and Beijing followed suit. The technological renovation also began in 1997. In Sichuan, Hunan, and Zhejiang Provinces, state loans were obtained to transform old theaters into multifunctional and Panavision theaters. To solve the problem of a lack of funds, in 1997 the state launched an experimental program in Beijing, Shanghai, and Guangzhou to attract foreign funds to renovate theaters. By 2000, foreign funds had been used to update 30 theaters, and 166 theaters had been equipped with digital stereo systems. These theaters became the largest in terms of box office receipts, accounting for about 45 percent of the national total. However, the majority of the 5,000 theaters nationwide remained outdated and in poor condition by 2000 (see chapter 3).[37]

By exercising its enormous administrative power and strict censorship, the Chinese government hoped to use Hollywood to produce domestic films that toed the party line. By doing so, it expected to boost the growth of the indigenous film industry, win back the Chinese audience, and maintain its ideological legitimacy. Did it succeed?

## Assessment of the Government's Strategy and the Status of China's Film Industry

During the first few years after the return of Hollywood, several relatively successful domestically made movies sustained the hope and courage of Chinese filmmakers that they could do battle with Hollywood. Taking a lesson from Hollywood's investment and marketing strategy, they achieved success both cinematically and at the box office. These films include *Blush* (*Hong Fen* [1995]), which charts the journeys of two women in a brothel after the revolution brings an end to their old way of life. It won the Silver Bear Award at the Berlin International Film Festival and brought in more than 7 million yuan in domestic box office receipts. *In the Heat of the Sun* (*Yangguang canlan de rizi* [1994]), directed by the talented Wen Jiang, amassed more than 10 million yuan in receipts. With a touch of nostalgia, it depicts the restlessness and dreams of a group of wild teenagers during the era of the Cultural Revolution. This film won the Venice Film Festival's award for best actor in 1994, as well as multiple awards at the Golden Horse Film Festival of Taiwan in 1996. *Red Cherry* (*Hong Yingtao* [1995]) shows the horrors of war as seen through the eyes of some Chinese children studying at Moscow's International School; it made about 15 million yuan at the box office. Finally, *A Time to Remember*, also known as *Red Lovers* or *Shanghai Story* (*Hong se lian ren* [1998]), tells a story of revolution and romance through the eyes of an American doctor; it won awards at the Cairo International Film Festival and was the box office champion in 1998, earning 25 million yuan.

Among these movies, *Red Cherry* and *A Time to Remember* are considered main-melody films, but they represent a more humanistic, romantic, and market-oriented version of the genre. They also represent a genuine effort by both the government and filmmakers to improve the quality of such films in order to compete with Hollywood. *Red Cherry* tells about the war experiences of the children of senior Chinese Communist Party leaders attending school in Moscow, a novel and exotic subject for Chinese audiences. *A Time to Remember* is a moving love story about a leader of the Communist Party, another rare subject for main-melody films. He is portrayed as an ordinary human being dealing with his memories, mental confusion, and a desire to find true love. When placed against the backdrop of the grand Chinese revolution, his common human nature plus his dedication to the revolutionary cause make him a striking and noble character who shines through the entire movie. To attract audiences, both films employed new faces and well-known stars; *A Time to Remember* even hired famous Hong Kong actor Leslie Cheung. Their genuine and passionate performances gave the films an unprecedented humanistic touch, making them stand out from other cliché propaganda movies.

The humanistic trend in main-melody films continued up to 2013. The goal was apparently to humanize and commercialize propaganda movies and downplay political conflict, while foregrounding the vicissitudes and destinies of ordinary people. The official definition of main-melody movies also changed with this trend. In October 2006 SARFT declared that all films that reflect truth, virtue, and beauty could be labeled main-melody movies.[38]

In addition, in an effort to attract domestic audiences and compete with Hollywood, Chinese film director Feng Xiaogang created a new film genre—New Year celebration movies, or *He Sui Pian.* Based on a similar genre common in Hong Kong and Taiwan, and appealing to the popular mentality and festive atmosphere of Chinese New Year, this type of movie achieved huge market success from 1998 to 2000. Some critics have argued that Feng's New Year celebration genre is the only type of movie that can succeed in bringing audiences back to domestic films and competing with Hollywood.

The fifth generation of Chinese filmmakers, who began experimenting with their creative movies in the open and free political environment of the 1980s, was forced to confront Hollywood on a commercial level and at the box office. A few of them, including Zhang Yimou, tried to adapt to the market-driven reality and produced a few good movies, such as *Not One Less* (1999) and *My Father and Mother* (1999). Most, however, were gradually silenced after the return of Hollywood films. The emerging sixth generation of filmmakers produced primarily underground and art-house films during this period; these were not even allowed to be shown publicly, let alone compete with Hollywood movies at the box office. Thus, the most talented Chinese filmmakers were at a serious disadvantage in a market-dominant and profit-driven era.

Even those relatively successful domestic films were unable to compete with Hollywood blockbusters in terms of market share. Hollywood imports boasted an average of 42 million yuan in box office receipts, ranging from *Titanic*'s 359.5 million yuan in 1998 down to *Mickey Blue Eyes*' 6 million yuan in 2000.[39] Looking at the overall situation, a pretty gloomy picture of China's film industry is revealed. Except for the few films mentioned above, most domestic films were not successful. Box office receipts for domestic films had been steadily declining: in 1995, the year of the massive introduction of foreign megaproductions, 70 percent of domestic films were not even listed on the schedules of most theaters. From 1997 to 2002, China's yearly output was only 80 to 100 films, with 80 percent of them not being purchased or shown at all; only about 30 films made it to theaters.[40] In 1998 the gross box office receipts of the Chinese film market were 1.45 billion yuan, with *Titanic* accounting for nearly one-fifth of that total. Because of the NATO bombing of China's embassy in Yugoslavia, American films were banned for six months in 1999, leading to a drastic drop in annual box office receipts to 840 million yuan. That figure increased to 1 billion yuan in 2000 and dropped again to 800 million yuan in 2001. For a country with a population of 1.3 billion, the heavy reliance on American films to support its economy was embarrassing. One survey found that only three types of movies could attract audiences: Hollywood blockbusters, Hong Kong and Taiwan commercial movies, and Feng Xiaogang's New Year celebration movies. Most theaters were reluctant to purchase domestic movies at all, let alone show them.

As the date of China's reentry into the WTO approached in 2000, and as the foreign film quota increased to twenty, some commentators believed China's indigenous film industry would face a larger crisis. In an interview, Li Yiming, deputy director of the China Film Art Institute, said half of domestic films were still subsidized by the state or by CFEIC, which obtained part of its profits through Hollywood blockbusters. However, most domestic films kept losing money and were unable to repay CFEIC, resulting in a long chain of debt in the industry. Li commented that China's indigenous film industry was in a "most critical situation."[41] When Feng Xiaogang sought funds from Columbia Pictures Film Production Asia for *Big Shot's Funeral* (*Da Wan* [2001]), the Chinese filmmakers' dilemma was fully revealed, and the early experiment with filmmaking and the state's import policy seemed to be at a dead end.

In 2002 the elite newspaper *Nanfang Weekend* ran a special edition titled "An Elegy for Eight Years of the Hollywood Invasion." After reviewing the eight-year journey of Hollywood films in China and the corresponding performance of China's domestic films, it declared that the Chinese film market had been conquered by Hollywood.[42] In the same issue, radical film critic Dai Jinhua was quoted as saying: "I believe this eight-year invasion by Hollywood films has stricken a deathblow to China's national film industry. Moreover, the process has not finished yet, and is going to worsen with China's reentry into the World Trade Organization (WTO). If I once predicted 'the wolf is coming,' I now believe the wolves are here."[43]

If Dai was right, then one can conclude that the Chinese government's policy during this period was ineffective. Its original vision of using money earned from Hollywood imports to revitalize the domestic film market and film industry did not work. On the one hand, the film market had indeed improved, and audiences had been drawn back to theaters. On the other hand, audiences had been attracted back to theaters not by domestic films but by Hollywood imports. China's domestic film industry did not benefit much from this strategy, nor was its overall production quality enhanced. Why did this plan fail in spite of the unprecedented investment by the government and the enormous effort by filmmakers?

The Chinese government's ineffective cultural policy led directly to the unsatisfactory status of the indigenous film industry. This policy did not address the disjuncture between government-planned film production and audience-determined market demand, nor did it adequately define the status of the film industry. In addition, the policy, which was largely administrative and mandatory, was incompatible with the market forces the government itself had liberalized since the initiation of economic reform.

Although China's reformers have long suggested that the film sector should be considered both a creative venture and a moneymaking business, that sector never enjoyed the status of an independent artistic enterprise and was never operated according to market rules. More than two-thirds of all domestic films that were directly or indirectly funded and guided by the government were produced according to the government's plan rather than the audience's needs. In China, cinema remains an important propaganda tool and is heavily loaded with party-sanctioned ideology. The film sector's embarrassing status as a government tool that is nevertheless responsible for its own economic efficiency leads to fundamental problems in production, distribution, and exhibition processes.

First, the government failed to clearly define the function of cinema and the status of the film industry. In the context of China's reality before 2000, movies were unlikely to be considered either purely creative art or purely entertaining commodities; they had to carry out a propaganda mission that made achieving market popularity difficult and unpredictable. Thus, domestic movies often lacked entertainment value and were unable to compete with Hollywood genre films that are solidly based on audience taste and market demand.

Second, in guiding film production, the Chinese government neglected cinema's artistic nature. Its attempts to impose administrative order on the process of artistic creation and to exert strict censorship only served to repress the initiative and creativity of filmmakers and set up obstacles to the film production process. For instance, in 1997, immediately after the government adopted the strategy of promoting main-melody films, domestic film production dropped by 33 percent.[44]

Third, in terms of film distribution and exhibition, the government interfered excessively with the market through its administrative orders, failing to consider audiences' desires and preferences. In practice, the rule that movie theaters must reserve two-thirds of their screen time for domestic films was extremely hard to abide by, and most theaters did not follow this rule. Either they were unable to find enough attractive domestic films to fill two-thirds of their screen time or they found it too hard to resist the temptation of Hollywood imports because of their need to make a living.[45] As such, the government's strategy eventually worked against its original goal.

Fundamentally, the ineffectiveness of the government's policy can be traced to the inherent contradiction of importing Hollywood movies while promoting main-melody films. As a cultural commodity, movies integrate the dual functions of economy and culture. Inseparable from a film's economic value (box office receipts) is its cultural connotation and influence. To accept one and disclaim the other is difficult. The Chinese government was fully aware of this contradiction, and it intended to promote main-melody movies to counter the Hollywood influence from the outset. Meanwhile, it shunned any theoretical discussion of the ideological implications of Hollywood cinema and avoided any involvement in the theoretical debate launched by the press and the academic community, following Deng Xiaoping's developmentalist strategy of "to do without debate." However, the government's main-melody strategy was problematic. Frankly, it was a disguised method of maintaining the supremacy of the ruling party by misleadingly using the concepts of socialism and capitalism at the political-economic level, while failing to fully explore China's rich resources at the historical-cultural level.

At the political-economic level, China's socialism has largely become rhetorical, and its original components of a planned economy, public ownership, and the averaging of wealth have been fundamentally altered. In terms of economic determinants, Chinese-style socialism and Western or American-style capitalism are not absolutely opposite and mutually exclusive. What truly differentiates China from Western and American societies is not a rhetorical term like "socialism" or "capitalism" but a different political and social structure, as well as China's distinct cultural tradition. Accordingly, the only plausible and meaningful way to promote movies with Chinese characteristics is at the historical-cultural level. China's millennia of history, distinct cultural traditions, and colorful landscapes, as well as the true lives of ordinary people, could be abundant resources for film production. In particular, changing ideas and values, lost identities, confusion and anxiety, struggles and aspirations, tears and joy in a dazzling, evolving, rapidly globalizing world constitute a unique repository for filmmakers to draw on. A wise government would have allowed more freedom to encourage the production of realistic films to compete with Hollywood. Once again, the Chinese government's policy is crucial for domestic films to achieve a cultural and competitive edge.

China's membership in the WTO was formally approved in November 2001. The Chinese government agreed to double the annual quota for revenue-sharing imports to twenty films, to allow foreign investors up to a 49 percent share in operating theaters, and to permit foreign investment in joint video-distribution ventures.[46] Facing massive financial pressure and formidable challenges, the Chinese government reworked its strategy and proclaimed a series of new film regulations against the larger backdrop of a newly launched reform of its cultural industries. This time, Hollywood was not merely part of the distribution linkage; it was allowed to participate in film production.

## Reform of China's Cultural Industries

China's reentry into the WTO and the associated commitments it made led to a shift in its cultural policy. The Chinese made considerable concessions to the US side, and Hollywood's long-standing desire for a piece of the Chinese market seemed to be at least partially satisfied. However, the most notable reason for the film policy shift was internal: the Chinese government redefined the role of film after more than twenty years of ambivalence and reluctance and launched a reform of the cultural industries.

Prior to 2000, the status of the film sector in China had always been vague, dubious, and ambivalent. From the 1950s to the late 1970s, films served as the party-state's propaganda tool, responding to the party's political agenda. During the open, free reform era between 1984 and 1988, led by premier Zhao Ziyang, the film sector was redefined as "an integral part of cultural industries instead of political institutions for the (re)enforcement of the Communist Ideology."[47] With the launch of main-melody films in 1987, and especially after the bloodshed and repression of the 1989 Tiananmen student movement, the film sector once again became a propaganda tool and the conveyor of official ideology. After Deng Xiaoping's famous 1992 South China tour and the massive launch of a socialist market economy, reform in the film industry took off as well, starting in 1993. Yet not until 1997, when the establishment of a socialist market economy became the Communist Party's fundamental goal and marketization of the cultural sector was under way, did the official definition of the film sector undergo a remarkable change.

To meet the goals set by the CCP's Fifteenth National Congress in 1998—which called for an "all-round advance of 'socialism with Chinese characteristics' into the 21st century"—China's various sectors, including the film sector, accelerated the marketization process. At the 1998 Nan Chang film meeting, the party's propaganda minister, Ding Guangen, said, "The film sector must win the market in order to prosper. Under the condition of the socialist market economy, film as a cultural product cannot be independent of the market economy."[48] At the 1999 national conference of directors of state-owned studios and managers of distribution companies, the deputy director of SARFT, Zhao Shi, asserted that "film belongs to cultural industries."[49] She also vowed to lift state-owned film studios out of their plight by 2000 by deepening the reform and expediting the development of the film industry, based on the guidelines of the Fifteenth National Congress with regard to advancing innovative industries. At the same time, debate over the role and function of the film sector was ongoing. Some professionals from the film sector admitted that "it is ridiculous that up to now China's film sector still does not know if they should treat film as a propaganda tool, or as a commodity." They wanted the government to make it clear that "film is a commodity. It has a function of propaganda. But it is first of all a commodity. . . . The film sector should be operated as an industry and according to the principle of market economy, the requirement of the WTO, and the logic of arts."[50]

In August 2000 the party's deputy minister of propaganda and director of SARFT, Xu Guangchun, made an inspection tour of the Film Bureau and stated that the core issue was how to form a robust national film production capable of meeting the needs of 1.3 billion people. He reiterated that "political correctness" was the number-one consideration when making films, with the second being the audience's interests and likes. But if the audience did not like a film, meeting the strict criterion of "political correctness" would be of little use.[51] During the 2001 national film conference, Xu repeated that "film is a mass cultural product. Under the condition of the socialist market economy, the film sector must win back the market, win back the audience in order to prosper."[52]

By the year 2002, when the Sixteenth National Congress of the Communist Party of China convened and formally advanced the idea of "cultural industries," both official and unofficial voices had acknowledged the market value of the film sector and its role as a cultural industry. This cleared the way for massive transformation and the establishment of a new film industry. During the Sixteenth National Congress, Chinese president Jiang Zemin called for "deepening the reform of the cultural system." He added that the cultural system should be transformed to meet the requirements of the socialist market economy, and a system for administering cultural production that mobilized the enthusiasm and creativity of cultural workers should gradually be established.[53] During this meeting, the term "cultural industries" appeared in official documents for the first time, symbolizing a drastic turning point in the official status of culture and a historical milestone in the transformation of China's cultural system. As cultural scholar Wang Jing commented: "The state's rediscovery of culture as a site where new ruling technologies can be deployed and converted simultaneously into economic capital constitutes one of its most innovative strategies of statecraft since the founding of the People's Republic."[54]

To echo the call of the Sixteenth National Congress, the film sector held two national working conferences in 2002 and 2003. Xu Guangchun formally declared that "film is a cultural industry" and observed that the film sector should be liberalized from its original institutional system (*Shiye tizhi*) and operated according to market logic.[55] He also redefined film, stressed its entertainment function, and extended the definition of main melody to include all works beneficial to "economic development, social progress, national solidarity, and people's well-being."[56]

The party-state, pushed by various external and internal forces, finally acknowledged the market and entertainment functions of film and prepared to embark on a wholesale transformation of the cultural industries. However, given China's one-party authoritarian system and strict censorship, film, like culture, can never be fully independent of political restraint and government control. It is not unusual for official utterances on the role of film to vary, depending on the context. Like Xu Guangchun and Zhao Shi, party officials might emphasize film's role as a cultural product on one occasion, while stressing its propagandistic role on another occasion. The status of film, like the status of culture, is always ambivalent or double-functioned and at the discursive disposal of the government. Accordingly, the film sector has to seek a balance between its different roles, negotiate its way through, and learn to "dance with shackles."

## Reform Policy, the Boom of the Domestic Film Industry, and the Inflow of Overseas Funds

Within the broader context of reform of the cultural industries, and amid the theoretical preparation to do so, several sets of new regulations for the domestic film industry were unveiled. The process of transforming China's domestic film sector into a cultural industry was, in fact, initiated by the government document titled "Some Opinions about Carrying out Further Reform in the Film Industry," issued by SARFT and the Ministry of Culture on June 6, 2000 (referred to as Document 320). The document clearly stated that the goals of transformation were "to meet the requirement of the socialist market economy and the WTO, while upholding the Deng Xiaoping Theory and the CCP's cardinal principles; to enhance 'Main Melody' and encourage diversity; to maintain the control of the CCP, the government, and state-owned economy while properly making use of private and foreign investment for our gains." In summary, the reform had to "ensure the socialist nature of the film industry" while properly dealing with the relationship between control and market demands.[57] From the contradictory rhetoric of the document, it is clear that the party-state struggled to seek a balance between its ideological control and the demands of the market and WTO, and between its socialist legacy and the direction of reform.

Based on these guidelines, the document announced that the major reform measures included the establishment of media groups; the trial implementation of a shareholding system for film production, distribution, and exhibition; the active promotion of theater chains; and permission for foreign investment in the renovation of cinemas. In 2004 Document 320 evolved into SARFT Document 41, dealing with the development of the film industry and thus serving as a fundamental guideline for the industry's transformation.[58]

In December 2001 the State Council issued "Film Managerial Regulations," another crucial document that covered every aspect of the domestic film industry. Although that document reiterated the government's policy of encouraging private and foreign investment in film production and theater construction, it devoted much space to the film censorship system and the harsh penalties for violating the regulations. For example, any studios or individuals found to be engaging in unauthorized cooperation with overseas partners in film production, importation, distribution, or print processing would be subject to fines of up to 300,000 yuan and would have their licenses revoked. Individuals who participated in foreign film festivals without the proper authorization would be forbidden to engage in the film business for five years.[59]

Based on these guidelines and regulations, starting in 2003, SARFT released Documents 18, 19, 20, and 21, and it issued additional supplementary regulations in 2004 and 2005. The gist of these documents was that foreign and private capital investment was permitted in both film production and theater construction. However, foreign investors were not permitted to establish solely owned studios and theaters or participate in joint ventures with non-state-owned companies. Foreign investors could establish joint ventures only with state-owned companies or hold shares amounting to no more than 49 percent. Yet, in several major cities, including Beijing, Shanghai, Guangzhou, Xi'an, Chengdu, Wuhan, and Nanjing, foreign shareholders were allowed to own as much as 75 percent of theaters and to have cooperative terms of no longer than thirty years on a trial basis. The same terms applied to Hong Kong and Macau investors.[60] Although the state changed the foreign ratio from 75 percent back to 49 percent in August 2005, Hong Kong and Macau investors were still allowed a 75 percent share.

SARFT also loosened the rules on film censorship by revoking its review of screenplays before the start of filmmaking. As long as filmmakers submitted a synopsis of no fewer than 1,000 words to SARFT, their films could be listed in the annual plan. In the past, film producers had to have their screenplays reviewed and approved by SARFT and obtain permits before moving forward. However, the screenplays for Sino-foreign cooperative films, films with "important revolutionary historical themes, and films with sensitive themes" still had to be reviewed by censors.[61]

The supplements issued in 2004 and 2005 granted greater rights and market access to Hong Kong and Macau investors, following the guidelines of the closer economic partnership arrangements (CEPAs) between the mainland and Hong Kong and Macau.[62] The two CEPAs are considered the first free-trade agreements aimed at eliminating customs tariffs between mainland China and its special administrative regions. They allow Hong Kong–produced films, upon passing censorship, to be distributed in the mainland without quota limitations. For distribution purposes, mainland–Hong Kong coproductions are treated as domestic films. Through the CEPAs and related film regulations, the Chinese government granted more rights to "Greater China" investors while limiting the rights of foreign investors.

Between 2003 and 2013, the Chinese government's reworked policies achieved astonishing outcomes and resulted in fundamental changes in domestic film production, distribution, and exhibition. First of all, China's film output consistently increased, reaching a record high of 745 films in 2012.[63] In 2004, immediately after implementation of the new policies, the output of feature films (excluding documentaries and cartoons) jumped to 212, a 50 percent increase over the 140 films produced in 2003; this broke the record high of 170 films set in 1992. The number climbed to 260 in 2005 and 330 in 2006, making China the third largest film producer in the world, trailing only the United States and India.[64] Film output continued to skyrocket between 2007 and 2012.

Accordingly, box office receipts nationwide rose as well, with an average annual increase of more than 25 percent between 2003 and 2013. In 2012 China boasted gross box office revenue of more than 17 billion yuan (approximately US$2.74 billion).[65] Although film output decreased to 638 in 2013, box office revenue increased by 27.5 percent to reach 21.77 billion yuan (approximately US$3.51 billion).[66] See figures 1.1 and 1.2.

The most drastic change, however, was the inflow of transnational capital. Transnational media conglomerates seized the opportunities offered by the policy shift and marched into China. Warner Bros. joined with CFEIC

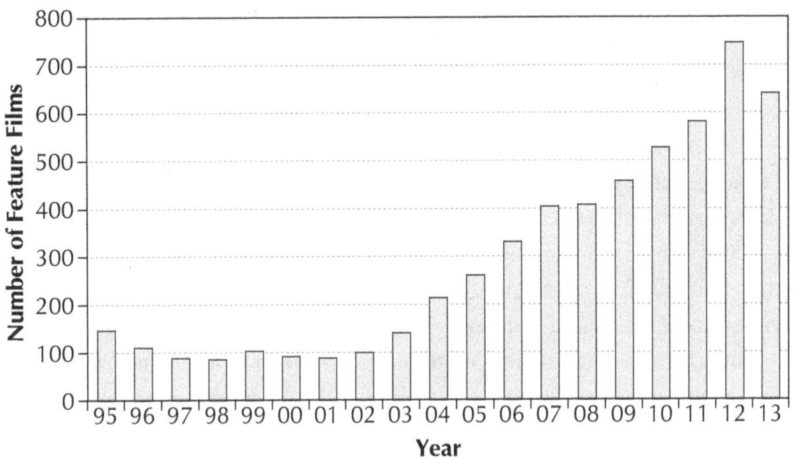


Figure 1.1. China's feature film output, 1995–2013

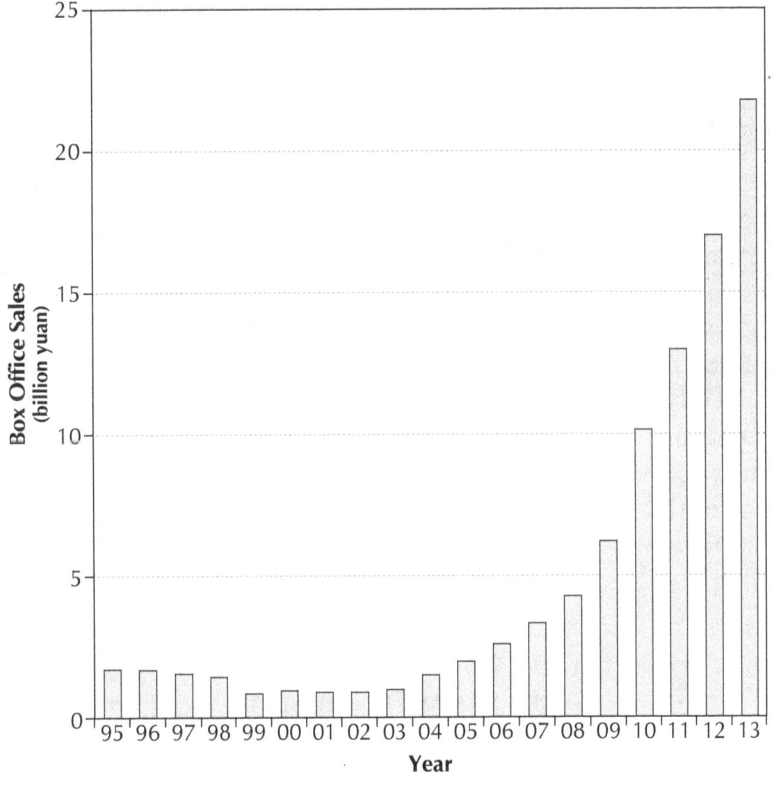


Figure 1.2. Box office sales (billion yuan), 1995–2013

and Hengdian Company to establish a large corporation that controlled seven theater chains with more than 35 percent of the market share. Sony Pictures Home Entertainment also set up a joint venture with CFEIC.[67] Viacom collaborated with Shanghai Wenguang Group to establish the first Sino-foreign cartoon production company, and Wenguang Group took part in another joint venture with the Japanese Dentsu Company.

Foreign investment also flowed into the renovation of theaters. In January 2004 Warner Bros. cooperated with Dalian Wanda Group to set up Warner Wanda International Theater, with Warner Bros. managing and providing technological support. Warner Bros. also planned to invest in more than thirty multifunction theaters in China in the years to come. Korea Orion and American Loews invested in a number of new theaters with a 75 percent foreign share and a 25 percent Chinese share.[68] By 2005, all seven major Hollywood film studios had set up offices in Beijing or Shanghai, awaiting further changes in state policy that would bring additional opportunities.

Before the 2008 global financial crisis, international funds flowing into China helped solve Chinese filmmakers' long-term financial difficulties. In May 2007 China Film Group Corporation and America's IDG jointly established the IDG China Media Fund, with plans to invest in the production of sixty to eighty films over a ten-year period while increasing the fund by a factor of ten. In addition, A3 International Film Fund was jointly launched by mainland China's nonstate sector and film producers from Hong Kong, Japan, South Korea, and the United States. Its goal was to raise US$100 million for investment in thirty Asian coproductions among China, Japan, and South Korea over a five-year period, with 60 percent of the fund invested in China. In October 2007 Weinstein Brothers announced the establishment of an Asian Film Fund of US$285 million, with more than 50 percent of the fund to be invested in twenty Chinese films over the next five years. It is estimated that the funds flowing into Chinese film production will reach US$60 million a year.[69] Accordingly, coproductions have become the major contributor to China's film revenue.

## Competitive Cooperation, Tug-of-War, and the WTO Lawsuit

While transnational corporations attempted to secure a greater market share and maintain a sound footing in China, the Chinese government heavy-handedly controlled the inflow of transnational capital and the expansion of foreign conglomerates into the domestic film industry. By allowing joint ventures only with state-owned companies such as China Film Group Corporation and Xinhua Media Entertainment, the government guaranteed its control of shareholding. In August 2005 the Ministry of Culture, along with four other state ministries, issued a document titled "Several Opinions on Foreign Investment in the Culture Industry." This new document nullified the regulation in Document 21 that allowed foreign shares in theaters in several major cities to be as high as 75 percent, stressing anew that "Chinese mainland investors must own at least 51% or play a leading role in their joint ventures with foreign investors." This new rule frustrated Time Warner's strategy in China; consequently, Warner Bros. International Cinemas (WBIC) withdrew from China in November 2006. WBIC's exit from China "shows the vulnerability of foreign media and entertainment companies to the country's policy changes."[70] At the same time, state-owned companies played a more active role in seeking opportunities to cooperate with foreign investors. In April 2008 the China Film Group Corporation and Xinhua Media Entertainment announced a strategic alliance to coproduce movies from offices in Beijing and Los Angeles. Xinhua Media Entertainment, a new subsidiary of Nasdaq-listed XFMedia, produces animated drama series and special effects for Chinese television.[71]

The battle for control of the Chinese market has been a central concern of the Chinese government, a major source of frustration for Hollywood studios, and the subject of frequent quarrels between the two sides. To maintain its grip on the domestic market, the Chinese government's strategy has consisted of quotas, policy protection, and shareholding control, while Hollywood studios have appealed to WTO rules to seek greater access to the Chinese market. In April 2007 the trade representative of the United States, in conjunction with the MPAA and two other professional associations, filed suit with the WTO against China's strict limits on the import of foreign movies and other media. The American side accused China of discriminating against foreign companies by imposing more restrictive conditions and of maintaining a monopoly in film importation and distribution controlled by state-owned enterprises and large joint ventures. After nearly three years of hearings and appeals, on January 21, 2010, the WTO found China in violation of international trade rules and mandated an end to the government's monopoly on the distribution of imported books, movies, and films by March 19, 2011. China disagreed with the ruling but indicated its willingness to comply. The lawsuit was considered a major victory for the US side. New MPAA chief executive Christopher J. Dodd has made the opening of China one of his top priorities, and he has been championing an increase in the annual quota of twenty foreign imports.[72] The Chinese side has expressed concern about Hollywood's aggressive stance. Mao Yu, deputy director of the Film Bureau, said at a 2010 conference in Beijing that once the quota is raised and more Hollywood movies flow into China, Hollywood will net 60 to 70 percent of the revenue earned from the Chinese market, rather than the 13 to 15 percent under the current revenue-sharing arrangement. This would result in considerably reduced returns for China's film sector and have a negative impact on the development of the domestic film industry.[73]

Once transnational corporations saw new opportunities in China, the capital started coming back. In March 2011 IMAX Corporation, the Canada-based big-screen theater chain, announced that it was setting up a joint venture with China's largest cinema operator, Wanda Cinema Line Corporation. IMAX planned to open 75 theaters in 25 locations by 2014, with the goal of bringing a total of 177 IMAX theaters to China in the years that followed.[74] Another top Hollywood finance and production company, Legendary Pictures, formed a joint venture with China's largest private and publicly listed entertainment conglomerate, Huayi Brothers Media Corporation. The joint venture, called Legendary East, will produce films in Hong Kong.[75] Other collaborations include Sony Pictures' 2009 remake of *The Karate Kid* in partnership with China Film Group Corporation; former News Corporation president Peter Chernin's launch of an entertainment and technology company in China, India, and Indonesia; and California-based theater chain UltraStar's plan to build digital cinemas and educate employees in cooperation with Xiamen Province of China.[76] In addition, Hollywood Movie Works announced in July 2011 that it will build a film production base in Beijing. This project will take ten years to complete, with a total investment of $3.3 billion. According to President John Roberson, the company aims to transfer all pre- and postproduction, special effects, and cartoon production to China, thus achieving a complete outsourcing of production to China.[77]

Despite pulling out of China in 2006, Warner Bros. also planned to return. In June 2011 Warner Bros. Entertainment announced that it would offer its movies on Chinese cable TV via a pay-per-view system. It expected

Table 1.1. Films Cofunded with Overseas Capital, 2003–2010

| Year | Total Film Output | Films Cofunded by Hong Kong and Taiwan Companies | Films Cofunded by Foreign Companies |
|---|---|---|---|
| 2003 | 140 | 36 (25.7%) | 16 (11.4%) |
| 2004 | 212 | 44 (20.8%) | 5 (2.4%) |
| 2005 | 260 | 34 (13.1%) | 9 (3.5%) |
| 2006 | 330 | 35 (10.6%) | 11 (3.3%) |
| 2007 | 402 | 26 (6.5%) | 15 (3.7%) |
| 2008 | 406 | 26 (6.4%) | 11 (2.7%) |
| 2009 | 456 | 25 (5.5%) | 7 (1.5%) |
| 2010 | 526 | 39 (7.4%) | 9 (1.7%) |

*Sources: China Film Yearbook 2005–2011* (Beijing: Zhongguo dianying chubanshe [China Film Press], 2005–2011); *The Research Report on Chinese Film Industry 2011–2013* (Beijing: Zhongguo dianying chubanshe [China Film Press], 2011–2013).

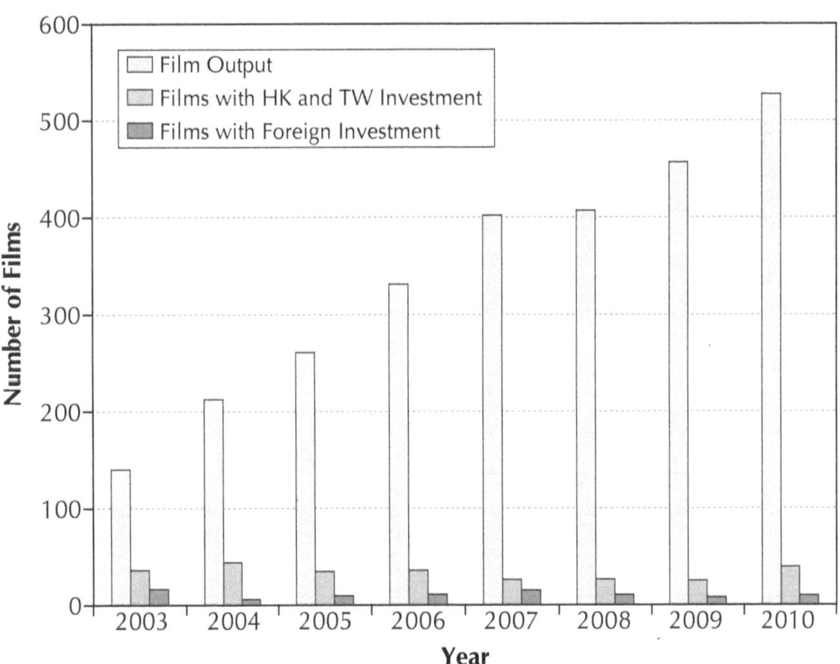


**Figure 1.3.** Film output and films cofunded by overseas capital (HK = Hong Kong; TW = Taiwan)

about 3 million Chinese households to have access to both recently released films and old titles. The company ultimately aimed to reach 200 million homes. Jim Wuthrich, Warner's president of international home video, said, "The opportunity of China is just too irresistible to most companies and particularly Warner Bros."[78] Global companies are eager to test China's waters, but up to now, they have all been subject to the Chinese government's strict restrictions.

A careful investigation of foreign investment in China's film production, based on *China Film Yearbook* statistics from 2004 to 2011, indicates that films cofunded by foreign capital constituted only a small portion of the total film output, and that portion was relatively stable during the eight-year period from 2003 to 2010 (see table 1.1 and figure 1.3). As such, although foreign capital flowed into China at an unprecedented rate, the number of films funded by foreign capital remained very small and stable. State-owned film studios maintained a strong presence and leadership through coproductions.

Official Chinese statistics show that, prior to 2003, more than 60 percent of revenue was earned from Hollywood movies, 30 percent from Hong Kong movies, and only 10 percent from mainland China movies. After 2003, domestic films, including both mainland and Hong Kong movies, shared the film market with Hollywood imports. It seems that the gov-

**Table 1.2. Market Share of Domestic Films, 2004–2013**

| Year | Market Share (%) |
|---|---|
| 2004 | 55 |
| 2005 | 60 |
| 2006 | 55 |
| 2007 | 54 |
| 2008 | 59 |
| 2009 | 66 |
| 2010 | 56 |
| 2011 | 54 |
| 2012 | 48 |
| 2013 | 59 |

*Sources: China Film Yearbook 2005–2011* (Beijing: Zhongguo dianying chubanshe [China Film Press], 2005–2011); *The Research Report on Chinese Film Industry 2011–2013* (Beijing: Zhongguo dianying chubanshe [China Film Press], 2011–2013).

ernment policy led to some positive outcomes. Accordingly, the Chinese government and film researchers cheered the triumph of domestic films and claimed that domestic films surpassed foreign imports in terms of box office receipts for eight consecutive years from 2004 to 2011 (see table 1.2).

Film Bureau director Tong Gang said: "It is not only a fact but an irreversible trend that state-owned studios, non-state and overseas investors jointly create domestic films."[79] However, are domestic films still *domestically made* films? Statistics from official documents indicate that most "domestic" films that boasted impressive box office returns were in fact coproductions with overseas producers and Hollywood stars. For example, the top five films of 2003 in terms of ticket sales were all coproductions funded by either Columbia Pictures Film Production Asia or Hong Kong companies. Among the top ten films that year, only three were solely produced by domestic and state studios. Similarly, the top eight films of 2004 were all coproductions funded by Columbia or by Hong Kong companies. In 2005 and 2006 the trend continued, and the scale of Sino-foreign cooperation expanded to an unprecedented level (see table 1.3). Producers of these top-ten films included Moonstone Entertainment and Ruddy Mor-

**Table 1.3. Number of Coproductions among Top Ten Films, Based on Receipts, 2003–2013**

| Year | Coproductions |
|---|---|
| 2003 | 7 |
| 2004 | 8 |
| 2005 | 8 |
| 2006 | 7 |
| 2007 | 10 |
| 2008 | 9 |
| 2009 | 7 |
| 2010 | 8 |
| 2011 | 6 |
| 2012 | 7 |
| 2013 | 5 |

*Sources: China Film Yearbook 2004–2011* (Beijing: Zhongguo dianying chubanshe [China Film Press], 2004–2011); *The Research Report on Chinese Film Industry 2011–2013* (Beijing: Zhongguo dianying chubanshe [China Film Press], 2011–2013).

gan Productions of the United States; Show East and Boram Entertainment Inc. of Korea; and Avex Inc., Gilla Company, and Toho Company of Japan. These films starred actors from mainland China, Hong Kong, the United States, and Japan. In 2007, all top-ten films were coproduced, cofunded, and globally distributed by overseas companies. As such, coproductions were major contributors to China's film revenue. Although they constituted a small percentage of the overall film output, their influence on audiences was tremendous, and their market share was enormous up to 2012.

The Chinese state has consistently tried to use global capital for the benefit of the domestic film industry and film market—whether using money earned from Hollywood imports to promote main-melody movies or allowing greater foreign investment. In the meantime, Hollywood has constantly pressured the Chinese government to lift the quota and open up the market. In 2012 the quota was increased to thirty-four imports and the shared revenue for foreign studios rose from 13 to 25 percent of ticket sales. These changes were cheered by major Hollywood studios and viewed as a significant victory for global Hollywood.

## Who Wins, and What Is the State's Role?

The Chinese government's evolving policy has resulted in a striking facelift for the domestic film industry. Chinese film professionals have not only emulated Hollywood's big-budget, high-tech model but also embraced Hollywood's distribution-exhibition system. Consequently, a strong market-oriented film industry has developed from production to distribution, and box office revenue has become the sole measure of a film's success. Replacing main-melody movies were overdone kung fu movies that combined spectacular Hollywood-style special effects with traditional Chinese cultural elements. This was the domestic film industry's most influential genre and its prime market attraction before 2013, and for the government, these films were an important component of Chinese "soft power." Works of social realism, in contrast, had been marginalized (I revisit this theme in chapters 4 and 5). Suffice it to say here that this trend significantly shaped the aesthetic tastes of the audience and the direction of the Chinese film industry. Accordingly, transnational, transregional coproductions have become the major contributor to domestic film revenue and the backbone of the domestic film industry to date. An intertwined partnership network is in the process of forming not only regionally in Asia but also globally.

The state actively engages in global communication, extensively advances its own agenda, and sustains the interests of the party-state. In its governance of the cultural industries, the Chinese state is characterized by its ability to bring both market forces and global capital under its control, its capacity to incorporate party ideology and the leadership of state-owned groups with private and global capital, and its status as both a policy maker and a market player—"both a referee and an athlete"—leading to a state monopoly of the film industry. Consequently, the state's essential role as a heavy-handed upholder of party-state interests surpasses its role as a market facilitator and industry regulator. During its long and complicated engagement with Hollywood, solidifying national identity and culture and maintaining the legitimacy of the ruling party have been the central concerns of the Chinese government. It is safe to say that the state has never lost control of either the domestic industry or the market. It is also safe to claim that the Chinese government was the biggest beneficiary of its own policy and a big winner in its tug-of-war with Hollywood-led global capital up to 2011. Between 1994 and 2011, the gross box office revenue from imported films totaled 22.468 billion yuan (approximately US$3.21 billion), including both American movies and movies imported from other countries. Even if *all* imported movies were considered Hollywood hits and revenue was shared at the rate of 13 percent, Hollywood took away only 2.9 billion yuan, or less than US$500 million, from China in total—significantly less than what it obtained from other parts of the world, thus demonstrating the Chinese government's negotiating capabilities.[80] Therefore, through its strategic and skillful negotiations, the Chinese government was able to prevent the domestic film market from being conquered by global media capital while making use of transnational partnerships to serve its own agenda. Through both an alliance and a tug-of-war with global capital, as well as the Greater China alliance, the Chinese state effectively consolidated its authoritarian and bargaining power.

Beginning in 2001, the state launched another round of reform, including the massive transformation of sixteen state-owned studios, as part of its overall updating of the domestic film industry. State-owned studios were first redefined as state-owned and state-controlled enterprises; they were then reorganized as film groups with shareholding companies. By 2007, the major state-owned studios had completed their entrepreneurial transformation, which involved personnel layoffs, enterprise group formation, and the establishment of their own theater chains. These reforms empowered state-owned studios to sharpen their competitive edge and ensured the backbone status of state-owned enterprises in an increasingly diverse and competitive world. For foreign studios, the reforms meant they would continue to face formidable challenges from Chinese studios and consistent and powerful state protection (I revisit this topic in chapter 3).

China's engagement with Hollywood is in fact a post–Cold War cultural war. Central to this war is who prevails and who maintains hegemony of the discourse. This is a fiercely contested battle. The Chinese state has fought very hard to negotiate its way through the general trend of going global. The difficulty lies in the fact that China has to observe the rules of the game imposed by its WTO membership, while it also tries to maintain control and protect its national identity and national interests. The latest agreement about lifting the film import quota indicates that, under the unrelenting pressure exerted by Hollywood capital, the Chinese state has had to compromise and make concessions. Although we can claim that the Chinese state was a bigger winner than Hollywood up to 2011, it is still too early to declare a win-win competition or the final victor. What we can be certain of is that the state has shaped both the domestic societal structure and the global cultural landscape. The Chinese state has also managed to reverse the power relationship in global communication.

# 2

# The Debate about Hollywood

The Chinese government and the Chinese nation are always concerned about the possible erosion of national culture and national identity. This central concern is evident in China's encounter with Hollywood and is typically reflected in the extensive debate over the symbolic meanings of Hollywood cinema. It should be noted that, from China's perspective, Hollywood movies are considered a "total cultural package" rather than a collection of diverse, individual products.[1] There are different interpretations of these films' symbolic meanings and their general connotations as a whole; accordingly, there are different understandings of American culture as represented by Hollywood movies. This has led to different cultural policies and strategies, which have tended to complicate the modernization of China's film industry.

## The Hollywood Cinema and Americanism

An explanation of the American way of life and the American spirit—or Americanism—is in order. According to Berndt Ostendorf, "Americanization *used to mean* a forcible assimilation to Euro-American standards" whereby immigrants who arrived in the first quarter of the twentieth century were implanted with American ideals, traditions, and ways of life. After the end of the Cold War, "Americanization implies a tacit and, increasingly, not so tacit exceptionalism which has been stabilized by the collapse of all other alternatives. In 1989 America moved from being *a* city upon a hill to the *only city* upon a hill, the only viable model of political (and perhaps cultural) modernity in the world." Ostendorf agrees that Americanization contains basic elements such as "westernization," "modernization," "technical innovation," and the "liberal market economy," as well as cultural industry and "American-style commodification"—all of which "gradually expand and fan out into globalization."[2]

Globalization has long been associated with Americanization. Many believe that globalization is merely a euphemism for US imperialism. From the perspective of political economy, global communication and the Americanized global culture represent the advancing army of American corporate capitalism.[3] The assumption here is that American popular culture in general, and Hollywood films in particular, explicitly and actively advocate American values and the American way of life, thereby threatening other national and local cultures. Therefore, Hollywood cinema becomes a key symbol of the American spirit. This association can be traced back to the inception of the motion picture industry. As early as 1923, Will Hays, president of the Motion Picture Producers and Distributors of America, stated: "Every film that goes from America abroad, wherever it shall be sent, shall correctly portray to the world the purpose, the ideals, the accomplishments, the opportunities, and the life of America. . . . We are going to sell America to the world with American motion pictures."[4] After the Second World War, the United States was emerging as a superpower, and the motion picture industry responded to the government's Marshall Plan to help promote the American way of life around the world.[5]

In 2001 Meryl Marshall, chairman of the board and CEO of the Academy of Television Arts and Sciences, declared: "Throughout the twentieth century, democratic and free market ideals were the cornerstone of American films successfully produced, exhibited, and distributed throughout the world. . . . Many of these American films and television programs have helped promote freedom and democratic values, the same values that encouraged throngs of people throughout the world to rise up and challenge repressive governments, contributing to the end of the Cold War, the destruction of the Berlin Wall, and the events in Tiananmen Square before the crackdown."[6]

It is clear that motion pictures, seen as "a consciously constructed liberal and popular New World utopia," are the most significant and successful ideological exports from the United States and an ideal instrument for Americanizing the world.[7] Therefore, the symbolic meanings of Hollywood movies, and the interpretation of the norms, values, and culture reflected in them, represent another focus of the debate in China. This focus is closely related to the thesis of cultural imperialism and the central theme of globalization theory—global cultural homogeneity and heterogeneity.

## Cultural Homogeneity versus Heterogeneity

The notion of cultural imperialism spread widely and influenced a variety of fields from the mid-1960s to the late 1970s. Advocated primarily by Latin American scholars and heavily influenced by Louis Althusser, Antonio Gramsci, and the Frankfurt School, this theory focuses on the relationship between the expansion of American capitalism and the extensive exportation of American mass culture. Proponents argue that American communication and cultural industries support the expansion of transnational corporations and become the advancing army of capitalism. Typical is Herbert Schiller, who claims that mass media are seen only as vehicles for corporate manipulation, and audiences are passive receivers for such manipulation and domination.[8] Although this notion has been widely criticized since the early 1980s, especially by "active audience" theorists and those espousing the idea of "resistance" supported by the ethnographic work of I. Ang and T. Liebes and E. Katz on *Dallas*,[9] Schiller has proposed the idea of a "total cultural package" rather than a single program or a particular genre to deal with the power of capitalist culture. He advocates study of the present-day "transnational corporate cultural dominance," in view of the intense opposition and resistance to such dominance. He believes that "today, the United States exercises mastery of global communication and culture."[10] Joining Schiller are other cultural critics who maintain that cultural imperialism is "a multi-faceted cultural process" that affects people through the "export and institutionalization of European ways of life, organizational structures, values and interpersonal relations, language and cultural products." Cultural imperialism is thus "the systematic penetration and domination of the cultural life of the popular classes by the ruling classes of the West in order to reorder the values, behavior, institutions, and identity of the oppressed peoples to conform with the interests of the imperial classes."[11]

Critics of the thesis of cultural imperialism claim that it "overstates external determinants and undervalues the internal dynamics," "conflates economic power and cultural effects," makes wrong assumptions about passive audiences and underestimates "local and oppositional creativity," and holds "an often patronizing assumption that what is at risk is the 'authentic' and organic culture of the developing world under the onslaught of something synthetic and inauthentic coming from the West."[12]

British cultural critic John Tomlinson proposes four ways of talking about cultural imperialism: as "media imperialism," as a discourse of nationality, as a critique of global capitalism, and as a critique of modernity.[13]

Despite much criticism, recent research has maintained that cultural imperialism's "most important contribution transcends criticism: the argument that power pervades in international communication processes."[14] Some argue that the general framework of cultural imperialism should not be dismissed. It is against this background that China's debate over Hollywood unfolded and quickly converged with the central theme of globalization theory: global cultural homogeneity and heterogeneity. This theme is closely related to the thesis of cultural imperialism, in the sense that global cultural homogeneity is considered a direct consequence of US cultural domination.

The discourse of cultural homogenization presents this state as "a consequence of globalization" and indicative of a global culture of "uniformity and ubiquity." This uniform and ubiquitous culture contains a common essence and is manifested in "a standardized consumer culture."[15] Whether globalization is considered an outcome of modernity or modernity is considered an outcome of globalization,[16] global culture is necessarily built on Western modernity based on the Enlightenment vision. This global trend theoretically assumes "the fundamental superiority and universal applicability of the project of modernity."[17] While acknowledging important elements of Western modernity such as reason and science, industrial capitalism, state administration through the rule of law, and citizenship rights as universal values, the discourse often implies that a free-market economy and liberal democracy are the cornerstones of a universal culture.

The discourse of cultural heterogeneity, in contrast, embraces notions of cultural complexity and interculturalism and corresponds to the postmodern criticism of the universal claim of the metanarrative of the Enlightenment vision. From this view, the triumph of Western modernity is merely the domination of one particular culture over another, and various local cultures are weighed equally in their paths to modern society. As Dilip Parameshwar Gaonkar has concluded, elements of "alternative modernities" are in fact embedded in every national and cultural site.[18]

Regarding the relationship among a global culture, American hegemony, and Hollywood films, cultural theorist Mike Featherstone has provided the best summary:

> Here a global culture was seen as being formed through the economic and political domination of the United States which thrust

> its hegemonic culture into all parts of the world. From this perspective the American way of life with its rapacious individualism and confident belief in progress, whether manifest in Hollywood film characters such as Donald Duck, Superman and Rambo, or embodied in the lives of stars such as John Wayne, was regarded as a corrosive homogenizing force, as a threat to the integrity of all particularities. The assumption that all particularities, local cultures, would eventually give way under the relentless modernizing force of American cultural imperialism implied that all particularities were linked together in a symbolic hierarchy. Modernization theory set the model into motion, with the assumption that as each non-Western nation eventually became modernized it would move up the hierarchy and duplicate or absorb American culture, to the extent that ultimately every locality would display the cultural ideals, images and material artifacts of the American way of life.[19]

Put another way, on the one hand, "homogenizers" privilege the temporal transition from tradition to modernity and more or less believe in convergent development; on the other hand, "heterogenizers" stress and cherish cultural difference and disclaim a universal system.[20]

In contrast to a sharp dichotomy between homogeneity and heterogeneity, I believe that the most plausible approach to the global cultural trend is one that emphasizes global interdependency, connectivity, and complex processes that involve "all sorts of contradictions, resistances and countervailing forces."[21] During these complex processes of cultural resistance and amalgamation, a new culture that is not easily incorporated into either the master (Western) cultural model or diversified local cultural traditions might be expected to emerge. Some scholars have used the term "new transnational third cultures" or "hybridity" to conceptualize this trend.[22] It remains to be explored what these third cultures mean to individual nation-states, their citizens, and global cultural exchanges.

Many theorists working in the globalization field agree that the fundamental issue is the relationship between cultural homogeneity and heterogeneity. For example, Arjun Appadurai contends, "The central problem of today's global interaction is the tension between cultural homogenization and cultural heterogenization." Roland Robertson and John Tomlinson share the same concern and insist on the centrality of the "global-local dialectic." Fredric Jameson raises the issue of universalization and particularization by discussing the experience of Americanization and American mass culture. He suggests that in Third World countries, where postmodernism, postcolonialism, and modernity often coexist, Americanization and American mass culture can be experienced as both a source of "liberation" from "hidebound state and national forms" and "a threat and a force of disintegration of traditions from which new and alternative possibilities might otherwise have been expected to emerge." He also suggests that, since the state power in Latin America, Asia, and Africa is often an unenlightened and oppressive one, Hollywood films sometimes become "the source of resistance to internal hegemony as well as the form external hegemony ultimately takes."[23]

The different interpretations of Hollywood films by China's various communities speak to this fundamental issue of cultural homogeneity and heterogeneity. Basically, there were two attitudes and discourses related to Hollywood cinema in China: left-wing intellectuals displayed completely negative attitudes toward Hollywood culture and often made derogatory comments about Hollywood movies, whereas audiences and liberal intellectuals had largely positive attitudes toward Hollywood and often expressed unreserved praise for Hollywood films. As time went on—and especially after 2001, when China joined the WTO—more scholarly studies of Hollywood culture began to appear.

## The State Policy on Hollywood Imports: Pro and Con

For the first six years of the Hollywood inflow (from late 1994 to 2000), various social forces competed for dominance of the discourse, the market share, and audience attention. Key players in this battle were the Chinese government, film distributors and exhibitors, filmmakers and directors, left-wing and liberal professors, journalists and film critics, and college students, as well as ordinary moviegoers who were largely urban dwellers. These social groups took different positions toward the state policy of importing Hollywood movies: Film distributors and exhibitors cheered market revitalization and economic gains, while ordinary moviegoers embraced Hollywood blockbusters and welcomed the competition. The majority of China's filmmakers and left-wing intellectuals, however, strongly opposed the importation of Hollywood cinema and advocated protection of the indigenous film industry.

Most Chinese film distributors and exhibitors strongly believed that Hollywood blockbusters would help revive the Chinese film market and raise national revenue through huge box office sales. Some journalists and liberal film critics also cheered the market revival brought about by Hollywood imports. They all allied with the Chinese government in the sanction of market supremacy, which served to justify the state policy of importing Hollywood movies.

The main player in the importation of revenue-sharing American movies was Wu Mengchen, general manager of the China Film Export and Import Corporation. Wu maintained that market success was the best reason to import Hollywood megaproductions. Once this economic benefit was acknowledged, all quarrels would subside and all sides would calm down. In addition to this economic triumph, the Chinese audience would benefit from Hollywood imports: "Now the Chinese audience are no longer second-class citizens in terms of their access to the world's outstanding movies," Wu said. "They can have access to excellent foreign films synchronously with foreign audiences. The history of the Chinese audience watching only outdated foreign films is gone."[24]

*Beijing Youth Daily*, the most popular newspaper among Chinese youth, was frequently overwhelmed by positive Hollywood reports from 1995 to 1998. Its main tone was that of hailing the success of the film market and the satisfaction of the Chinese audience. Its public forum for readers' opinions was often filled with praise for Hollywood movies. It championed the media coverage of Hollywood and became an unfailing supporter of the state policy on Hollywood imports.

Overall, those in favor of Hollywood imports considered Hollywood films a commodity, and transactions involving such a commodity could be expected to follow the rationale of a market economy and free trade. Box office success was therefore viewed as a success of the market economy. "The inflow of Hollywood films is a free market trade based on the freedom of choice of audiences," one film critic wrote. "The introduction of Hollywood films into China symbolizes social progress. Any restriction on free trade and on the freedom of personal choice is unreasonable."[25] Because Chinese-made films were generally of very poor quality, it was natural for Chinese audiences to turn to Hollywood films to satisfy their aesthetic and entertainment needs. Furthermore, most theaters and distribution companies were on the brink of bankruptcy, so the big gain in box office receipts from Hollywood movies would help them become financially self-sufficient and make quite a contribution to the national revenue.

The majority of ordinary Chinese moviegoers welcomed competition from Hollywood and believed in "the survival of the fittest." Their main arguments were as follows: China's film industry could benefit from Hollywood by learning its advanced skills and technology as well as its marketing and business strategies. At the same time, Chinese audiences could enjoy wonderful movies and broaden their knowledge of the outside world.[26] They believed Hollywood movies benefited China both economically and culturally and that the state's import policy was justified.

In contrast, the majority of China's filmmakers and left-wing intellectuals strongly opposed the importation of Hollywood cinema. They believed the inflow of Hollywood films would be disastrous for China's film industry and that the state should take responsibility for protecting it. As early as February 1994, soon after China's Ministry of Radio, Film, and Television announced the decision to import ten foreign megaproductions each year, prestigious Chinese director Xie Jin commented at the first conference of the Association of Chinese Film Directors that the competition was no longer among Chinese film directors but between them and Hollywood. "We are going to fight Hollywood together!" he said.[27] In the meantime, several hundred college students from the Beijing Film Academy, the most prestigious college in China for the education of film directors, cinematographers, and actors, issued an open letter calling for "resisting Hollywood!"[28]

## Hollywood Movies: Sex, Violence, and Moral Degradation?

Left-wing intellectuals severely attacked both the content and the monotonous format of Hollywood movies. According to these critics, Hollywood movies are, at best, stereotyped genre movies driven by huge capital investments, similar story lines or plots, popular movies stars, and spectacular gimmicks such as special effects. These movies cater to audiences' poor taste, providing only audiovisual pleasure and superficial satisfaction. Most Hollywood movies fail to provoke audiences to think profoundly about human beings and society or to explore the deeper meanings of life; they rarely display lofty human spirit or ideals. They are vulgar and clichéd commodities lacking in aesthetic value and philosophical depth—

merely "an entertaining fast food that aims to produce temporary fantasy and stimulations."[29]

At their worst, Hollywood movies are "spiritual opium," full of sex and violence. One critic wrote: "Western movies and television shows, represented by the United States, are fraught with pornography, violence and crimes in the name of reflecting social problems and exploring distorted human lives. After providing sensational stimulations, what these films leave for us is only restlessness, fear and lost hearts." Whereas Hollywood was once a world art center that portrayed things genuine, virtuous, and beautiful, contemporary Hollywood is immersed in exaggerated depictions of base human nature and serious social problems, including economic recession, violence, sex crimes, homosexuality, and drug addiction. "Among ten imported foreign megaproductions . . . , seven were from Hollywood. Except for *Forrest Gump* and *Lion King,* the others are all full of bloody murders, gunfights, and sexual temptations."[30]

The most derogatory comments about Hollywood were made by the authors of *China Can Say No.* In the chapter titled "Burn Hollywood," the authors describe the horrible scenes in the film *Natural Born Killers,* assail the moral degradation brought about by violent Hollywood movies, and call for "saving the children!" They write: "Violence comes to Hollywood movies as a natural manifestation of individual acts of heroism, while individual acts of heroism reinforce violence. This is the most common way of expression of Hollywood movies. Accompanying individualism is degraded hedonism. Because of serious social problems, like financial crisis, family crisis, racial discrimination, violent crimes, sex liberation and drug addition, American people are extremely pessimistic, confused and self-abandoned. All these down moods are tapped and exaggerated by Hollywood for profits."[31] These authors equate Hollywood movies with sex and violence, and they consider Hollywood cinema the epitome of degraded American culture.

## Hollywood Movies: Ideological Deception and American Hegemony?

Beyond the ubiquitous sex and violence, Chinese critics' deepest concern is the American cultural values and American way of life promoted by Hollywood movies. Critics argue that almost all American films attempt to spread the American spirit and the American dream. "American movies, collectively speaking, serve America's state interests," writes one critic. "There is hardly a single American movie that does not glorify Americans and propagate American values and the American way of life."[32]

In an article titled "How I View Hollywood," well-known film critic and theorist Dai Jinhua analyzes the negative impact of Hollywood on the indigenous film industry and calls for the Chinese to be alert to the imperialist nature of Hollywood's cultural invasion. Drawing on the thesis of cultural imperialism, Dai analyzes Hollywood's global strategy and points out that Hollywood movies are one of the major products of American transnational capital, supported by US political and military power. Hollywood has long coveted the huge Chinese market and wants to reap big money from it. Witnessing the great popularity of *The Fugitive*, *True Lies*, and other films, Dai writes, "Hollywood is the product of the 'U.S.-made' DreamWorks. It is the carrier of the 'American Dream' that is wrapped in 'the universal dream of human beings,' which is nothing but the American way of life and American ideology. . . . If there is an export called ideology, Hollywood is no doubt the most successful exporter. On the vast territory of developing countries, Hollywood has always been the advancing army of American transnational capital."[33]

Other researchers have gone deeper to explore the ideological implications of the American way of life. They argue that classic Hollywood movies usually have two deep-level structures to propagate American values: the manifestation of the American spirit, and the introduction of the "hero myth." This second structure serves the first by describing the United States as a "paradise on earth" where freedom, equality, and fraternity are achieved and justice is promoted by heroes. The purposes and ideals of these heroes are always correct and represent not only the wishes of the American people but also the desires of the peoples of all nations; "Independence Day" becomes the festival of the whole world. The exploitation and pillage, the huge disparities between rich and poor, classes, nations, and genders, are all masked by this splendid illusion. Calling these deceptions "an ideological illusion, a magic dream and a long-lasting myth," critics believe these images are intended to promote Americanism to a global audience and establish the hegemony of the American system. As such, the key mechanism of Hollywood ideology is "American supremacy." Boasting American exceptionalism, Hollywood movies always portray Americans as the world's police force and saviors, and they always exaggerate American-style glory and dreams.[34]

In the eyes of these critics, the American way of life and the American dream are ideological illusions that fool the Chinese people, endanger the Chinese cultural tradition, and destroy the spiritual home of the Chinese people. They worry that through such cultural infiltration, the Chinese people will lose both their collective national identity and their direction in a globalized world. Central to their concern is a deep-rooted "cultural anxiety" that can be summarized as follows: "If the American-style myth produced by Hollywood would undermine the Chinese people's self-identity while creating an "'American Complex'; if American-style individualism represented by Hollywood would deconstruct a national cohesion necessary for national development; if the trend for spectacular Hollywood movies would repress the concern for domestic living conditions; if consumerism promoted by Hollywood would exert a negative influence on cultural values of Third World countries; if the Hollywood model would completely replace Chinese narrative tradition; and if Hollywood would thoroughly destroy China's indigenous film industry."[35]

Simply put, the conflict between Hollywood cinema and China's indigenous cinema was a clash of cultural values and national identities. Therefore, Chinese intellectuals considered the safeguarding of indigenous films their top priority. With the goal of saving the Chinese film industry from being destroyed by Hollywood, some Chinese organizations launched a campaign of spontaneous resistance.

## Resistance to Hollywood

Conflicts between the top-down state policy and the bottom-up response to American movies are notable in the process of China's reception of Hollywood culture. One remarkable attempt to resist Hollywood power was made by China's influential magazine *Popular Cinema*. The magazine not only actively participated in the debate about the importation of Hollywood cinema but also consciously introduced various strategies to counter US hegemony. Starting in January 1997, *Popular Cinema* published a series of articles about the measures adopted by Australia and various countries in Europe, Latin America, and Asia in their battles with Hollywood. The first article, which featured the sensational headline "Be Alert to the Hollywood Invasion—European Filmmakers' Outcry," spotlighted the actions taken by France, Britain, Germany, Italy, and Sweden to protect their national film industries and resist Hollywood domination. These articles maintained that the battle between Hollywood and other nations' film industries was a conflict between different cultures, traditions, and values and therefore reflected a clash of civilizations.

Furthermore, the magazine attempted to desanctify the Academy Awards. Between 1996 and 1997 it ran two columns that exposed the dark side of Hollywood and its Oscar-related scandals. The editors stated explicitly that their intention was to remove the aura of the Academy Awards and give the Chinese people a comprehensive picture of Hollywood, in the hope that this would reverse their obsession with Hollywood movies and their overzealous admiration of American culture. Among the cases exposed were the following: the shocking purge of communists in Hollywood during the McCarthy era; the framing of Hollywood magnate Alexander Pantages for rape, orchestrated by his business rival Joseph P. Kennedy between 1929 and 1931; the dirty history of Kennedy's capital accumulation in Hollywood; the racketeering case against studios by the gangster-controlled Hollywood union between 1934 and 1941; the lascivious gatherings of teenagers hosted by famous Hollywood actor Lionel Atwill in 1941; and Marilyn Monroe's suicide. These events strikingly revealed the dark and dirty side of Hollywood and its stars, alerting the Chinese audience to these deceptive images.

The resistance launched by *Popular Cinema* came to an end in June 1997 with a published interview with the deputy director of the Film Bureau, Dou Shoufang. In the interview, Dou repeated two state policies: the Chinese government strongly endorsed the activities launched by various nations against American cultural hegemony, and the Chinese government intended to learn from the successful experiences of foreign countries in developing a national film industry. Developing China's film industry would require opening up to the outside world without ostracizing foreign culture, and the Chinese government had already taken steps to protect the national film industry. Dou held that it was reasonable to import foreign movies, as long as they accounted for only a small portion of all films circulated on the Chinese market. The importation of excellent foreign films would both entertain the Chinese people and enhance the national revenue.

## The Chinese Audience's Response to Hollywood Hits

Liberal film critics and journalists, as well as ordinary moviegoers and movie fans, strongly endorsed Hollywood movies and the values and humanist ideals they portrayed. Specifically, critics acknowledged the following universally sanctioned values: the humanism and humanitarianism displayed in Steven Spielberg's *Saving Private Ryan* and *Schindler's List;* the heroism, goodwill, and struggle for freedom portrayed in *Braveheart, Titanic,* and disaster films like *Twister* and *Deep Impact;* and other cardinal virtues such as honesty, loyalty, friendship, family responsibility, and love featured in films like *The Bridges of Madison County, Toy Story,* and *The Lion King.*

Spielberg's blockbuster *Saving Private Ryan* was a perfect example for a discussion of humanitarianism. The Chinese audience commented that despite the realistic demonstration of the bloodshed, cruelty, misery, and inhumanity of war, the film still portrays human nature at its best and great humanitarianism. Deeply touched by the movie and the story, they commented that the film provoked them to rethink their values and the meaning of life. "It is not the issue of whether it is worth it to use eight lives to save one life," one moviegoer said. "It is the issue of humanitarianism that should be carried on. To save Ryan is to save a family's faith in America."[36] "The film is so shockingly human," said one journalist in an interview. "The whole story line is covered by the touching atmosphere of humanitarianism, manifested in the great respect for a mother, a family and for an ordinary life."[37] In after-show interviews, many movie fans strongly approved of the spirit of self-sacrifice and helping others reflected in the movie, and some of them explored the implications of the movie more deeply. One person commented, "To save Private Ryan is not only a task, a unique filmic plot. It should be our ultimate thinking at the end of the century—how to save human beings' souls in the war or in gray daily life from philistine materialism and insignificant desires."[38]

Chinese movie fans and reporters also highly praised the heroism and human spirit represented by outstanding Hollywood films such as *Braveheart* and *Titanic. Braveheart*'s serious theme, spectacular scenes, and heroic spirit garnered positive evaluations. Film critics argued that the Scottish people's heroic struggle for freedom, led by William Wallace, was an invaluable legacy for all human beings. Wallace's personality, spirit, and unyielding fight for freedom and justice will long be cherished by people all over the world.[39]

The global hit *Titanic* also created a huge stir in China. The film was covered extensively by the media, with *Beijing Youth Daily* contributing five articles on the film in one week. In addition to the moving theme of true love, the newspaper especially praised the film's striking individual acts of heroism in the face of disaster. The core ethic behind these acts is to value life and to uphold moral principles, yet to behave heroically by sacrificing oneself to save others. Examples include Jack's heroic death to save his lover; the insistence of a dignified, elderly gentleman that he would stay on the sinking ship; the captain's loyalty to duty; and the band's last performance as the ship went down. In summary, the film functioned as a "soul saver" to push audiences to reflect on their own inner worlds, confront ugly social phenomena, and meet the challenges of life's harsh journey.[40]

Disaster films like *Twister* and *Deep Impact* also provided good opportunities to dramatize the triumph of the human spirit when faced with a natural disaster. Besides the films' audiovisual shock, the characters' upbeat, optimistic, and persistent struggles with nature were highly approved by Chinese film critics. Such films illustrate that, when faced with a difficult and challenging environment, the best of the human spirit comes shining through and is glorified.[41]

The Chinese audience seemed to believe that Hollywood megaproductions reflect true human feelings and commonly held human values. Therefore, Chinese filmmakers should learn from Hollywood. As one movie fan concluded, "Only those films that speak directly to our heart can arouse deep resonance among us Chinese audiences. Chinese filmmakers, please care about human beings."[42]

Although a majority of the Chinese audience found Hollywood blockbusters very enjoyable and believed they represent universal human values, others contended that these blockbusters were merely carriers of the American ethos and full of American propaganda in disguise. Some of the reviews of *Saving Private Ryan* and *Forrest Gump* supported such an argument. Taiwan's Long Yingtai argued that *Saving Private Ryan* depicts the human nature of only Americans, not others, including Germans. She emphasized that a founding principle of the United States is individualism and individual dignity. However, "all praises to human nature are accompanied by flying American flags that appear both at the beginning and at the end of the film. Oh, it turns out that all praises are attributed to the State! What on earth do you praise? Individualism or state supremacy?" She wrote: "*Saving Private Ryan* is but another fine-made American propagandistic movie for patriotism. . . . American culture, American values, American self-feelings and worldviews are hereby transmitted to the whole world through such a commodity."[43] As such, Long Yingtai believed that American supremacy is the film's major theme, rather than humanitarianism.

In May 1999, because of NATO's accidental bombing of the Chinese embassy during air strikes in Yugoslavia, *Saving Private Ryan* came under severe attack. Chinese audiences, shocked and saddened by the death of three Chinese journalists during the bombing, felt betrayed. They believed the humanitarianism portrayed in *Saving Private Ryan* was hypocritical and propagandistic and that the United States employed a "double standard" in dealing with its own citizens and citizens of other countries. As a consequence of the bombing, American blockbusters were prohibited in mainland China for six months. This incident reflects the fragile relationship between the two countries and the close connection between cultural appreciation and sociopolitical contexts.

*Forrest Gump* also generated two distinct opinions. Radical film critics argued that the film reflects the mainstream ideology of American society and is a triumph of American conservatism. Dai Jinhua published a long article devoted to an ideological critique of the film. Drawing on the "state ideological apparatuses" theory of French Marxist Louis Althusser and the "hegemony" thesis of Italian Marxist Antonio Gramsci, Dai argued that *Forrest Gump* is the perfect instrument for the representation and reproduction of mainstream ideology. Through a detailed textual analysis, Dai pointed out that the film's review of forty years of American history deliberately downplays and distorts the two most important historical movements: the civil rights movement and the women's movement. For instance, the film makes absolutely no mention of the political murders of Martin Luther King and Malcolm X. And the feminist movement is negatively portrayed through the bitterly rebellious journey of Jenny and her redemption by Forrest's true love. Thus, these two movements are disdained in a subtle way, whereas the traditional values represented by Forrest Gump eventually triumph. Dai also argued that the film exaggerates the racial reconciliation between blacks and whites through Forrest's friendship with "Bubba"; it promotes a mainstream American dream through hard work while neglecting the existence of serious racial discrimination and other social problems. In conclusion, and citing similar American film reviews, Dai called the film a successful, timely, and sweet fairy tale that serves as a cinematic redemption of Americans' lost national identity and glory resulting from the US defeat in Vietnam and years of racial conflict.[44]

Other radical critics agreed that the film signals the return of American conservatism. It satirizes liberalism, identifies with traditional principles, and promotes patriarchal family values that eventually accommodate and recuperate feminist rebellion. They argued that the film directly and explicitly praises American conservatism and the American value of down-to-earth hard work, as represented by Gump. Further, it implies, through Jenny's son, that this American tradition will be passed on to future generations.[45]

However, most film critics and fans quite enjoyed *Forrest Gump* and found that it offered thought-provoking fodder for the Chinese people. They spoke highly of Gump's honesty, virtuousness, unconditional love, and loyalty to country and friends—values that are rarely seen in the morally degraded modern society yet are full blown in the mentally challenged Gump. Many Chinese audiences were deeply touched by the display of these attributes. They also praised Gump's positive attitude toward life and his persistent struggles with fate.[46] Finally, they explored the film's implications for contemporary China and even for global modern development. One reporter wrote: "In the contemporary society that is filled with naked hedonism, greedy pursuit of money and power, as well as rampant sex, drugs and violence, Forrest Gump's honesty, persistence, promise keeping, and loyalty to love set a great role model for people. China is now experiencing a similar path to a modern society like America did many years ago, and we often lose our direction and the code of conduct in a rapidly changing society. The film can provide us with profound implications as to how to live an honest life without greed and frivolousness."[47] The film was also considered an allusion to modern Western society's moral crisis and a reflection of the relationship between tradition and modern civilization, thus having profound implications for China. "Although China does not have a Protestant tradition and capitalist cultural background, the Chinese audience is deeply touched by the film," wrote one critic. "Perhaps this is exactly the film's significance to China. It serves as a signpost that points out a way for our consideration, that forces us to reflect on our own limitations, on the relationship between tradition and modernity, as well as on the assertion that history is a kind of lineal progression."[48]

The preceding analysis of *Forrest Gump* and *Saving Private Ryan* highlighted two distinct opinions about the meaning of Hollywood movies: one believed in the universality of Hollywood movies and their implications for China; the other emphasized the propagandistic and hegemonic nature of Hollywood movies. At this point, the Chinese government's stance was crucial in determining the fate of Hollywood movies in China, and it has maintained a very clear and relatively stable attitude toward Hollywood cinema and Western and American culture since its adoption of an open-door policy in the early 1980s. This attitude, which has prevailed for thirty years, is not fundamentally different from the Chinese government's attitude of the previous thirty years (1949–1979), despite economic reforms and social changes taking place in China and the world. The government's attitude has heavily influenced and even dictated ordinary Chinese people's understandings of Western and American culture. This stance, which has been held by different regimes since the Qing Dynasty and the Opium War, can be summarized as follows: "We'll take their technology and keep our culture."[49] In this regard, the stance of the Chinese Communist Party has been consistent with past regimes.

When former Chinese president Jiang Zemin commented on *Titanic* in March 1998, his remarks were highly publicized and widely cited. Jiang said the film portrays the relationship between money and love, between rich and poor, and it depicts the behavior of various people in times of peril and emergency. He also recalled that before 1949, when the People's Republic of China was established, he had watched quite a few "good" Hollywood movies such as *Gone with the Wind, Waterloo Bridge,* and *A Song to Remember.* He invited the members of the Political Bureau to watch *Titanic* not because he wanted "to promote capitalism" but for the purpose of "knowing your enemy better in order to beat him." Jiang reminded party officials, "We should never think that we are the only ones who know how to persuade people."[50]

Although it was widely believed that Jiang's comment exposed his preference for Hollywood movies, it also revealed Chinese leaders' deep-rooted preconception of the evil of capitalism. As discussed previously, they used state power to promote so-called main-melody films and warned the nation to be alert for "foreign cultural infiltration and poisoning." In this regard, the Chinese government and one side of the debate—radical film critics and intellectuals—actually reached an alliance, upholding the Chinese value system against the Western cultural invasion and cooperating closely in an effort to produce Chinese-value films.

Yet *Titanic* and other Hollywood blockbusters obviously taught the Chinese government how to improve domestic films and propagate the party ideology more effectively. Acknowledging the persuasive effect of Hollywood, Jiang and other Chinese officials admitted that capitalist propaganda may be even more powerful than China's socialist propaganda. Therefore, they hoped Chinese filmmakers would use Hollywood's artistic expression, diversified styles, and technology to promote main-melody movies that could beat American movies loaded with Western values. For example, Han Sanping, CEO of the China Film Group, mentioned years later in an interview that he greatly admired Mel Gibson's *The Patriot* and that this was the kind of film China should be making.[51]

After 1997, the debate on the validity of the government's policy on Hollywood imports subsided, yet the discussion and academic analyses of the symbolic meanings of Hollywood movies continued. At the turn of the twenty-first century, the discussion became heated again as China's reentrance into the World Trade Organization (WTO) approached.

## To Be or Not to Be? WTO and the Debate over China's Film Future

On December 11, 2001, China formally joined the WTO after years of negotiation with the United States. Under the term of the agreement, the annual quota for revenue-sharing imported films was increased from ten to twenty, and foreign investors were allowed to own up to 49 percent of the shares in Chinese film companies. Echoing Dai Jinhua's predication that the "wolves are here," another leading professor and film critic from the Beijing Film Academy, Zheng Dongtian, used Hamlet's famous soliloquy, "To be or not to be," as the title of his article about the critical challenges faced by China's film industry after joining the WTO.[52]

Joining Dai and Zheng, other leading Chinese communications researchers and film critics conducted many in-depth analyses of Hollywood's global hegemony and China's possible strategy. First, they pointed out that the United States, as the world's number-one "superpower," wields political, military, and economic might that supports Hollywood's global triumph. In global exchanges, a political and economic imbalance inevitably results in a cultural imbalance. US power helps establish the superior status of US culture and pushes other countries to identify with it. This imbalanced relationship is the driving force for the global diffusion of American culture.[53]

Second, they argued that the US government always serves as a "bodyguard" and a logistical support for Hollywood's global expansion. A review of Hollywood history reveals close cooperation between the Hollywood film industry and the US government. Between the establishment of the Motion Picture Export Association of America and World War I, the US government adopted a variety of means to promote American movies, pop songs, and other mass cultural products. During and after World War II, Hollywood films served the government's political agenda by artistically creating an antifascist and anticommunist atmosphere. Donald Duck and other Hollywood visual images were considered just as powerful as the Marshall Plan. By selling the American way of life to the world, Hollywood contributed to the US government's ideological battle, and the US government granted massive support to the film industry. With the end of the Cold War, Hollywood's global economic interest was put on the government's agenda during its attempt to build a new world political and economic order as well as a new international information order. Market access for Hollywood movies was a heated topic during WTO negotiations between the US government and other countries.[54] Obviously, the US government has always been a mighty supporter of global Hollywood.

Third, Chinese researchers analyzing Hollywood's global strategy, and especially its strategy in China, maintained that Hollywood studios are drawn to China's huge market and potential for economic profit, calling it an untapped "gold mine." China's place in this polarized world cannot be underestimated, with its irresistible market of 1.3 billion people. As entertainment analyst Jeffrey Logsdon commented in April 1994, "If only one percent of the [Chinese] people go [to movies] and you only charge one-fiftieth of the admission that you'd charge here, you still get to some pretty big numbers."[55] Hollywood magnates expected China to surpass Europe and Japan and become the world's second largest film market, with US$120 million a year in receipts and a fifteen-fold increase, by 2015.[56] Actually, by 2012, China had already passed Japan to become the world's second largest film market, behind only the United States. To access the China market, Hollywood has employed a series of strategies, including investing in film production, distribution, and circulation sectors; integrating Chinese cultural themes and characters into Hollywood movies; attracting talent from mainland China and Hong Kong to Hollywood; and cultivating Chinese audiences' taste for Hollywood movies. With these strategies, Hollywood expects to reap huge economic profits and eventually conquer the entire Chinese film market. Because this would result in the destruction of China's indigenous film industry, scholars have called for specific steps to prevent foreign films from overwhelming the domestic market.

If the domestic market is surrendered to Hollywood, they argued, China's national film industry will be beyond redemption.

However, another group called this concern about Hollywood "pathological paranoia" and questioned the necessity of building a cultural "Maginot Line" to resist Hollywood. Typically represented by Gui Qingshan, a professor at Beijing Normal University, this group included liberal film critics, journalists, and professors. In accordance with China's ordinary moviegoers' admiration for Hollywood hits, they believed Hollywood films are cultural treasures and an excellent representation of modern artistic masterpieces. They advanced several arguments. First, historically, Hollywood has depended on the participation and joint efforts of talented individuals from various countries—Charles Chaplin, Ingrid Bergman, Vivien Leigh, Audrey Hepburn, Nicole Kidman, and Ang Lee, to name a few. Artists from various nations have contributed colorful characters and added to the glamour of Hollywood. Therefore, to a certain degree, "Hollywood culture . . . is an epitome of world cultures. It is filmmakers and artists from western and eastern Europe, North and South America, as well as Japan, Iran, India, Hong Kong, Taiwan, even mainland China that co-create the contemporary universality of Hollywood."[57]

Second, Hollywood movies at different historical periods are representations of collective human wisdom and cinematic achievement. For example, in the 1920s Chaplin's progressive comedies profoundly revealed the evils of a capitalist society, depicted the alienation of human nature, and assaulted totalitarianism and despotism. During the 1930s and 1940s numerous outstanding movies, including *Casablanca, Waterloo Bridge, It Happened One Night,* and *Citizen Kane,* described lofty and genuine human feelings, praised patriotism and antifascism, and explored the meaning of life. During the 1940s and 1950s film noir (French for "black film") was popular, a type of Hollywood crime drama with a black-and-white visual style. Other films, such as *Rebel without a Cause* and *The 400 Blows,* portrayed the so-called lost generation and included a strong touch of social criticism, reflecting the deep conflicts within American society. During the 1970s and 1980s films like *Kramer vs. Kramer* and *Terms of Endearment* described ordinary people's life journeys, while *Platoon* and *Born on the Fourth of July* profoundly reflected the wounded and divided American psyche caused by the Vietnam War. Entering into the 1990s, blockbusters like *Forrest Gump, Schindler's List, Braveheart,* and *Titanic* were all zealously welcomed by people all over the world. In other words, good Hollywood movies describe true human feelings and represent universal values and moral standards that are shared by all human beings without regard for national boundaries.

In conclusion, this group contended that culture cannot be "invaded"; "culture can only exchange, integrate and transform through its own logic." If a foreign culture is well received by other nations, it must contain factors that speak to those other nations' cultural consciousness and spirit. The successful diffusion of Hollywood culture worldwide is attributable to the common ground shared with other nations. "Modern thoughts can only triumph through wide resonance in those factors that accord with the trend of social history and with basic human nature. . . . No matter Western or Eastern cultures, superpower culture or developing countries' culture, traditional culture or modern culture, they all share some common grounds on which modern society and modern civilization are built."[58]

Other researchers have tried to compromise, arguing that Hollywood cinema is the carrier of both the American spirit and a universal cultural legacy. In *Chinese Movies in Post-Hollywood Ages* and *Hollywoodism,* university professor Lan Aiguo analyzed the symbolic meanings of Hollywood genre films and outlined the mechanisms through which Hollywood ideology works. He argued that in addition to American supremacy and American spirit, another mechanism of Hollywood ideology is Western values and standards, including democracy, freedom, humanism, and individualism. These are, in fact, universally sanctioned notions. However, "once these notions become an absolute judgment imposed on any social circumstance, they are turned into a kind of language hegemony and a suppressive force to complex social realities."[59] Hollywood makes use of this ideological hegemony to repress independent film productions whose themes are incompatible with mainstream ideology and to marginalize nonmainstream films such as *Apocalypse Now.* Therefore, Hollywood is a fiercely contested venue as well. Wrapped in these universally sanctioned forms, these notions have become Hollywood's method of camouflaging America's state interest and imposing American hegemony.

A third mechanism, and the core of both Hollywood ideology and Americanism, according to Lan, is individualism and individual acts of heroism. American supremacy, American spirit, and a sense of being the world's savior are all reflected in Hollywood heroes' charisma and individualism. Patton, Superman, Rambo, John Wayne, and others, particularly in westerns, represent the ideal stereotype of the American hero and rugged individualism: they are brave, determined, honest, filled with integrity, selfless, hardworking, and fighters of the bad guys; they always serve justice and ensure law and order. They are the safeguards of the American dream, the practitioners of the American spirit, and the achievers of the American way of life. In Hollywood movies, conflicts between these individuals and the system are solved, and the American way of life is saved. After a series of battles, American individualism eventually prevails.

Lan and other scholars also contended that, from its birth, Hollywood absorbed elements of other cultures and became a melting pot for international talent and capital. However, Hollywood products are always "distinctly imprinted by American culture and spirit."[60] It is this sophisticated nature that determines the complexity of global cultural exchanges. "On one hand, the cultural power of Hollywood movies is manifested in its effective adoption of world cultures and in the fact that they have become all human beings' cultural legacy; on the other hand, Hollywood movies are a carrier of American culture, American spirit and Western values."[61]

Furthermore, film historians have pointed out that during the early period of republican China (1919–1949), Hollywood represented advanced culture and modernity. The birth and development of China's indigenous film industry, in this view, were directly influenced and stimulated by Hollywood. In addition to being a school where China's first and second generations of filmmakers were self-trained, Hollywood movies constituted an important part of China's urban life. Going to the cinema "became both the source and symbol of modernity" during the 1930s and 1940s.[62] At that time, the cultural values and worldview reflected in Hollywood films were in accordance with modern Shanghai's cosmopolitan mentality, satisfying the needs of an urban lifestyle. Some values even accorded with traditional Chinese ethical and moral standards. "Therefore, as 'The Other' of Chinese culture, Hollywood both deconstructed and reconstructed traditional Chinese culture. As an important medium, Hollywood films to a larger degree became a driving force of China's modernity."[63] Hollywood cinema was thus a double-edged sword—exporting the American way of life, on the one hand, and accelerating the nascence and development of China's indigenous film industry, on the other.[64]

The question became, how could China's film industry survive, given that Hollywood functioned as both a "savior" for China's film market and a "teacher" for China's filmmakers? Gradually, researchers acknowledged the universality of Hollywood and observed that Chinese movies would also have to reflect universal themes in order to compete in the world market. In a 2002 book titled *Globalization and the Fate of Chinese Film and Television,* Chinese scholars agreed that multiculturalism and universality were the main cultural reasons for Hollywood's successful global diffusion. The key for Chinese movies' success, it was argued, was the adoption of universally appealing themes and common human concerns—life and death, love and hatred, civilization and nature, war and peace, and so forth.

The debate gradually subsided, but there appeared to be no agreement. With the new government policy and newly emerging circumstances, opinions shifted gear.

## "Dancing with Wolves" or a Win-Win Situation?

Between 2001 and 2005, the Chinese government issued several sets of new regulations to ease limitations on film production and distribution by private and overseas investors. As a result, transnational film corporations flowed into China, and both film output and revenue reached record highs. Meanwhile, the distinction between "domestic" and "foreign" films became increasingly blurred, and "transnational cinema" prospered.

This trend created confusion and new challenges for those who advocated resisting Hollywood and protecting the domestic film industry. "Hollywood's transnational production mode and its development in China will result in a situation of 'dancing with wolves.' The so-called 'resistance to Hollywood' and 'the protection of national cinema' will face a dilemma and confusion," one scholar wrote. "The wolf is already in the blood of sheep, and the wolf's genes will change the attributes of sheep. The concept of national cinema or domestic films will be challenged by a concept of transnational cinema or a concept of 'Greater China' cinema; and Chinese cinematic culture will undergo a fundamental change."[65]

Others predicted a win-win situation, or "copetition" (cooperation in competition), which speaks directly to the intertwined nature of coproductions between Hollywood and China. Under these circumstances, both Hollywood and China would benefit and make money together. "Chinawood" might even challenge Hollywood.[66]

Starting in 2003, China launched a wholesale program to transform its cultural industries. The state called for emancipating cultural productive forces and developing a "socialist advanced culture." It later (2006) borrowed Harvard professor Joseph Nye Jr.'s concept of "soft power" to refer to the significance and influence of Chinese cultural industries. The government hoped to enhance Chinese cultural power and facilitate China's strong global presence by expanding its cultural influence, compatible with China's economic power.

The Chinese film industry and researchers had to adjust their positions to toe the state policy line and justify the relationship with Hollywood once more. From 1995 to 2000, the mainstream tone had been confrontation and protection, and the thesis of cultural imperialism prevailed. After 2001, the mainstream tone became "dancing with wolves," and an emphasis on universality seemed more prominent. After 2006, in accordance with the idea of "soft power," even scholars who had originally advocated protecting the domestic film industry against Hollywood hegemony held that Chinese films should reflect universality, common values, and human nature. Furthermore, they supported "compromise" and "yielding" to foreign producers to achieve a larger national benefit in return.[67] This theoretical shift resonates with the uncertainty of the state cultural policy and indicates China's ambivalent and vague cultural vision.

## *Kung Fu Panda* and Its Opponents

The thesis of cultural imperialism has had a profound and long-lasting impact on China and is deeply embedded in the mentality of left-wing Chinese intellectuals. Although the Chinese government, the domestic film industry, and the media all shifted gears to welcome Hollywood imports and to make strategic use of Hollywood capital for the purpose of national development in the twenty-first century, anecdotal resistance to and attacks on American imperialism have led to eye-catching stories during China's irreversible process of globalization. These are typified by the responses to *Kung Fu Panda, Kung Fu Panda 2,* and *The Karate Kid.*

The director of *Kung Fu Panda,* Mark Osborne, allegedly worked on the story line for five years and spent more than thirty years studying Chinese culture. He referred to *Kung Fu Panda* as "a billet-doux to China." The movie is a marriage of two distinct Chinese cultural elements—kung fu and the panda—as well as a brilliant and humorous animated film. It led foreign imports in China in box office receipts in 2008, netting more than 180 million yuan (roughly US$25.7 million) from China and US$630 million from the world.[68] *Kung Fu Panda 2* continues the warm and humorous style of its predecessor with a new story line involving the Chinese tai chi philosophy of "inner peace." On the day it premiered in Nanjing, May 28, 2011, the film netted more than 40 million yuan (about US$6.35 million). The filmmaker disclosed that the goal was to make 600 million yuan in the Chinese market (US$95.2 million).[69]

The extremely popular film and its sequel evoked a nationalist response among a few Chinese leftist intellectuals, both in 2008, after the Wen Chuan earthquake in southwestern China, and in 2011. The leader of the two resistance events, Zhao Bandi, an avant-garde artist, organized a protest in front of the office building of the State Administration of Radio, Film, and Television on the morning of June 16, 2008. The protesters held a banner with the slogan "No Tolerance to Hollywood Gold Grubbers in Aftershock China! *Kung Fu Panda* Goes to Hell!" Zhao submitted an open letter to SARFT in which he lashed out at Hollywood celebrities such as Sharon Stone, who had infuriated millions of Chinese by saying that China's earthquake was "karma." Zhao charged that "Hollywood is a place that applauds the arrogance, hypocrisy and immorality of people like Sharon Stone" and noted, "Hollywood has never changed during the past decades; it has always been a cultural hooligan and cultural bandit." He went on to say that the screening of *Kung Fu Panda* in China's theater chains was akin to "grubbing necklaces and watches from earthquake victims." Referring to *Kung Fu Panda* as "stealing Chinese national treasure and kung fu to make money," Zhao called for its immediate cancellation. Tong Gang, director of the Film Bureau, met with Zhao and other protesters and talked with them for twenty minutes. Tong said that although the bureau understood the protesters' feelings, since *Kung Fu Panda* had cleared the censor, the decision to screen the film was up to the distribution and exhibition units. Zhao later indicated that the protesters were satisfied with the official response, but he suggested that the film's screening be delayed or canceled in the Sichuan earthquake area out of respect for the people there. On June 19, 2008, Zhao announced on his blog that Zhou Baolin, the Film Bureau's director of marketing, had informed him that all theaters in Sichuan Province would temporarily delay the screening of *Kung Fu Panda*. Accordingly, at 8:30 p.m., five theater chains in Chengdu announced that the animated film would not be shown. Echoing Zhao's protest, a small number of people had gathered in front of one Chengdu theater to oppose the screening of the cartoon. However, the majority of messages posted on Zhao's blog were against his resistance. One person from Sichuan stated that he had been looking forward to watching *Kung Fu Panda* and was very disappointed by the delay. Others accused Zhao of attempting to obtain personal gains by attacking an American film.[70] Other parts of China were not influenced by Zhao's protest, and the film opened nationwide on June 22, 2008.

Many considered Zhao's protest radical and ridiculous. Film director Lu Chuan said in his blog that "the cartoon brings overwhelming joy. The laughter it sent is so precious in disaster-packed China. When can our Chinese cartoon industry produce a good film like this? *Kung Fu Panda* is almost perfect from the perspective of film production." He also asked Zhao Bandi to "spare Panda Po."[71] A TV anchor argued that the cartoon's universal values and cherishing of Chinese culture made it an upbeat, thought-provoking film that resonated with Chinese audiences. He ridiculed Zhao for using the cartoon to make a name for himself, saying that Panda Po had actually helped make "a celebrity from a third-class artist." The anchor concluded that Zhao's attack on *Kung Fu Panda* had more to do with personal gains than art. Finally, the anchor lamented the domestic film industry's inability to represent Chinese culture, commenting that *Kung Fu Panda* should make all Chinese filmmakers and fans feel ashamed because, this time, Hollywood truly understood Chinese culture.[72]

Zhao Bandi launched another protest when *Kung Fu Panda 2* was scheduled to open in China in the summer of 2011. In May he sent letters to managers of theater chains all over China, asking them not to show the film. He also placed advertisements in newspapers that called for audiences to resist this 3D blockbuster. This time, his efforts were joined by a leftist professor from Beijing University, Kong Qingdong, and the director of the Beijing Film Academy's School of Animation, Sun Lijun. Kong Qingdong wrote in his blog, "Hollywood robs Chinese symbols and uses your own symbols to conquer you. . . . Hollywood not only makes money out of you, it also intends to brainwash you and conquer your heart." Sun Lijun said, "*Kung Fu Panda 2* grubs Chinese elements and fools Chinese in the name of loving Chinese culture. Its so-called 'billet-doux to China' and 'protection of Chinese culture' are all lies."[73] At the Tenth Cartoon Award ceremony held by the Beijing Film Academy on May 29, Zhao, Kong, and Sun issued a joint letter to parents and children, urging them to "go outside to see Mother Nature, but not *Kung Fu Panda 2* on June 1st, Children's Day." They were opposed not to Panda Po, they claimed, but to the invasion of foreign culture. "We cannot let our children develop an instinctive dependence on American culture from very young ages," said Zhao. But similar to three years earlier, their protests did not create much of a stir. Most fans disagreed with them, and some brought their entire families to watch the movie; most theater chains ignored them. The Chinese official voice, meanwhile, was silent.

Press and intellectual circles continued to view Zhao's acts as motivated by personal gains. *China Youth Daily* referred to the resistance as "Utopians' coquetry and favor-currying" by resorting to outdated ideological criticism.[74] Cheng Manli, deputy director of the School of Journalism and Communication at Beijing University, wrote in an article, "When we are not able to do our own job well, the so-called resistance to 'cultural imperialism' sounds like an excuse to escape responsibility."[75] Dr. Li Kaisheng from Xiangtan University in Hunan Province commented in an interview with *Voice of America* that *Kung Fu Panda*'s popularity can be attributed to the integration of Hollywood technology and Chinese cultural elements that resonate with the Chinese audience. The film is a superior exemplar of the marriage between the East and the West. Another famous Chinese writer told *Voice of America* that a few people's negative attitudes toward the cartoon should not be viewed as a common phenomenon and a mainstream trend. *China Review News,* a Hong Kong–based digital news agency, published a long article stating that the resistance to *Kung Fu Panda* is "fake patriotism" because it is, in fact, "protecting one's own commercial interest in the name of patriotism." The Hong Kong–based *South Morning China* also published an article arguing that no one can ultimately possess a culture; the most popular culture will transcend national boundaries.[76]

History often repeats itself. The debate over Hollywood movies and American culture in China may go on for several more decades. The latest resistance speaks to the lingering influence of the long-standing conflict between Western-American "universal" values and local Asian-Chinese values—or the conflict between so-called universalism and particularism. Another debate over Hollywood hits involved the remake of *The Karate Kid,* which was harshly criticized by some Singaporeans. The film relates the journey of an African American boy (Jaden Smith) as he learns Chinese kung fu, fights bullies, develops friendships, and eventually wins a kung fu contest. Those Singaporeans considered the film "a disgrace to the Chinese" because a black boy is depicted as a hero who defeats all the Chinese boys, while the Chinese boys are portrayed as cold-blooded bullies.[77] This disapproval did not gain wide acceptance and had few repercussions in mainland China.

## China's Search for a New National Identity

Arjun Appadurai once pointed out the disjunctures between different global flows, which create an uncertain landscape in a rapidly globalizing world. The disjuncture in global cultural flows is the most remarkable one. China's debate displays this cultural disjuncture, even as the country seeks to be integrated into the global economic system. The different positions taken in the debate foreground this cultural disjuncture and theoretical issue.

Among the different interpretive communities in China, the radicals highlight the negatives about Hollywood; they criticize Hollywood cinema's representation of US hegemony and express anxiety over the Americanization of Chinese culture and the loss of national identity. The liberals emphasize the positives; they cite the universality of Hollywood culture and modernity and believe that Hollywood might enlighten the national cinema and national culture. These dissenting positions also resonate with Professor Zhao Yuezhi's suggestion of a clash between "the Chinese nationalist and culturalist perspective" and "the liberal democratization perspective."[78]

However, if one looks a little deeper, one finds that no matter which perspective a group of people holds, they are all painstakingly seeking a better solution for China's cultural vision and national direction. My contention is that China's debate over Hollywood cinema actually serves as a reference for the Chinese people to make sense of their own modernization process and national identity. The debate, in a broad sense, has little to do with Hollywood cinema in the US context, but it has much to do with the implications for China. Different groups of Chinese at different times have used Hollywood cinema to define what China is and where it should go in the future. Therefore, the entire debate is about China's quest for a new, modern national identity and how the Chinese people can draw on the American experience to build a modern China. The fundamental theme hidden beneath this great debate is, in fact, the issue of modernity and alternative modernities. The debate is about different social groups in China searching for a new national culture, national identity, and Chinese alternative modernity in a rapidly globalizing world. Is there any alternative to Western, American, capitalist modernity? This question has long been a focus of left-wing intellectuals around the world. In China, Mao's revolution opened up a path to an alternative modernity beyond capitalism—

socialist modernity. The communist party-state set up a goal to accomplish the so-called four modernizations—namely, agriculture, industry, national security, and science and technology—to catch up with the United Kingdom and the United States. Through a planned economic system and a centrally controlled administrative power, a modern industrial system was established during the 1950s and 1960s. However, the socialist experiment with modernity largely failed owing to endless and extremely brutal political persecutions, power-related strife, and the fanatical and preposterous "economic leap forward." All this led to the collapse of China's national economy by the end of the 1970s and forced Deng Xiaoping to adopt a reform-oriented open-door policy to gradually integrate with the global capitalist system. In the West, left-wing intellectuals, witnessing the alienation of human beings, the rampant power of global capital, and the widening gap between the rich and the poor, are also sincerely looking for an alternative. What, then, is the implication of China's debate and its search for an alternative?

Since 1949, China's cultural front has never been independent of politics; it has always been part of the country's political ideology and has always served the official propaganda agenda. From 1950 to 1978, Mao Zedong employed a revolutionary cultural policy that stifled cultural diversity and plurality. During the reform era initiated by Deng Xiaoping—from the anti–bourgeois liberalism campaign and the anti–spiritual pollution campaign of the 1980s to the bloody repression of the 1989 student democratic movement—China's cultural policy has consistently attempted to repress any liberal democratic views and to uphold official Marxist-Maoist ideology, and the culture industry served this purpose. The New Enlightenment movement, initiated by intellectuals, played a major role in the cultural debate in the 1980s, during which time most Chinese intellectuals showed unreserved admiration for the Western Enlightenment view and modernity. The cultural debate and the movement, however, were brought to an end by the political repression of 1989.

Some scholars have claimed that Deng Xiaoping's strategy was to integrate China into the capitalist world system only in the economic and technological sectors, that there was never a clear acknowledgment of capitalist norms and values in the political, social, and cultural spheres.[79] Furthermore, Deng banned any theoretical discussion of the ideological nature of reform in his 1992 tour of South China. Consequently, China's cultural policy was inconsistent and ambiguous entering the 1990s.

Because the decision to import Hollywood movies was based largely on economic considerations, the cultural and political implications were underplayed by the state, either unintentionally or deliberately. Therefore, the state policy lacks "cultural vision, ideological assertiveness, and political legitimacy."[80] This circumstance not only provides China's "cultural workers" room to maneuver but also makes the debate on the meaning of Hollywood cinema possible. Accordingly, the debate as a site of the reception of American culture discloses China's cultural dilemma and its confusing national identity. Consequently, the entire Chinese society is in a state of disorientation. The debate went nowhere, and the same can be said of China's cultural and ideological direction, up to now. This theoretical confusion has become a practical dilemma that has severely affected the development of China's indigenous film industry and reflects China's ambivalent perspective on globalization.

# 3

# The Film Industry as Negotiation of Space

Both China's cultural policy and the debate about Hollywood can be viewed as instances of resistance to the domination of global capital and American culture. This chapter traces the formation of mainland China's film industry, embodying production, distribution, and exhibition. I argue that this has been a government-sponsored, top-down process combining market forces and heavy governmental intervention. The process is another counterhegemonic strategy adopted by the Chinese government in its confrontation with global Hollywood to negotiate operating space for the domestic film sector. The growth of the domestic film industry has profoundly impacted China's development and reshaped the global cultural landscape. On multiple occasions, Chinese officials have used the phrase "going to sea by borrowing a boat" (*jie chuan chu hai*) to refer to their strategy of making use of global production and distribution networks to promote Chinese films. By taking advantage of Hollywood's networks, theater chain system, and capital, while maintaining control of state-owned studios, China has successfully advanced its domestic film production.

## Chinese-Style Theater Chains: The Reform of Film Distribution and Exhibition

After 1949, China's film sector copied the Soviet Union's model of state-owned film studios and a vertical, multilayered system of distribution and exhibition characterized by many administrative and regional barriers. People living in countries with free-market economies and private ownership often find it difficult to understand how this model worked. Under this system, film production studios and distribution-exhibition units were not independent, profit-making enterprises; they were subordinated to state administrative entities at various levels and received operating funds allocated by the state. Before 1993, the system was configured in a four-tier vertical layout: the top level was the state-franchised China Film Export and Import Corporation (CFEIC); the second tier comprised film distribution companies at the province and autonomous region level; the third tier consisted of film distribution companies at the city level; and the fourth tier included film distribution companies at the county level. To be exhibited in theaters, a film had to pass through all four tiers of this distribution structure. The revenue earned from ticket sales was shared among these tiers, as well as with the film studios and theaters. Because the distribution units received larger shares of revenue, film studios and theaters were frustrated and discouraged by this model. Nevertheless, this system fed the distribution companies' more than 500,000 employees and benefited their affiliated state administrative departments during the long period of a planned economy.

However, many problems arose after the nation's intensified marketization reform. Although Document 3, issued in 1993, aimed to end the forty-year model of vertical distribution, studios still faced strong regional protection and local monopolies and found it very difficult to recover production costs and make profits. The distribution companies at every level were backed by local governments that wanted their share of film distribution revenue. For example, CFEIC usually purchased its quota of ten foreign imports from foreign distributors and then gave these movies to distribution companies at the provincial level, which in turn delivered the movies to distribution companies at the city level, which delivered them to theaters. Through this multilayered distribution process, CFEIC secured 46 percent of the gross box office revenue, including the royalties paid to foreign distributors and CFEIC's fee for the distribution rights. The disbursement of the remaining 54 percent was determined by negotiations among provincial and city distribution companies, as well as theaters. On average, theaters and city distribution companies retained 36 to 42 percent of the revenue, while provincial distribution companies, which did nothing but serve as middlemen, acquired 12 to 18 percent. Provincial and city distribution companies were dependent on each other: The provincial companies had no theaters; they were franchised by the state only to purchase and distribute movies. The city distribution companies had their own theaters, but they were not allowed to purchase movies directly; they could receive prints only from provincial distribution companies. This odd relationship sustained the film distribution system for many years before 1993. Predictably, Document 3, which aimed to eliminate these layers and allow studios to bypass the provincial distribution companies and issue prints directly to city distribution companies and theaters, encountered strong resistance from the provincial distributors throughout the country, making it almost impossible to implement.

A typical example of local resistance to Document 3 is the short-lived "Jiangsu breakthrough." In 1993 the state-owned Beijing Film Studio negotiated—unsuccessfully—with the Jiangsu provincial distribution company to distribute the very popular Jet Li kung fu film *Once upon a Time in China III: The Invincible Shaolin.* Recognizing the film's market potential, four third-tier distribution companies in Jiangsu Province, including the Suzhou city film distribution company, negotiated with Beijing Film Studio to distribute the film in Jiangsu. As a result, both Beijing Film Studio and the four distribution companies earned remarkable box office returns. The four distribution companies then established the Suzhou Film Service Center to distribute films at a low service charge. This initiative bypassed the provincial distribution company and negotiated directly with film studios, which professionals in the film industry considered a breakthrough. Nevertheless, the Jiangsu Provincial Cultural Administration sided with the Jiangsu provincial distribution company and prohibited the four city-level distribution companies from becoming film distribution agents. Consequently, the "breakthrough" was short-lived, and both film studios and distribution companies nationwide remained in financial crisis.[1]

While the government took a pragmatic stance with regard to importing Hollywood blockbusters to pay for domestic film production, a structural overhaul of the film sector started in the mid-1990s as well. At that time, the Film Bureau under the State Administration of Radio, Film, and Television (SARFT) faced a divided and disjointed national market that had been carved into various regional administrations under the protection of local governments. Determined to get rid of the financial burden and improve the performance of the film sector, the Film Bureau resolved to "fight bloodily for a path" leading to reform of the distribution-exhibition chain, aiming for a radical breakthrough that would establish a unified national film market and eliminate regional and administrative barriers.[2]

This radical breakthrough came with the introduction of the theater chain system in mainland China. Originally invented by Adolph Zukor, head of Paramount from 1915 to the 1930s, the theater chain system is a central component of Hollywood's studio system. Under this arrangement, film producers align with a number of theaters to exhibit their films, sharing costs, profits, and risks. It is Hollywood's primary mode of film distribution and exhibition and constitutes Hollywood's "vertically integrated power."[3] After 1993, when Document 3 mandated an intensified institutional reform of the film sector, Chinese distribution companies in various provinces made numerous attempts to break through the monopoly of local governments and form chains to profit from film distribution. The earliest example was the successful experiment with theater chains in Shanghai. China's biggest metropolis had once been a film production center, and Hollywood movies accounted for almost 75 percent of the local film market before 1949. The introduction of theater chains clearly speaks to the influence of the Hollywood business model.

With 13 million permanent residents and, by 1995, an additional 3 million migrant workers, Shanghai constituted a huge film market. It also had fifty-eight well-equipped theaters, a unique advantage for the establishment of a unified film distribution mechanism. In the early 1990s two major film distribution companies, Yongle and Dongfang, started to experiment with theater chains. The Shanghai Municipal Film Distribution Company was transformed into the Yongle Shareholding Company Ltd., with the approval of the Shanghai government, in late 1992. By then, 75 percent of its shares were owned by the state, 18.1 percent by legal persons, and 6.9 percent by former employees. It had nearly twenty subcompanies and was the first shareholding company in mainland China's film sector.[4] It developed four affiliated theater chains based on different audience segments, film genres, and theater conditions: Heavenly King, with six superb theaters; Star, with nine major theaters; Sunlight, with fifteen newly built theaters; and Moonlight, with fourteen small theaters. At the same time, Dongfang aligned with seven cinemas and six theaters to form its own chain. By July 1995, Yongle and Dongfang had become the two major theater chains in Shanghai, competing with each other and breaking the local monopoly. The Shanghai experiment first shocked and then enlightened the country, laying the foundation for the implementation of theater chains nationwide.[5]

Meanwhile, in Beijing, the New Film Alliance Distribution Company, a joint venture of the Beijing Municipal Distribution Company, CFEIC, and dozens of theaters, was established on a trial basis in 1996. The new company distributed prints directly to Beijing theaters, thus breaking the monopoly previously held by the Beijing Municipal Distribution Company. Since the Municipal Distribution Company was one of the shareholders of the new company, and since most of its employees were rehired by the new company, the transition went smoothly, with little discord.[6]

In addition, Beijing Zijincheng Company, a joint venture of the Beijing television station, Beijing Television Art Center, Beijing Film Distribution Company, and Beijing Literature and Art Video/Audio Press, was established on April 9, 1997, with the sanction of the government. Beijing Zijincheng was allowed to combine production, distribution, and exhibition, which broke the monopoly of sixteen state-owned studios and created a new model of film production based on "production on demand."[7] This model targeted local markets and produced films based on market demand. It prioritized distribution and exhibition and guaranteed the market return on investment. However, the model remained subject to regional barriers and operated only in the local area.

These experiments in Shanghai and Beijing were later labeled the first stage in the trial reform of the film distribution system. The ultimate goal was to break through local monopolies.[8]

The second stage of experimentation focused on restructuring film distribution companies and creating competitive theater chains. Beyond Beijing and Shanghai, distribution companies throughout the country actively engaged in market-oriented trials in an attempt to transform the multilayered distribution system. In Jiangsu Province, the Jiangsu Changjiang Film Company Ltd. was set up in the first half of 1996, integrating the provincial distribution company with eleven city distribution companies, with the aim of moving toward a group that combined production, distribution, and exhibition. The new company strengthened its competitive power when CFEIC became a shareholder at the end of the year. In Zhejiang Province, eleven new large-scale theaters were built to form a theater chain, and the provincial distribution company agreed to grant a portion of its revenue to city companies and theaters. In Fujian Province, twenty-three theaters and the city distribution company established a joint venture, with 70 percent of the investment contributed by the provincial distribution company.[9]

Sichuan Province in southwestern China was among the first to reform its distribution system. Sichuan Southwest Film Company Ltd. was established in October 1995; its twenty-three shareholders included distribution companies at the provincial, city, and county levels. As such, the established hierarchical relationship among distribution companies was transformed into a reciprocal partnership. In 1999 the new company developed its own theater chain with twenty-three theaters. In 1998 a second distributor, the Sichuan Ermei Film Distribution Company, was established by shareholders Ermei Studio, Chendu Municipal Film Distribution Company, and Chendu Huaxie Theater. The two distribution companies engaged in a fierce competition that involved renovating theaters, reducing ticket prices, and providing better service to audiences. This provided a valuable model for launching similar reforms nationwide.[10]

The third stage was the launching of a cross-provincial theater chain. For example, the Northeast China Theater Chain was established in April 2001, comprising seventy distribution companies in three provinces. In inland China, the Hebei Zhonglian Theater Chain Company Ltd. was set up, joined by seven distribution companies, one film studio, and seventeen exhibition units in Hebei, Shanxi, and Inner Mongolia Provinces.[11]

To better learn from Hollywood's business model, the Film Bureau sent a delegation of theater managers to the United States and Singapore between September and October 1997. The delegation visited Warner Bros., Sony-Columbia, Disney, and Universal, as well as five multipurpose theaters. Upon its return to China, the delegation made the following recommendations to SARFT: Transregional shareholding theater chains should be established in China as soon as possible, and film groups combining production, distribution, and exhibition should be set up on a trial basis. Meanwhile, multipurpose theaters should be built along freeways, and old theaters in big cities should be renovated. Foreign investment in both film coproduction and theater construction should be permitted and more actively pursued, and the government should enact more accommodating and supportive policies to create broader, freer space for domestic film production.[12] In addition, the Film Bureau sponsored a number of lectures and seminars aimed at educating film professionals about the theater chain system.[13]

These experiments provided valuable insights into how a Chinese-style theater chain system might work. With the formidable challenges facing China after joining the WTO, the prolonged crisis in the film sector, and the swift reform of cultural industries in the twenty-first century, the theater chain system was formally and forcefully implemented by the state at the end of 2001.

In June 2000 SARFT and the Ministry of Culture jointly issued Document 320, proposing the establishment of film groups and the implementation of a theater chain system.[14] On December 18, 2001, the two entities jointly promulgated Document 1519, covering regulations to implement the structural reform of film distribution and exhibition.[15] Document 1519 makes a number of stipulations. First, CFEIC, now affiliated with the newly established China Film Group, would be the sole company authorized by SARFT to import foreign movies. A second shareholding distribution company, Huaxia, would be established to share the responsibility with CFEIC of distributing domestic movies overseas; this new company would not be allowed to import films, however. The two companies' main mission was to promote domestic films by taking advantage of the revenue earned from imports. They were required to distribute at least twenty domestic films each year, including twelve major main-melody films. The two companies were also obligated to turn over 7 percent of the total box office revenue of every imported film to CFEIC to support the production of special categories of films made for peasants, for children, and for educational purposes.

According to the explanation provided by the Film Bureau, the Huaxia Film Distribution Company had been established to break CFEIC's monopoly and encourage competition, as the earlier experiment had found that a market monopoly hindered the development of Chinese films. But because CFEIC was the sole company allowed to import movies, it still had a monopoly. It was the sole source of imports for distribution companies nationwide, which often paid CFEIC fees of up to 90 million yuan. The Film Bureau rationalized that without the compensation earned from imports, local distribution companies would be reluctant to distribute domestic films, and financially, CFEIC was unable to shoulder all the responsibility for promoting domestic films. However, in reality, Huaxia was only allowed to distribute domestic films overseas, and CFEIC's status did not change. Huaxia, chaired by the former CEO of CFEIC, did not pose any real challenge to CFEIC. The only benefit of this move was to add one more company to promote domestic films; it did not encourage competition so much as it supported the overseas distribution of domestic films.

Second, Document 1519 required that the theater chain system be implemented to eliminate multiple layers in distribution networks and to remove administrative and regional barriers. It mandated that two or more theater chains be set up in each province or each big city, and it encouraged cross-provincial theater chains. Those regions that had not established theater chains by June 1, 2002, would be denied access to any revenue-sharing film imports. The regions of Beijing, Shanghai, Jiangsu, Zhejiang, Hubei, Hunan, Guangdong, and Sichuan were required to set up two theater chains by October 1, 2002, or be denied film imports.

Third, the document provided that nonstate capital investment was permitted in shareholding theater chains, and foreign capital investment was allowed for theater renovations. The Film Bureau declared that "no time can be wasted in implementing the theater chain system as a breakthrough of market reform. We must fight bloodily for a path."[16]

The establishment of a theater chain system in China was a top-down measure sponsored, mandated, and forcefully implemented by the government. This led to an odd marriage between governmental power and market forces. Various provincial and city distribution companies, urged by SARFT's working teams, were quickly restructured into theater chains before the deadline set by Document 1519. Some of these chains were formed by merely changing the names of the original distribution companies. Mao Yu recalled that from January to June 2012, supervisors and cadres from the Film Bureau frequently flew around the country to expedite the transition of local distribution companies into theater chains and to negotiate terms with local governments. These supervisors often met one another during their travels and exchanged details about their respective experiences.[17]

The Film Bureau claimed that the theater chain system was an ineluctable imperative for the reform of China's film market. This system was a complete rejection of the multilayered distribution model of the planned economic system. However, because of the government's heavy and direct intervention, Chinese-style theater chains did not emerge naturally out of market competition, as the Hollywood studios and Hong Kong's Shaw Brothers had; rather, they came about through governmental maneuvering. The weak market contribution and strong governmental regulation of the Chinese-style theater chain system resulted in some remarkable problems in the early stages. Newly established theater chains took over the previous market share with their change of title, but private companies could not really challenge the major theater chains because resources were still controlled by the former state-owned distribution companies turned theater chains. Theater chains lacked autonomy because they had no right to distribute imports and share revenue. Indeed, they could not even select which films to show; they had to accept whatever prints CFEIC and Huaxia issued to them.[18] Unlike Hollywood and Hong Kong studios, mainland China's theater chains were not an inseparable part of the studio system and did not contribute to its vertically integrated power at an early stage of their development. Vertically integrated power was truly explored only a few years later, when both state-owned and private studios underwent restructuring and established film groups to integrate production, distribution, and exhibition.

Most professionals in China's film industry acknowledge the necessity and significance of the theater chain system. They believe it has had a positive impact on China's film market. First, the system breaks through regional and administrative barriers that existed under the planned economy, eliminating the multiple layers and operating based on market demands. Second, the system enables a more reasonable redistribution of revenue among the production, distribution, and exhibition sectors. Theaters have the right to join chains and retain more revenue. Third, the additional revenue enables theaters to implement technological renovations; more multifunctional cinemas have begun to emerge, and they account for the biggest box office receipts. Fourth, as revenue increased, the distribution companies paid off debts of approximately 30 million yuan owed to the China Film Group, and they helped raise 2 million yuan for a special film fund. Further, a computerized ticket-sale network is installed in every cinema that joins a chain, which prevents theaters from falsely reporting receipts and evading taxes. By 2003, one year after the implementation of the chain system, thirty-five theater chains, comprising 1,106 cinemas and 2,197 screens, had been set up in twenty-five provinces and cities. However, despite all these benefits, the national film market remains polarized, with 20 percent of theater chains taking in more than 80 percent of box office receipts. Theaters that were unable to join a chain before the deadline, as well as 80 to 90 percent of old cinemas in poor, remote, and rural areas, were excluded from the system and could not benefit from imported and domestic hits.[19]

In January 2004 SARFT promulgated a new document encouraging cross-provincial chains and nonstate shareholders in order to accelerate the restructuring of theater chains.[20] In the same year, the number of theater chains increased to thirty-six, with 1,188 participating cinemas and 2,396 screens. This growth increased the demand for film production and more effective film distribution, which encouraged private film distribution companies and led to the rapid rise of private film companies such as the Bona Film Group. A new round of film policy reform between 2003 and 2004 led to a new wave of theater renovation and foreign capital investment, which greatly enhanced the competitive edge of various theater chains and facilitated the quick emergence of large-scale film exhibition groups such as Wanda, Xingmei, and Xin Ganxian. With the initial three-year contract signed by participating theaters set to expire in 2005, the time for restructuring theater chains nationwide had finally arrived.[21]

The turning point for China's theater chain system was reached between 2005 and 2006. Before 2002, no single cinema had annual ticket sales of more than 30 million yuan, and fewer than ten cinemas boasted sales of more than 10 million yuan. By 2005, however, four cinemas had ticket sales of more than 30 million yuan, and forty-one surpassed 10 million yuan.[22] Beginning in April 2005, eleven theater chains, 31 percent of the nationwide total, underwent restructuring and reorganization, which led to the emergence of several major regional theater chains: Xingmei, which was affiliated with CFEIC, covered nineteen provinces; Shanghai Lianhe encompassed six provinces and twenty-two cities; the Beijing-based Xinyinglian extended to northern China; and the northeastern-based Wanda aimed for a broad national market.[23]

In 2003, the first year the theater chain system was mandated, only two chains had annual box office receipts of more than 100 million yuan—Shanghai Lianhe and Xinyinglian. In 2004 CFEIC-affiliated Xingmei joined them. Two years later, the number increased to eight with the addition of Nanfang Xinganxian, Wanda, Jinyi Zhujiang of Guangzhou, Shidai of Sichuan, and Taipingyang of Sichuan. By 2009, the number had skyrocketed to fourteen, and Wanda led the pack with 830 million yuan in box office revenue. In 2010 twenty registered theater chains, 57 percent of the total, boasted annual box office receipts of more than 100 million yuan; Wanda again topped the list with 1.4 billion yuan. Thus, in 2010, a single theater chain's receipts surpassed the entire country's gross box office revenue from just eight years earlier.[24]

The development pace of the theater chain system and the market potential unleashed by it have been astounding. The number of cinemas joining chains jumped from 827 cinemas and 1,581 screens in 2002 to 2,107 cinemas and 6,256 screens in 2010, a growth rate of 106 and 239 percent, respectively. The number of 3D screens increased from 82 in 2008 to 2,020 in 2011, and there were 27 IMAX cinemas in 2011, compared with only 1 in 2003.[25] Statistics indicate a 17.9 percent increase in the number of theater chains in 2012, with the total number of theater chains and screens nationwide reaching 46 and 13,118, respectively.[26] In 2013 the number of screens increased by 5,077, or nearly 40 percent, to reach 18,195 nationwide.[27] In 2013 the top ten theater chains with more than 700 million yuan in box office receipts were Beijing Wanda, Shanghai Lianhe, Xingmei (with CFEIC), Guangdong Dadi, Nanfang (with CFEIC), Guangzhou Jinyizhujiang, Zhejiang Shidai, Beijing Xinyinglian, Zhejiang Hengdian, and CFEIC Digital.[28]

The state has used its administrative power to mandate the establishment of the theater chain system in China and intervene heavily in the creation of a national market. As Chinese media scholar Michael Curtin notes, "markets are made, not given."[29] The difference is that the Chinese state is directly involved in and is a key facilitator of the national market. As a result, the flourishing theater chain system created a huge demand for movies, and the limited number of Hollywood imports became the major supply and a source of competition among theaters. As mentioned earlier, domestic film production had not benefited much from reform of the film distribution system. Accordingly, the state's next move was to take action in the production sector. The goal was to revitalize state-owned studios and bring in private capital in order to exploit the vertically integrated power and bridge the severed links between production and distribution.

## The Reform of State-Owned Studios

From the 1950s to the early 1980s, China's film industry followed the Soviet model. Under the planned economic system, state-owned studios did not engage in film distribution and were not concerned about selling their films. CFEIC had full responsibility for the distribution of films, and studios received state subsidies to pay for film production.

The state-owned studios functioned as a "big and whole" (*daerquan*) unit within the planned economy. Each studio was composed of various film production departments as well as various logistics departments covering a number of diverse areas, including housing and accounting services, hospitals, cafeterias, grocery stores, and kindergartens. Studios were said to have "everything but a crematorium."[30] In addition to the daily expenses of film production, overburdened studios had to cover the salaries and provide for the welfare of a large number of employees. For example, Changchun Film Studio, the oldest state-owned studio in China, employed about 4,570 people in the early 1980s. Among them, only 800 were film professionals who produced an average of seventeen movies a year; the others were workers and administrative assistants in logistics departments. The studio's daily expenses reached nearly 40,000 yuan. Similarly, Shanghai Film Studio had 2,574 employees, including 555 film professionals who produced fifteen films annually. Even if not a single film was produced, the studio needed operating capital of 15 million yuan.[31] After the initiation of economic reform, the film sector was redefined by the state in 1984: studios were still considered public institutions, but ones that should use entrepreneurial management.[32] Film studios were now responsible for their own economic efficiency and received only limited government subsidies to cover their operating capital. By the end of the 1980s, the average production cost for each movie had reached nearly 1 million yuan, but state subsidies for studios did not increase. For example, Beijing Film Studio received a state subsidy of 3.8 million yuan in 1984, based on production costs of 380,000 yuan for each feature film, and the subsidy was frozen at that level. In 1988 the studio faced a shortage in operating capital because the gap between rapidly rising production costs and the state subsidy had reached 10 million yuan. Furthermore, the studios' share of profits from film distribution were inadequate, with the largest portion going to the multilayered distribution units. Between 1985 and 1988, studios' gross profits dropped by 76 percent—from 63.83 million yuan to 15.28 million yuan; the number of debt-ridden studios rose from one to six. The average production cost for each feature film increased by more than 67 percent during these four years, whereas the sale price increased by less than 10 percent. In 1989 more than one-third of studios, more than 900 of the 2,300 county-level distribution companies, and about 1,000 of the 3,100 urban theaters were in debt.[33] Six thousand film-related enterprises either closed or converted to other businesses. Take Changchun Film Studio as an example: from 1997 to 2004 the studio was able to pay its employees a monthly wage of only 300 yuan (less than US$40).[34] Even worse, the number of tickets sold dropped by 12.6 billion from 1979 to 1991, leading the entire domestic film industry to the brink of bankruptcy. Although many attempts were made to turn things around in the 1980s and 1990s—from the redistribution of print profits to the introduction of Hollywood blockbusters to compensate domestic studios—the domestic film production sector did not undergo a fundamental overhaul until China rejoined the WTO.

To fulfill its WTO promises and overcome the financial bottleneck of state-owned studios, China finally addressed reform of the film production sector in 2000 with Document 320.[35] In this document the state proposed a shareholding system to transform state-owned studios and establish large-scale film groups. The essence of the document's provisions was to speed up the establishment of major conglomerates through the restructuring of affiliated institutions and the relocation of resources, using former state-owned studios as their cores. The film conglomerates would employ a vertical integration model, combining production, distribution, and exhibition. The document also clearly stipulated that conglomerates would be under the control of the Communist Party and that party secretaries would sit on the board of directors or act as legal representatives of the state-owned and state-controlled shareholding conglomerates. This document marks the wholesale commencement of reform in the film sector, and it was entirely state initiated and state-designed. During two conferences held in January and March 2001, SARFT mandated the establishment of three major film groups in the north, east, and northeast, using the extant Beijing Film Studio, Shanghai Film Studio, and Changchun Film Studio as their cores. Another three film groups would follow based in Guangdong, Sichuan, and Shaanxi Provinces, extending the reform into central, southwestern, and northwestern China.[36] The China Film Group was the first to be established, in February 1999; three more film groups were created by June 2003—Shanghai Film Group, Changchun Film Group, and Xiaoxiang Film Group. By June 2008, the Western Film Group and Zhujiang Film Group had been established, bringing the total number of large state-controlled conglomerates to six.[37]

SARFT issued a series of mandates designed to guide the transformation. These regulations stressed the state-owned nature of film studios while pushing the studios to address market competition. These regulations reflect the dual status of state-owned studios as both representatives of state interests and for-profit entities, commensurable with the general goal of promoting cultural industries as an important part of a "socialist market economy." During this long and painful period of transformation, the state employed a variety of administrative measures, mandatory orders, market layoffs, and state compensation. The transformation included enterprise licensing, studio restructuring, and personnel and payroll changes. The last exacted the greatest human toll on the path toward marketization.

The goal of personnel and payroll changes was to transform former socialist state employees into free-market laborers. A market competition system was introduced to employ and reemploy filmmaking professionals and actors, while the retired, the disabled, and nonprofessionals were provided for through a combination of layoffs and state compensation. In China, a "layoff" is not the same as a layoff in capitalist market economies; workers who are laid off are not unemployed but are transferred to other positions, sometimes at a reduced salary. For example, China Film Group currently has 2,400 active workers on its payroll and 1,500 retired workers. Every year the group allocates more than 26 million yuan to pay the salaries and medical and living expenses of its retired employees, while reemploying most of the professionals. During the transformation, the Shanghai Film Group reassigned more than 1,000 people, the largest personnel shuffle in its history. The Changchun Film Group reassigned 1,300 people; in addition, 580 retired early and 418 were laid off, thus reducing the group's personnel from 3,000 to 800. The Zhujiang Film Group laid off almost half its original 596 employees, but it received significant funding from the Provincial Financial Department to pay for their medical and living expenses.[38] Through a semisocialist welfare approach and a semicapitalist layoff approach, state-owned studios were rapidly transformed into market-based enterprises.

Following these personnel changes, institutional restructuring got under way. Almost all state-controlled conglomerates were restructured, employing the vertical integration model to combine production, distribution, and exhibition. They diversified their production lines by adding digital production, coproductions, postproduction marketing, and cine film processing and printing. For example, in 2004 China Film Group launched a wholesale transformation of the shareholding system and developed an industrial linkage that extended to production, distribution, exhibition, printing, and processing. By 2010 the group held fifteen solely funded companies, was a shareholder in an additional thirty companies, and had one movie channel, bringing its total assets to 2.8 billion yuan. To enhance its vertical integration power, the group established seven theater chains through either share control or shareholding. Among them, the Xingmei chain had 107 member theaters covering twenty-three provinces and perennially ranked among the top three chains nationwide in terms of box office revenue. In 2007 the group increased its share control in Xingmei from 40 to 60 percent and established absolute control of Xingmei. Taken together, the China Film Group's 438 participating cinemas accounted for 40 percent of the national market, and its box office revenue accounted for half the box office receipts nationwide.[39] Beginning in 2004, China Film Group launched a series of high-investment films that earned huge box office returns, including *The Search* (*Wuji*), *The Warrior*, and *Red Cliff*. Of the seventy-seven Chinese-language films on the schedules of China's major theater chains in 2008, China Film Group produced or coproduced ten. These ten films generated almost 800 million yuan at the box office and accounted for nearly one-third of Chinese-language films' box office receipts that year. One name appeared in the credits of all of them: Han Sanping, CEO of China Film Group. In an interview, Han expressed his strong faith in state-owned enterprises. Rather than being doomed to fail, he believed state ownership would prevail and proudly claimed that "China Film Group is outstanding and strong."[40] Han Sanping also argued for state protection and the responsibility that should be shouldered by large-scale state-owned enterprises like China Film Group. He asserted that a "free capitalist market economy sometimes makes enterprises more vulnerable when facing an aggressive Hollywood." Therefore, although film companies with multiple owners should be encouraged and are important, there is room for state-owned enterprises to operate and lead the economy under the beneficial policies enacted by the state.[41]

To foster state-controlled film groups and secure market shares of state-owned enterprises, the Chinese government set aside large sums to compensate these state-controlled conglomerates. As early as September 1987, the Ministry of Broadcasting, Film, and Television and the Ministry of Finance jointly established a state fund to subsidize feature films with "significant themes." In May 1991 that fund was incorporated into the State Special Fund for Film Production by using 5 percent of national box office revenue. This special fund was used for eight categories of film industry development, from subsidizing films with significant themes and rewarding film professionals to renovating theaters. In March 1996 another special fund for fostering excellent films was established by collecting 3 percent of the advertising revenue from CCTV and television stations at the provincial level. This special fund was used to subsidize the production of "significant" films, rural film exhibition, children's films, science-related educational movies, documentaries, and movies produced for minorities. In 2007 the two funds reached 150 million yuan and 120 million yuan, respectively. In addition, local governments set up various cultural development funds to subsidize film production. CCTV's Movie Channel also contributed tens of millions of yuan every year to film production. The state subsidized the technological updating of state-owned studios, investing more than 3 billion yuan in the past decade.[42] In 2007 China Film Group successfully went public, with 500 million bonds issued to build the national digital movie production base and digital cinemas, symbolizing the debut of state-controlled film conglomerates in the financial market.[43]

Furthermore, between 2001 and 2005, the film sector continued to enjoy three beneficial state policies: the exemption of prints from sales taxes, the exemption of distribution revenue from sales taxes, and the subsidizing of film and television productions through funds collected from the distribution of imports. In addition, the tariff on imported films (which are used to subsidize the production of significant films and educational films) was reduced from 35 percent to 5 percent.[44]

As such, the state hopes to maintain its leadership of state-controlled conglomerates by investing in and fostering their film production. Through the China Film Group, the state has helped create a state-owned enterprise that exploits the full potential of vertical integration. However, outside the China Film Group and the Shanghai Film Group, movies produced by other state-controlled groups have not landed in the top thirty in terms of box office revenue. State studios can survive and prevail only by taking advantage of the state's protection and generous resources; thus, they are not on an equal footing with private companies and do not engage in fair competition. Furthermore, they are subject to state intervention and follow the government's administrative orders, without much autonomy. The domestic market is thus divided into the top state-controlled film groups and the private companies with their flexibility and competitive edge.

## ENCOURAGING PRIVATE AND FOREIGN INVESTMENT

Because of the severe financial crises experienced by state-owned film studios during the 1980s and early 1990s, they had to come up with various ways to fund film productions. The earliest investments in coproductions came from Hong Kong and Taiwan. Between 1988 and 1994, there were 147 coproductions with Hong Kong and Taiwan.[45] Meanwhile, in the mid-1980s, domestic private and independent investment started to flow into film production. Early private film production companies included the Nanchang Film and Television Institute; Jindao Film and Television Production Company; Xiejin-Hengtong Film and Television Development Company, which was cofunded by well-known director Xie Jin; and Chuangshiji Film and Television Company, which was funded by well-known director Teng Wenji.[46] In the 1990s more and more private institutions began to invest in film production, and debt-ridden state-owned studios solicited funds from private companies. By 1993, more than half of China's domestically made movies were being funded by private capital.[47] The 1990s box office successes *Red Cherry, Red Rush,* and *In the Heat of the Sun* were all funded by private capital.

After the issuance of Document 3 in 1993 and a series of reform measures undertaken between 2002 and 2005, the state provided a strong boost to private film production. Among each year's top ten movies in terms of box office receipts, 80 percent have been funded by private and overseas capital. Private film companies have become the backbone of domestic film production and coproduction. The major players include Huayi Brothers, New Pictures, Boli Bona, and Shiji Yingxiong. According to Wang Zhongjun, CEO of Huayi Brothers, the biggest difference between state-owned studios and private studios is that state-owned studios possess state resources such as fixed assets, personnel, and production bases, and they enjoy state protection, while private studios are market targeted and profit driven and have the advantage of a simplified decision-making process. In addition, state-owned studios are sometimes subjected to heavier burdens imposed by the state, such as making main-melody propaganda movies, which can lead to greater restrictions.[48]

New Pictures Company Ltd., the longtime sponsor of China's most well-known director, Zhang Yimou, is another big name in film production. In 2002 and 2004 New Pictures released two box office smashes, *Hero* and *House of Flying Daggers,* making it China's top film production company. In 2006 New Pictures and Huayi Brothers became the top two domestic box office earners with *Curse of Golden Flowers* and *The Banquet,* respectively.

Since 2001 Huayi Brothers has been China's top earner in terms of box office receipts. Originally an advertising company established in 1994 by two brothers, Wang Zhongjun and Wang Zhonglei, with an investment of US$100,000, the company began investing in movies in 1997 and created Feng Xiaogang's New Year celebration film series. In March 2000 Huayi Brothers Taihe Film and Television Investment Company Ltd. was established. The company has gradually created its own industrial chain that includes studios, agencies for actors, and advertising and distribution subsidiaries. By 2003, the company was garnering 30 percent of domestic box office receipts. In 2004 that number rose to 35 percent, and its output accounted for one-third of all domestic films. It also cooperates with foreign companies such as Sony-Columbia and has produced many profitable movies, including *Cell Phone, A World without Thieves, The Banquet,* and *Kung Fu Hustle.*[49]

Since its shares have gone public, Huayi Brothers has been hailed as the top company in China's entertainment industry, with a gross market value of 10 billion yuan and more than 100 movie stars under contract. Many other private studios have emulated its management framework and operating and financing models. Huayi was the first film studio to adopt a private financing strategy. By using a fund-raising model of "shareholding finance plus shareholding mortgage," Huayi secured more than 400 million yuan from big companies like Yahoo! and Tom. It later employed other methods such as royalty mortgages, credit mortgages, and share listings to obtain more than 1.2 billion yuan in bank loans. Huayi's operating model has provided a framework for independent producers. In addition to film studios, it has eleven TV studios, each of which is fully autonomous and responsible for the production of its own TV programs. Huayi shares these studios' production risks and profits.

Huayi invested US$60 million in its subsidiary Huayi International in 2011, with the intention of cooperating with Hollywood studios to make English-language movies and set up joint ventures with both European and Asian companies to engage in film production, distribution, and exhibition and the training of talent.[50] In addition, on June 10, 2011, the US company Legendary Pictures announced that it would set up a Legendary Oriental Company in partnership with Huayi to make movies. Legendary Oriental planned to produce one or two movies a year, with Huayi responsible for film distribution in China and Warner Bros. handling distribution globally.[51]

As the largest private film distribution company in China, Boli Bona had a 15 percent national market share for five consecutive years between 2005 and 2009. Unlike Huayi, which initially focused on film production and gradually extended its business to distribution and exhibition, Boli started in film distribution and expanded into film production in 2003 and exhibition in 2005. By 2009, Boli had organized its industrial infrastructure to encompass film production, distribution, and exhibition. Because of its broad distribution network, Boli has a great advantage over other companies. It claimed that its ultimate goal is to "become China's Paramount." In 2009 box office revenue from movies that Boli invested in and distributed reached 850 million yuan, accounting for 14 percent of China's gross box office receipts of 6.2 billion yuan.[52]

Enlight Media Group, comprising Enlight Media Company and Enlight Film Company, is another large private media company. Backed by the group's 300 TV stations and 600 TV channels nationwide, Enlight Film Company has quickly become one of China's largest film investment and distribution companies, specializing in commercial films. In 2009 its gross box office revenue totaled 180 million yuan, which accounted for 5 percent of the national market.[53]

Wang Jianlin, the CEO of Wanda and the richest man in China, has also played a crucial role in the China-Hollywood connection, in part through his purchase of the AMC theater chain and his US$20 million donation to the Academy of Motion Picture Arts and Sciences Museum, but in other ways as well. Wanda has dispatched a number of delegations to meet with Hollywood studio heads as the collaboration between China and Hollywood becomes closer. Wang has a great deal of government support for a variety of reasons, one of which is his conscious promotion of Chinese soft power overseas.

Other private companies have enjoyed success as well, including Beijing Galloping Horse Media Company Ltd. and Zhejiang Huace Film and TV Company Ltd. The former was established in 1998 and conglomerated in 2007. In 2012 it purchased America's digital domain to advance its capacity for digital and online movie production. The latter is headquartered in Hangzhou and was granted a series of favorable financial, land, and tax breaks in May 2012 in order to establish the China (Zhejiang) International Film and TV Cooperation Zone, encompassing Shanghai, Nanjing, Wuxi, Suzhou, and Hangzhou. The goal is to industrialize Chinese film and TV production by introducing Hollywood's advanced technology and business model and by encouraging collaboration and coproductions.[54]

Through their flexible business models and sensible market strategies, private companies have become major film producers and major contributors to box office revenue. As table 3.1 indicates, starting in 2004, more than 80 percent of movies have been funded by private domestic and overseas capital. Starting in 2009, privately funded movies constituted half the total film output, while the number of movies produced by state-owned studios has declined significantly since 2003. Meanwhile, coproductions

**Table 3.1. Source of Funding for Films, 1995–2010**

| Year | Total Film Output | Output of State-Owned Studios (Percentage of Total) | Output of Privately or Collectively Owned Studios (Percentage of Total) | Number of Coproductions: State-Owned, Privately Owned, and Overseas (Percentage of Total) | Number of Top Ten Box Office Earners Produced by State-Owned Studios | Number of Top Ten Box Office Earners That Were Coproductions |
|---|---|---|---|---|---|---|
| 1995 | 146 | 74 (50.7%) | 3 (2.1%) | 69 (47.3%) | — | — |
| 1996 | 110 | 67 (60.9%) | 0 | 43 (39.1%) | 4 | 6 |
| 1997 | 85 | 45 (52.9%) | 0 | 40 (47.1%) | 6 | 4 |
| 1998 | 82 | 52 (63.4%) | 0 | 30 (36.6%) | 6 | 4 |
| 1999 | 99 | 58 (58.6%) | 4 (4.0%) | 37 (37.4%) | 4 | 6 |
| 2000 | 83 | 38 (45.8%) | 0 | 45 (54.2%) | 4 | 6 |
| 2001 | 71 | 36 (50.7%) | 0 | 35 (49.3%) | 2 | 8 |
| 2002 | 100 | 43 (43.0%) | 2 (2.0%) | 55 (55.0%) | 3 | 7 |
| 2003 | 140 | 39 (27.9%) | 14 (10.0%) | 87 (62.1%) | 2 | 8 |
| 2004 | 212 | 37 (17.5%) | 54 (25.5%) | 121 (57.1%) | 0 | 10 |
| 2005 | 260 | 43 (16.5%) | 81 (31.2%) | 136 (52.3%) | 2 | 8 |
| 2006 | 330 | 48 (14.5%) | 151 (45.8%) | 131 (39.7%) | 0 | 10 |
| 2007 | 402 | 59 (14.7%) | 164 (40.8%) | 179 (44.5%) | 0 | 10 |
| 2008 | 406 | 34 (8.4%) | 181 (44.6%) | 191 (47.0%) | 0 | 10 |
| 2009 | 456 | 52 (11.4%) | 228 (50.0%) | 176 (38.6%) | 0 | 10 |
| 2010 | 526 | 45 (8.6%) | 292 (55.5%) | 189 (35.9%) | 0 | 10 |

*Source: China Film Yearbook 1996–2011* (Beijing: Zhongguo dianying chubanshe [China Film Press], 1996–2011).

have dominated the top ten box office hits. In 2007 all top ten revenue earners were coproductions. These statistics illustrate the remarkable structural changes occurring in the Chinese film industry.

## New Challenges Facing the Burgeoning Chinese Film Industry

The Chinese film industry is still in the early stages of its configuration. Its overall industrial structure is very uneven and needs adjustment, and the production quality remains substandard. The problems confronting the Chinese film industry include the state monopoly, the disjuncture between production and exhibition, hostile competition among studios, and the threat of Hollywood movies.

In reality, local governments at various levels have continued to treat film as a propaganda tool. As a result, film production in many provinces is still a government act instead of a business enterprise. Local governments, mainly local party propaganda departments, often allocate large sums of money to foster main-melody film production in response to the requirements of the central government and SARFT. Film production is frequently seen as a mandatory task rather than an artistic endeavor or a profit-seeking venture. Local governments have also promulgated a number of regulations that encourage the production of main-melody movies. If a film producer's movie falls within the content range prescribed by the government, he can obtain a number of financial rewards that cover production costs and may even yield a profit. Consequently, 300 to 400 low-budget, low-quality movies are produced each year at the expense of the state, with no possibility of getting into any of the theater chains. In a July 2010 interview, famous film director Tian Zhuangzhuang posed this question: "Who is going to pay for the Chinese film industry?" Zhou Tiedong, general manager of the China Film Overseas Promotion Company, noted in a July 2011 interview that he had offered a suggestion to Han Sanping of CFEIC that would allow him to fund unprofitable main-melody movies: "Take the Chinese government as a big market to profit from."[55] If the government wants to make main-melody movies, the government must provide the funds. But where do the government's funds come from?

In addition to the 3.3 percent sales tax collected on movie tickets, the majority of the government's funds that are used to subsidize the domestic film industry, especially the production of main-melody movies and theater construction, are derived primarily from the State Special Fund for Film Development and the Movie and TV Mutual-Aid Fund. The State Special Fund was established by SARFT and the Ministry of Finance in 1996; all theaters at thc county level and above must contribute 5 percent of their box office revenue, including money earned from imports, to this fund each year. With box office revenue growing more than tenfold between 1996 and 2011, this fund has grown at a fast pace, reaching 610 million yuan in 2011. The Movie and TV Mutual-Aid Fund was also established by these two governmental entities; TV stations nationwide must turn over 3 percent of their annual advertising profits to this fund, amounting to 150 million yuan every year. The State Special Fund financed 202 main-melody movies between 1996 and 2002. After 2002, when reforms intensified and various investors began contributing to film production, this fund shifted its main focus to theater construction. The Movie and TV Mutual-Aid

Fund now shoulders the main responsibility for financing main-melody movies and government-sponsored film festivals.[56]

At the annual conference of the People's Political Consultative Committee in 2011, famous film director Feng Xiaogang complained about the large sums film producers were required to turn over to the state. According to Feng, Huayi Brothers, China's largest private film company, contributed as much as 40 million yuan to the State Special Fund in 2010, accounting for 50 percent of the company's profit that year and imposing a huge financial burden. Feng suggested that the government abolish the 5 percent levy and finance the fund on its own.[57]

Data provided by the administrators of the State Special Fund disclose that between 2008 and 2011, out of a total of 1.136 billion yuan, 582 million yuan was returned to local film funds, 333 million yuan was invested in approximately 1,000 new theaters, 110 million yuan was used for the technical renovation of more than 200 older theaters, 17.53 million yuan went to assist nine companies in translating Mandarin and foreign movies into minority dialects, 15.86 million yuan was used to computerize ticket-sale systems nationwide, 63.9 million yuan paid for the installation of digital projectors, and 13.72 million yuan was used to reward provincial film administrations that had good records in main-melody film production. Film professionals, meanwhile, continue to demand a more transparent system that informs the public how the State Special Fund and the Mutual-Aid Fund are allocated by the state.[58]

These figures indicate that the state redistributes film profits for various uses, ranging from theater construction to film production. The lion's share of the profits earned by film studios, however, goes toward the production of main-melody movies. As such, the film industry and the market are not autonomous. The state dictates the market with its administrative measures, protects state enterprises, and collects a large percentage of box office revenue for the production of politically correct movies that reinforce the state ideology. Under these conditions, the burgeoning Chinese film industry faces severe problems and new challenges. The most notable problem is the disjunction between production and distribution. As the preceding analysis shows, film production in many provinces remains a government-funded activity that lacks market appeal. However, theater chains nationwide are primarily profit-oriented businesses that operate according to market logic. Theater chains are reluctant to exhibit these unappealing government-sponsored movies, many of which are never screened and audiences have never heard of. The film producers manage to recoup their production costs only by receiving government funds. These movies, therefore, are not made for audiences; they are made for the government.

The second notable problem with the Chinese film industry is monopoly, which leads to a problematic industrial structure and uneven development. Powerful film groups with affiliated theater chains, such as the China Film Group and Huayi Brothers, have become near monopolies that are capable of exploiting their vertical integrated power to the fullest. The vast number of smaller film producers are unable to compete with them and cannot get their movies into major theater chains. Driven by market profits and judged by box office records, the Chinese film industry has entered an era characterized by the pursuit of quick success and instant profits at the expense of artistic pursuits. Consequently, major theater chains accept only movies made by big names in the field and with a good chance of turning a profit; they are reluctant to screen low-budget movies that may be unappealing to audiences or lack a profit-making potential. Although the state has succeeded in transforming the film sector from its original propaganda and public-service role into a market-based industry, it has not done enough to support artistic experimentation, foster young and inexperienced talent, and enact antitrust laws to create an environment that is conducive to fair competition.

Among the 526 movies produced in 2010, less than 20 percent were accepted by major theater chains. Many low-budget movies were screened for only one day and then removed from the schedule. Two big hits, *If You Are the One II* and *Let the Bullets Fly*, directed by Feng Xiaogang and Wen Jiang, respectively, dominated 90 percent of the major theater chains' screening schedules. Although box office receipts reached 10.17 billion yuan in 2010—a 63.9 percent increase over 2009—and placed China among the top ten film markets worldwide, less than 20 percent of the movies were profitable. Twenty-six movies, each with box office receipts of at least 10 billion yuan, accounted for 65 percent of the total box office revenue. The lion's share of movies lost money and ended up being broadcast on CCTV's Movie Channel. Zhang Hongsen, deputy director of the Film Bureau, said that only a few directors, a few film studios, and a few big-budget movies managed to make money. Low-budget movies and young directors have become the victims of market forces.[59]

This situation continued into 2011 and 2012. Among the 580 movies produced in 2011, only 160 were added to the schedules of major theater chains, with total ticket sales of 7 billion yuan; only 20 of the 580 were profitable. Meanwhile, 60 imports earned ticket sales of 6 billion yuan, and the top three box office winners were all Hollywood blockbusters.[60] Among the 745 feature films produced in 2012, only 231, or 31 percent, were listed on the schedules of theater chains. This percentage, however, was the highest since 2005, when the screening percentage hit a low of 16.5.[61]

So far, the Chinese film industry resembles a pyramid: a few hits and a few producers reside at the top of the pyramid and take 80 percent of gross box office revenue, while the majority of middle- and low-budget movies and their producers form the base of the pyramid and earn less than 20 percent of the total revenue. A healthier structure, analysts have argued, would resemble a spindle, with a large number of middle- and low-budget movies serving as the major contributors to film revenue.[62]

Xie Xiaojing, deputy director of the Beijing Film Academy, has recommended the implementation of state policies that provide a platform for young film directors and encourage competition. He believes that if there is no policy to foster low-budget movies and train new talent, the entire film industry will suffer. He also acknowledges the unbalanced distribution of film resources and the monopoly of powerful film groups and theater chains.[63]

Associated with this monopoly is the conflict of interest between theater chains and production studios in their fight for greater shares of the domestic film market. Two events demonstrate the intensity of this conflict: the quarrel between New Pictures and eight major theater chains that arose in November 2011, and a similar conflict between five major film studios and ten major theater chains in November 2012. Both events were triggered by film producers' requests to increase their share of box office revenue, which met with strong resistance from the theater chains. In the 2011 conflict involving New Pictures, Zhang Weiping, the company's president, requested a hike in the ticket price for his big-budget movie *The Flowers of War* to 40 yuan, as well as a 2 percentage point increase in shared revenue. (The film tells the story of thirteen prostitutes who sacrifice themselves to save female students during the rape of Nanjing in the 1937 war with Japan; it stars Hollywood actor Christian Bale.) Otherwise, Zhang would not allow theaters to show the film. Zhang's firm stance infuriated the managers of eight major theater chains, and they joined forces to resist his demands. At the same time, Yu Dong, president of Boli Bona Group (a competitor of New Pictures), sent a letter to major theater chains indicating that Boli Bona would decrease to 30 yuan the ticket price for its big-budget movie *Flying Swords of Dragon Gate,* a martial arts movie starring Jet Li and a sequel to the classics *Dragon Inn* and *New Dragon Inn.* As such, the conflict also involved hostile competition among film studios.

The revenue-sharing ratios for film studios and theater chains had been changing since the start of film marketization and the creation of chains in the early twenty-first century. To expedite the development of theater chains, the original ratio had been set at 33 percent for film studios and 67 percent for theater chains. Between 2001 and 2011 the film studios' cut gradually increased to 43 percent, for the purpose of supporting domestic film production. In 2002, when the film *Hero* came out, Zhang Weiping secured a ratio of 40 percent through negotiations with theater chains. The film *House of Flying Daggers* helped New Pictures negotiate a ratio of 41 percent in 2004, and it received 42 percent for the film *Curse of the Golden Flower* in 2006.[64] Zhang Weiping's request for an additional 2 percentage points for *The Flowers of War* meant that his studio's share would reach 45 percent, and some theater chains could lose money. If Zhang's film was not screened by the eight major theater chains that controlled 70 percent of the nationwide film market, neither side would be a winner. To resolve the conflict, on November 22, 2011, representatives of the Film Bureau invited both sides to lunch and eventually negotiated a compromise under which the ratio would be 45 percent for New Pictures and 55 percent for theater chains if box office revenue remained below 500 million yuan, meaning that New Pictures would net an extra 10 million yuan. Once receipts exceeded 500 million yuan, the ratio would shift to 41 percent for New Pictures and 59 percent for the chains. The Film Bureau played the role of mediator and tried to balance the interests of both sides, but it leaned slightly toward the film studio in order to show its support for domestic film production. The Film Bureau also stipulated that in this particular case, if the film studio's ratio rose to 45 percent, income from advertisements would go to the theaters.[65]

During the second conflict, in November 2012, five major film producers and distributors—China Film Group Corporation, Huayi Brothers, Enlight Pictures, Bona Film Group, and Xingmei Distribution Company—joined forces to request a 45 percent share for nine New Year's celebration movies.[66] After negotiations, the five distributors were successful in obtaining a 45 percent share.

These two events speak to the urgency of structural adjustment and profit redistribution for the development of a healthy film industry. For film studios, the rapid rise in production costs, including skyrocketing salaries for movie stars, has made it increasingly difficult to recoup investments. Additionally, the large portion of revenue that goes to theaters discourages studios and film professionals from making more and better movies. For theater chains and theaters, the rising operating costs, including rent, utilities, and salaries, pose a heavy burden. The annual rent for a medium-sized theater ranges from 2 million to 8 million yuan, but on Guangzhou's busiest street, the annual rent for theaters is 12 million yuan. According to an analysis by Qin Hong, CEO of the Xingmei theater chain, if a movie earned 40 million yuan in box office receipts, the theaters would make less than 20 million yuan. To achieve 40 million yuan in box office receipts, a theater must have at least 1,500 seats and an annual rent in the range 7 million to 8 million yuan. The investment in a single seat ranges from 8,000 to 20,000 yuan. Even in midwestern provincial cities, the investment for a single seat in a luxurious theater is 20,000 yuan. Therefore, it takes at least three years for a theater to earn any profit.[67] Although the number of movie screens in China exceeds 10,000, that is still only one-fourth the number available to US moviegoers. According to He Ping, a well-known film director, China's 10 billion yuan in box office receipts for 2010 was earned at 6,000 screens, compared with the United States' $11 billion in box office revenue earned at 40,000 screens. Thus, some people are concerned that any loss in revenue would deal a blow to theater construction, given that only 200 of China's 1,600 theaters earn more than 2 million yuan in revenue, while the majority are in debt.

Others worry about passing along rising costs to audiences via higher ticket prices. Movie tickets in China are already notoriously expensive. If the share ratios change, theaters will have no choice but to raise ticket prices in order to maintain their profit margins. China's well known economist Lang Xianping severely criticized overpriced film tickets in an article published in 2011. When he and his classmates went to see the movie *Shaolin Monks* in 1982, the ticket price was ten cents; by 2007, a ticket for the Hollywood movie *Transformers* cost 80 yuan—an increase of 800 percent in just twenty-five years. Statistics show that the ticket price of ten cents in the early 1980s accounted for 0.5 percent of the average monthly income of 20 yuan. By the end of the first decade of the twenty-first century, the ticket price had risen to 50 yuan on average, accounting for 2.5 percent of the average monthly income of 2,000 yuan. By comparison, a US ticket costs 0.25 percent of an American's average monthly income, and a ticket in Singapore costs 0.5 percent. Clearly, the relative cost of attending a film in China is far greater, and movie tickets are notoriously unaffordable for average Chinese citizens. Film professionals believe it would be more reasonable to limit the ticket price to less than 15 yuan.[68]

There was a new development in the conflict between theater chains and production studios in October 2013, when Huayi Brothers announced a change in the revenue-sharing ratios for its blockbuster *Young Detective Dee: Rise of the Sea Dragon.* It proposed a 30 percent–70 percent split rather than the conventional 43 percent–57 percent share for film studios and theater chains, respectively. Huayi's new strategy was intended to encourage theater chains to prioritize *Young Detective Dee* in their schedules at the expense of its own profit margin, which was believed to be a good marketing strategy for the movie.[69]

The conflict between studios and theater chains will become more intense over time as new and old interests compete for a market that is expanding by 30 to 35 percent a year. This tension is also part of a larger conflict in the industry. As China Film Group CEO Han Sanping has commented, the biggest weakness of the Chinese film industry is a lack of producers. Producers are absolutely essential to the development of the industry, and they are an important aspect of its privatization. However, the growing power of producers is fueling new conflicts between government control and market development. Moreover, this debate and its solution have important implications for Hollywood imports. Because both Chinese producers and Hollywood studios want their blockbusters to be shown on the most upscale digital screens in the most successful theater chains, this has led to a good deal of animosity and the increasing marginalization of small and medium-sized films.

The Chinese state has always interfered in the distribution of film revenue and profits, while leaning toward the support of domestic film production. Thus, the state acts as an invisible hand that pushes each side to move in the direction it wishes. Some believe state intervention is necessary when a conflict of interest leads to confrontations among the production, distribution, and exhibition sectors, while others argue that negotiation is crucial to maintain trust and preserve profits for all parties.[70] To balance the interests of these different groups, on November 22, 2012, the administrative committee for the State Special Fund for Film Development adopted four measures to support both studios and theaters and ease their concerns. These measures included awarding as much as 10 million yuan to film producers whose high-tech movies earn more than 500 million yuan in ticket sales and returning portions of the theaters' contributions to the State Special Fund back to them, based on the number of domestic movies screened. Through these measures, the state has eased the tension between film studios and theaters in their fight for revenue share.[71]

In addition to the state monopoly, the disjuncture between production and exhibition, and the conflicts of interest, other problems are noticeable. The booming Chinese film market results in the unregulated inflow and outflow of large sums of money. In 2010 China's gross box office revenue reached 10 billion yuan, a 60 percent increase over the previous year, and the projected returns for one movie were as high as 160 percent. With such a huge profit incentive, many investors with little knowledge of the movie industry, who had earned their money in real estate, industry and trade, coal mining, and land exploration, blindly rushed into the film industry in the hope of making a fortune. However, as detailed earlier, between 2005 and 2012, less than 31 percent of domestic movies were screened by the major theater chains, and 70 to 80 percent of movies lost money, making film production a high-risk investment. Many investors were unable to recoup even their basic principal. The tragic suicide of Chen Weimin, director of two companies in Zhejiang Province, due to his financial losses in film investment speaks to the harsh realities of the contemporary film industry.[72]

Hollywood imports were strong performers in the Chinese market during the first half of 2012. As a direct consequence of the increase in the film quota to thirty-four, facilitated by soon-to-be-president Xi Jinping's visit to the United States in February 2012, the 7.25 billion yuan (approximately US$1.17 billion) box office revenue earned by imports during the first three quarters of 2012 overtook the revenue from domestic movies by more than 2.3 billion yuan (US$371 million), making the conditions for domestic film production even more difficult.[73] Among more than eighty domestic movies screened in the first half of 2012, only 5 percent managed to recoup their initial investment, and none of them earned a profit. Accordingly, investors began to abandon film production, leading to a drastic decline in film investment and a further decrease in the scale of film production. This situation was reflected in the size of China's largest film production base (Hengdian), which had less than half the number of film production teams working in 2012 compared with 2011. Gao Jun, general manager of the Beijing Shengshi Huarui Film Investment Company Ltd., described the China-Hollywood competition as one between "eggs and stones."[74]

The Film Bureau responded to this situation by extending the protection period for domestic movies to the end of August; originally, this period was supposed to run from June 20 to the end of July. Although this move allowed domestic movies to recoup some investment and earn some profits, it also led to intense competition among domestic movies.[75] To ensure that Hollywood films accounted for no more than 50 percent of the market in any given year, the Film Bureau enacted a series of measures, including imposing blackout dates, opening two Hollywood films on the same day, and manipulating the box office for certain films. Additional measures were taken in 2013, such as a value-added tax system that taxed the revenue share of foreign producers rather than gross box office revenue, which led to an 8 percentage point decrease in foreign producers' share of revenue and caused a conflict between CFEIC and 20th Century–Fox over the distribution of *Life of Pi.* Another example of governmental intervention was the removal of *Django Unchained* from the running schedule on the day it opened.[76]

In 2013 the Chinese film industry rebounded robustly, at Hollywood's expense. Chinese domestic movies accounted for 59 percent of the gross box office revenue of 21.7 billion yuan, while imports accounted for 41 percent.[77] The Chinese state has higher priorities than the market, and it often resorts to administrative measures to manipulate the market performance of movies.

Other problems related to the training of talent, limited educational resources, and the lack of postproduction professionals have all hindered the development of the Chinese film industry and testify to the early stage of its industrialization. For example, in a number of recent Chinese megaproductions, the credits include a long list of foreign special-effects professionals. Feng Xiaogang's film *Aftershock* employed more than seventy foreign experts for eight months to reproduce the 1976 Tangshan earthquake. Two-thirds of the film's budget, or 50 million yuan, was spent on these foreign experts. According to Feng, Chinese film technicians were incapable of mastering the imported film production equipment and were able to use only 500 of the equipment's 5,000 functions. The extreme shortage of film technicians with expertise in audio and video techniques and cinematography, the corresponding shortage in educational staff, and the low quality of professional training have severely hindered the advancement of the domestic film industry.[78]

The Chinese state has negotiated much operating space for its domestic film industry. However, the concessions it has made to Hollywood have direct negative consequences for the further development of that industry. The state has tried to strike a balance and negotiate for national interests throughout the Hollywood siege. Although it introduced capitalist theater chains and transformed the socialist propaganda film system into a market-based film economy, the state has also made every effort to maintain its authoritarian control over the industry and uphold the leadership of state-owned studios. The domestic film industry may benefit from the conditional inflow of capital, technology, and skill permitted by the state, but it also suffers from the state's heavy-handed control and censorship. While the state facilitates the establishment of theater chains and the consolidation of the domestic film market, to a large degree it also continues to subject film production to its ideological control and fails to grant freedom of expression to the industry. As a result, film producers remain caught between market demand and a state censorship system intent on maintaining the party-state's supremacy. The very film market the government helped build often betrays the party-state's mission. Only a small number of domestic movies are placed on the running schedules of theater chains, leading to a vast waste of funds and the unbalanced development of the domestic film industry. This poses a new challenge to the state, which has tried very hard to balance its dual roles as party upholder and market facilitator. Even if we claim that the Chinese state is a bigger winner than Hollywood in its negotiations with global capital, it is doubtful that the state can be a successful mediator between an authoritarian political structure and a market economy. The industrialization process of China's film industry still has a long way to go.

# 4

# Artistic and Critical Cinema under a Triple Threat

## *Marketization, Hollywoodization, and State Censorship*

The latter half of 2012 was characterized by four stirring events in China's film industry—all of them related to state censorship. These events did not happen in isolation; they represented film professionals' newest attempt to challenge the authorities and China's censorship system.

The first event was a film symposium held at the Fifteenth Shanghai International Film Festival on June 18. Film director Lu Chuan, famous for *Nanjing! Nanjing!*, was near tears as he spoke of the withdrawal of his film *The Last Supper* from the summer schedules of the major theater chains for what he called a "noncommercial special reason." "I cannot say anything," he said. "If I disclose anything here, the film will most likely not be permitted to be released in the latter half of the year." He added, "Film is culture, not politics, not a propagandistic tool. I hope someday film can be considered an entertaining medium for the public." The producer of *The Last Supper*, Qin Hong, echoed this sentiment, saying he hoped the state system could create a more lenient and tolerant environment for film production. Qin Hong had invested approximately 90 million yuan in the film, and its withdrawal would result in a huge financial loss. *The Last Supper* eventually passed the censors and was released on November 29, 2012.[1]

The second event was film director Lou Ye's September 7 announcement on his blog that he would publicize all the censorship details related to his film *Mystery*. Lou Ye had been banned from making movies since 2006, when he took his film *Summer Palace* to the Cannes Film Festival without SARFT's permission. *Summer Palace* touches on the sensitive theme of the 1989 Tiananmen

Square incident, and it has many sexual and nude scenes that are objectionable to a Chinese audience. He made an underground film, *A Night Deeply Drunk on the Spring Breeze,* in Nanjing in 2009 and the film *Love and Bruises* in France in 2011. *Mystery* was his first movie made in China since the lifting of the ban. *Mystery* originally passed the censors and was scheduled to be released nationwide on October 19. Only forty-one days before the release date, however, SARFT demanded further cuts and plot revisions before it would issue the screening license. Outraged at this unexpected intrusion, Lou Ye announced that he would disclose all the details concerning the censorship of *Mystery* and added that he sincerely hoped SARFT would respect individual film directors' dignity and their right to have the final say about their own movies.[2]

The third event, one that resonated broadly and garnered widespread support, involved a long public letter posted to the blog of famous film director Xie Fei on December 15, in which he called for "substituting a film rating system for film censorship." Citing films that had been censored and banned in the past and the disappointing fact that only 200 of 791 censored films had been shown in 2011, Xie Fei criticized the censorship system for violating filmmakers' constitutional right to freedom of expression. The censorship system, he declared, "is a corrupt system that restricts the prosperity of the cultural product market, stifles artistic exploration, and wastes financial and administrative resources."[3] Xie Fei's letter came one day after CCTV announced on its own blog that *V for Vendetta,* long banned in China, would be shown on CCTV-6, the movie channel. *V for Vendetta* tells the story of what would have happened if Germany had won World War II and the United Kingdom had been turned into a fascist state where people have no political rights or freedom. A security officer called "V" wanders the streets and attempts to mobilize people into an antifascist movement. The film's themes include rebellion, resistance, and revolution, and many of the actors' lines sound very provocative in a Chinese context—for example, "The people should not be afraid of the government; the government should be afraid of the people," and "The thoughts are not afraid of bullets!" The movie was shown on CCTV without any cuts.[4] Many blog postings wondered what this meant and whether it signaled a reduction of censorship. It was in this context that Xie Fei posted his public letter. Within a few days, other filmmakers and film industry heavyweights, such as directors Wang Xiaoshuai, He Ping, Zhang Yuan, and Zhang Yang, as well as Yu Dong of Bona, expressed their support of Xie Fei and spoke against censorship restrictions.[5]

Finally, on December 26, 2012, award-winning film director Jia Zhangke announced on his blog that he would "go underground" again, stating, "it is unbearable and I don't want to endure anymore!"[6] Although Jia did not specify the cause of his anger, his post sparked widespread speculation that his latest commercial movie, *In the Qing Dynasty* (*Zai Qingchao*), had failed to pass the censors.

These four events foreground a recurring conflict in China's film history: the battle between filmmakers and state censorship. This conflict is nothing new, and it has often been the subject of eye-catching stories on various media outlets. This chapter, however, discusses some new questions: How has state censorship evolved and changed with a market economy? Does China's market reform serve as a check on the state's censorship power? How does state censorship address both domestic and international pressure? What strategies do domestic filmmakers employ in dealing with state censors? According to well-known independent film director Wang Xiaoshuai, many filmmakers in China exercise "self-censorship" and avoid sensitive political themes in order to secure more funding and box office revenue. Therefore, he believes the censorship system is no longer the primary problem in China's film industry.[7]

In addition to conflicts among the state, the market, and filmmakers, global media capital and Hollywood constitute another threat to domestic film production. After 2012, when the import quota was increased to thirty-four films a year, there was an immediate impact on China's domestic film market. In April 2012 Hollywood blockbusters such as *Battleship*, *Ghost Rider: Spirit of Vengeance*, *Titanic 3D*, and *New York Assassination* once again occupied more than 80 percent of China's film market, and Chinese filmmakers found it very difficult to get their films added to the schedules of major theater chains.[8] Film Bureau statistics indicate that in 2012, domestic movies accounted for only 48 percent of gross box office revenue, showing how hard it is for domestic movies to compete with Hollywood.[9]

These cases reveal the unprecedented problems facing Chinese filmmakers since the initiation of reform and the Hollywood import policy. As summarized by film director He Ping at the 2012 Shanghai International Film Festival, the Chinese film industry is currently facing three conflicts: (1) between the entire film industry and the state film administration, including the censorship system; (2) between Chinese films and Hollywood imports as they compete for market share; and (3) between artistic moviemakers and market and audience tastes.[10] A similar situation occurred two decades ago when Hollywood blockbusters first landed in China. After years of struggle and effort, film producers once again find themselves fighting the same enemies, albeit at a different level, now that a Chinese film industry and a national market have been established and are in the process of being regulated and improved.

Whereas previous chapters focused on the external China-Hollywood conflict, this chapter analyzes the two internal conflicts: film producers' struggles with the state censorship system and with market and audience demands. Externally, the Chinese state functions as a mediator between global capital and local agency; it is a negotiator between national interests and the interests of transnational capital. Internally, it serves as an authoritarian, heavy-handed upholder of the party-state. During the state's long tug-of-war with Hollywood, it has sought to reinforce its ideological control and reassert a consolidated national identity. To many liberal-minded filmmakers, this cause has been more of a detrimental and repressive force than a liberating and conducive one. In this chapter, therefore, I analyze the intertwined relationships among the state, Hollywood capital, and China's domestic film producers. I discuss film professionals' strategies to counter state repression, their subtle relations with global capital, and their unfailing efforts to pursue their art while trying to satisfy market demands. Here, I argue that under a state-market alliance without democracy, filmmaking in China has become a constant negotiation with state power and a desperate struggle for market survival. Contemporary artistic and critical Chinese films reflect fractured national identities and moral collapse, a strong sense of dislocation and disorientation, and a "no way out" dilemma. Hollywood movies may unexpectedly and temporarily meet the aesthetic needs of the Chinese audience and fill the ideological vacuum resulting from the failed socialist experiment and empty official propaganda, but they cannot substitute for indigenous experience and domestic humanistic concern. Trapped by both ideological disorientation and the untrammeled power of global Hollywood, the Chinese film industry's long march to modernity has yet to be completed.

## China's Film Censorship System under the Market Economy

The People's Republic of China is notorious for its censorship, which is imposed on almost all media ranging from print to the Internet. Because the film sector was nationalized and functioned as an important propaganda tool during the planned economy period from the 1950s to the 1980s, the censorship system was implemented with "political and ideological correctness" as its dominant criterion.

China's first film regulations were the "Five Temporary Methods of Administrating the Film Industry," issued by the Ministry of Culture in the 1950s. The regulations stated: "Whether it is domestic or imported, new or old, if elements of a film are found to oppose world peace and popular democracy against the interests of the Chinese people or to spread licentious, pornographic, superstitious or terrorist messages sufficient to disrupt order in the new society, such sections should be cut out, or the film could be banned and prevented from public screening."[11] The party-state's interests and principles dominated every other pursuit. Consequently, China's film history is replete with bitter literary and political persecutions that occurred during campaigns ranging from the Anti-Rightists Movement of 1957 to the Cultural Revolution of 1966–1976. During political turmoil, the Communist Party's various resolutions usually assumed the authority of law.

After the initiation of reform and the open-door policy at the end of the 1980s, the first formal regulation was the Film Censorship Ordinance, promulgated by SARFT in 1988 and refined in 1993 and 1997 and renamed the Film Examination Regulations.[12] On May 1, 1989, SARFT also issued "The Circular on Implementing the Censorship and Rating System for Some Movies," as the government's response to film marketization reform and the inflow of movies from Hong Kong and Taiwan. The circular clearly prohibited four types of movies from being publicly screened to children and teenagers: movies with plots involving rape, robbery, prostitution, drug addiction, and trafficking; movies depicting violence, murder, and fighting; movies exhibiting sexual activities; and movies with "ugly/abnormal social phenomena."[13] The first movie regulated under this circular was a thriller directed by Liang Peng and Mu Deyuan entitled *The Lonely Spirit in an Old Building* (*Heilou guhun*), which tells the story of a ghost taking revenge on her murderer after the Cultural Revolution. When it was released in 1989, the opening credits began with the message: "Inappropriate for children." The thriller was a box office success, earning 3.5 million yuan—five times its production cost. However, the circular was nullified a few years later without any explanation.[14]

China's first law related to films, the Film Administrative Regulations, was approved by the State Council in June 1996. Chapter 3, "Film Censorship," stipulated the procedures studios had to follow to pass the censors and clearly listed seven types of prohibited content.[15] The 1997 revisions to the Film Examination Regulations listed eight categories of banned content and sixteen plots or scenes that required revision or excision.[16] These regulations were replaced by the Film Managerial Regulations, promulgated by the State Council in December 2001; they specified ten categories of prohibited content:

> First, content that opposes the cardinal principles of the PRC's Constitution;
> Second, content that endangers national unification, sovereignty and territory integration;
> Third, content that discloses national secrets, endangers national security, or defames the nation and damages national interests;
> Fourth, content of sedition and discrimination against minorities, that endangers solidarity among minorities, and distorts customs and rituals of minorities;
> Fifth, content that promotes superstition and heresy;
> Sixth, content that undermines social stability and social order;
> Seventh, content that propagates obscenity, gambling, violence or abets the commission of a crime;
> Eighth, content of libel and slander;
> Ninth, content that undermines social norms or Chinese civilization;
> Tenth, other content prohibited by state laws and regulations.[17]

In December 2011 the State Council promulgated the China Film Industry Promotion Law (Discussion Draft), which clearly outlined what the state sought to promote and prohibit in the twenty-first century and suggested that it had no intention of introducing a ratings system. In addition to the ten prohibited categories from the 2001 regulations, there were three new categories: content that promotes religious fanaticism and undermines the solidarity between religious followers and nonbelievers, content that instigates and teaches criminal behavior, and content that undermines the interests and the physical and mental health of children and adolescents.[18] The latest law also highlighted three types of films it aimed to promote: films that uphold "socialist core values," films that are conducive to the healthy growth of adolescents, and films that demonstrate artistic creativity and advance artistic progress. Following the 2001 guidelines, the law stipulated that foreign companies, institutions, and individuals are prohibited from independently making movies in Chinese territory, although they are allowed to coproduce with domestic studios. Before production begins, domestic Chinese filmmakers must submit their film script synopses for approval by SARFT. The law also banned films from being shown at or sent to film festivals without a license. Those who break the rules are subject to fines of 50,000 to 500,000 yuan, and the film company's license may be revoked.

In practice, a Film Censorship Committee and a Film Reexamination Committee are responsible for censoring all films, including imports. According to an official circular published on the SARFT website, members of these two committees serve two-year terms. In 2006 the Film Censorship Committee was headed by Tong Gang, the director of SARFT, and two deputy directors—Zhang Pimin and Zhang Hongsen. The rest of the committee's thirty-four members held positions in governmental departments, people's courts, civilian federations, and universities. The twelve-member Film Reexamination Committee was headed by Zhao Shi, deputy director of SARFT; Tong Gang; and Yang Zhijin, director of the Administration for Literature and Arts under the Ministry of Propaganda. Other members had similar jobs and positions as those on the Film Censorship Committee, including three film directors—Yu Yang, Li Qiankuan, and Xie Tieli.[19]

It is clear that the state is both a lawmaker and an enforcer. The state is actively involved in the entire process of film production, from topic and theme selection to promotion to postproduction censorship. Facing increasingly acute criticism and market pressure, the state has sometimes made minor adjustments to its regulations. For example, SARFT loosened its restrictions in 2003 by revoking its mandatory review of screenplays before the start of filmmaking. Now, rather than submitting entire screenplays for approval by SARFT, filmmakers can submit a synopsis of no fewer than 1,000 words and have their films listed in the annual plan. However, coproductions and films with "important revolutionary historical themes and films with sensitive themes" are still required to have their screenplays reviewed by censors.[20]

Another change has been the implementation of the so-called double censorship system, which began on July 1, 2011. The administrations for broadcasting, radio, and film at the provincial level are now required to keep records of all film scripts submitted by filmmakers within the provinces and send those records to SARFT. Provincial administrations are also responsible for the preliminary censoring of films made by local filmmakers, which are then submitted to SARFT for final examination.[21] This double censorship system was, in fact, first announced in 2003 and implemented in seven cities, including Beijing, Shanghai, and Guangdong, on a trial basis in 2004. Some believe this system has turned out to be more beneficial to filmmakers than a centrally controlled system because local censors tend to be more flexible and lenient. However, this double censorship has also raised concerns about the lack of standardized criteria for the evaluation of movies.[22]

In China, censorship works primarily through the employment of administrative measures and mandatory orders to filmmakers. In reality, censorship is very unpredictable and dependent on the sociopolitical context. Some subjects, such as Tibet, human rights, and the 1989 Tiananmen Square protest, will forever be taboo for both domestic and imported movies. In 1997 two Hollywood films that angered the Chinese government were prohibited in mainland China. The first, *Seven Years in Tibet,* stars Brad Pitt as Heinrich Harrer, an Austrian mountaineer who befriends the young Dalai Lama while crossing the Himalayas in the 1940s. The other, *Kundun,* directed by Martin Scorsese, is a Disney-financed film that follows the life of the fourteenth Dalai Lama through 1959, when he fled Tibet for India. Both films depict communist China as a brutal tyranny attempting to crush Tibet's religious and political traditions. China had already warned Disney in 1996 that the release of *Kundun* would damage the company's efforts to expand into China. Fearing the loss of the potentially powerful Chinese market, Disney chairman Michael Eisner even hired Henry Kissinger to secretly fly to Beijing to smooth over the situation.[23]

Films are sometimes censored based on the specific sociopolitical context. In 2006 the Chinese government canceled the showing of *Memoirs of a Geisha,* starring Zhang Ziyi and Gong Li, on the grounds that it might spark public anger and rekindle anti-Japanese sentiment.[24] In 2008 China blocked the production of *Shanghai,* a Hollywood film about an American who investigates a friend's death in Japanese-occupied Shanghai, even though a large sum of money had already been spent on production.[25] Ang Lee's *Lust, Caution* was also banned because it shows sympathy for a traitor, and lead actress Tang Wei was banned in China for five years. She is now back in the government's good graces, and her 2013 film *Finding Mr. Right* (*Beijing yushang xiyatu*) was very successful, showing that bans are normally temporary, not permanent. Martial arts movie star Jet Li once complained about the strict censorship in his blog, noting that his 2000 film *Romeo Must Die* had been banned for featuring gangsters, and his 2001 film *Kiss of the Dragon* had been banned because his character, a Chinese policeman, kills people overseas. He wrote, "If gangsters aren't appropriate and police officers aren't appropriate, then what type of character can there be that wouldn't start an argument? . . . It leaves only the ancient Chinese stories to be produced."[26]

Filmmakers have sometimes been forced to go underground to bypass the censorship system. In October 2011 the Sixth Beijing Independent Film Festival had to change venues twice due to police visits to the event. The festival was screening more than fifty cutting-edge feature films, documentaries, experimental works, and animated films in Songzhuang, a village on the outskirts of Beijing that "is known as a hub for the avant-garde artistic community." These works are considered "independent" because they are not submitted to SARFT for approval.[27]

Chinese filmmakers originally expected that the newest law would allow more creative freedom, but they were disappointed again. Film critic Tan Fei has been very outspoken, commenting that the so-called promotion law sounds more like an "obstructive law."[28] China's well-known film director Feng Xiaogang openly attacked China's film censorship system at the Chinese People's Political Consultative Conference in 2012. He said the strict censorship system severely shackles filmmakers and restricts their imagination and creativity. To satisfy the censors, filmmakers avoid contemporary topics and rush to make movies with ancient themes, resulting in a lack of films that record the great transformation of contemporary Chinese society. In response to Feng's criticism, Zhao Baohua, a member of the Film Censorship Committee and the director and editor in chief of the magazine *Film*, said SARFT's censoring is merely a "bottom line" expurgation; most of the banned films were terrible. Zhao also denied the possibility of implementing a ratings system, saying, "China has a different national situation than Western countries. If we adopt the rating system, then X-rated, obscene, murderous, and violent movies can be publicly screened."[29]

The censorship system has also had serious conflicts with film production and distribution companies. Yu Dong, chair of the Bona Film Group, disclosed that among 520 domestically made films and coproductions in 2010, only about 100 passed the censors and obtained screening licenses. Various film production companies invested approximately 5 billion yuan in total but managed to recoup only 2 billion yuan. In addition to rising production costs, the censorship system is believed to be one of the major reasons for these financial losses.[30]

Conflicts between the state censorship system and Chinese filmmakers continue. Ying Liang, a leading figure in the world of independent Chinese cinema, faced police threats following a screening of his most recent feature, *When Night Falls,* at the Jeonju Film Festival in South Korea. The controversy raises important questions about creative freedom in filmmaking and citizen surveillance networks in China.[31]

## The Local-Global Alliance and Strategies against Censorship

Although a few horror, martial arts, and spy movies, such as *The Lonely Spirit in an Old Building* (*Heilou guhun*) and *Mystery Buddha* (*Shenmi de dafo*), caused some concern for the Film Bureau in the 1980s, after the initiation of reform and the open-door policy, the entertaining nature of these movies posed no serious threat to the official ideology. The earliest conflicts between the state censorship system and filmmakers occurred in about 1992. The emergence of underground and dissident movies, which led to a direct confrontation with state censors, can be attributed to three causes. The first is the debut of fifth-generation (and later sixth-generation) film directors, who grew up during the turbulent era of the Cultural Revolution of the 1960s and 1970s. Unlike their predecessors in the fourth generation, who were trained in China's educational system and, to a large extent, observed official ideological guidelines, these individuals had the experience of being sent to work in the remote countryside or in factories. The poor living conditions of peasants and workers and their shattered dreams under the socialist system were deeply imprinted on their memories. These experiences provided them with unforgettable life lessons and profoundly affected the way they looked at party history, the state, and society. For them, the camera was both a tool and a weapon to be used to express their personal views of China's history. Well-known fifth-generation director Zhang Yimou's *To Live* (1994) and Tian Zhuangzhuang's *Blue*

*Kite* (1992) are typical examples of dissident views that were banned by the state. Among sixth-generation directors, Zhang Yuan's *Mama* (1991), *Beijing Bastards* (1993), and *East Palace, West Palace* (1996); Jia Zhangke's *The Pickpocket* (1997) and *Unknown Pleasures* (2001); and Wang Xiaoshuai's *The Days* (1993) and *Beijing Bicycle* (2000) are on the list of banned movies. They focus on the living conditions of socially marginalized and underprivileged groups who have been largely neglected or forgotten by mainstream society and are traditionally absent from main-melody films, including migrant workers, poor peasants, criminals, drug addicts, prostitutes, gays, urban hooligans, and people who are HIV-positive. At the same time, these movies touch on sensitive issues and political taboos such as moral collapse, corruption, land seizure, power-money transactions, child labor, and crime.

The second cause of the rise of underground filmmaking is that the rapid transition to a globalized market economy after 1989, the concurrent film marketization reform, and the quick emergence of a consumer culture have led to a relatively liberal political and social environment, which makes individual artistic expression possible and acceptable. Third, financial support from foreign film funds and international film festivals has played a crucial role in fostering an alternative film culture. It has become customary for young filmmakers to participate at international film festivals, win awards and recognition, and attract the attention of foreign investors.

The first incident symbolizing the direct conflict between filmmakers and the state censorship system is known as the "Seven Gentlemen" event of 1994. On March 12 the Ministry of Broadcasting, Film, and Television prohibited seven film directors from making films because of their unsanctioned participation in the Chinese movie exhibition at the Rotterdam Film Festival. The "Seven Gentlemen" were Tian Zhuangzhuang, Zhang Yuan, Wang Xiaoshuai, Wu Wenguang, He Jianjun, Ning Dai, and Wang Guangli.[32] Since then, confrontations with state censors have become a routine part of Chinese filmmakers' daily lives.

The state censorship system evolved along with China's film industrialization and marketization reforms. Censorship was strictest between 1992 and 1997, in accordance with the state's plan to promote main-melody films to counteract Hollywood's influence and tighten ideological control after the 1989 student democratic movement. The Changsha Conference and the 9550 Project spoke to the state's tight censorship and control. In

1995 a number of independent films, including Wang Xiaoshuai's *So Close to Paradise,* Lu Xuechang's *The Making of Steel,* Wang Shuo's *Father,* and Huang Jianzhong's *Rice,* were prohibited. It took four and half years and many rounds of negotiations with the Film Bureau for these movies to be revised and approved for release. These years also witnessed tension and cold relations between filmmakers and the Film Bureau. Before 2000, the state's strategy to promote main-melody movies was ineffective, and film production continued to decline. The Ministry of Propaganda and the Film Bureau held the Nanchang Conference in 1998 and solicited filmmakers' opinions in an official effort to make amends. The relationship with filmmakers improved after the conference, and some fourth-generation directors began to make movies in accordance with the state's main-melody plan.[33]

Critical filmmakers in China are often forced to go underground to make films. Underground or independent films are those that have been banned by the government and are shown only overseas, or those that have been produced specifically for international film festivals and overseas art-house viewers and critics. In contrast, aboveground films are those the government allows to be publicly screened. Underground movies are independent in the sense that they are independent of official ideology, state funding, and the state's production and distribution system. Nonofficial domestic capital and foreign investment are major sources of funding for underground films. Foreign distribution and exhibition networks are the major channels through which underground movies reach audiences. From the latter half of the 1990s to 2005, about 150 independent fictional and documentary movies were produced, in addition to approximately 100 experimental or dramatic shorts.[34] To maximize their creative freedom and reach a broader domestic audience, most filmmakers work both aboveground and underground, in constant negotiation with the state.

A subtle change of attitude among state censors began to appear in the early twenty-first century, after China's reentry into the WTO in 2001 and the launch of reform in the cultural industries. Film marketization reform pushed Film Bureau officials to acknowledge the market value and the cultural role of the film sector. This change in attitude toward underground filmmakers accompanied the regulations that opened up film markets to foreign and private capital. On November 13, 2003, the Film Bureau invited a number of underground filmmakers, including Jia Zhangke and Wang Xiaoshuai, to take part in an internal conversation. Subsequently, the Film Bureau changed its policy toward underground films from one of prohibition to one of guidance and administration.[35]

Although it is clear that the market economy and reform of the cultural industries have gradually and conditionally transformed the strict and uncompromising Chinese censorship system into a more flexible and accommodating one, it is still unclear under what circumstances and about which criteria the censors are willing to compromise. Is the market now the true master? Or do the party-state's interests still transcend everything? The answer is probably the latter. The state will occasionally adjust its stance under the pressure of market demands for the purpose of economic gain, if those demands pose no real threat to its rule. However, when the interests of the party-state and the market are in conflict, the former will usually prevail.

The latest example is the fate of the Beijing Independent Film Festival, which was forced to cancel its public screenings in September 2012 under pressure from local authorities. The film festival was sponsored by the Li Xianting Film Fund, which had helped organized independent film screenings in Beijing for more than a decade. In 2011, in the context of an increasingly sensitive political climate, the Film Fund's two events, the Beijing Documentary Film Festival and the Beijing Independent Film Festival, had both been shut down. In 2012 the two festivals merged to become the Ninth Beijing Independent Film Festival, which was scheduled to screen more than 100 titles over nine days. The event was interrupted by officials and by a power failure and was eventually canceled. According to Li, he simply wanted to help artists obtain more freedom of expression, not political freedom. But even this simple mission seems hard to achieve.[36]

The government's censorship is sometimes unpredictable, reflecting a lack of standardized criteria, the personal attitudes of the censors, and the changing political climate. In recent years, some movies exploring the dark side of contemporary Chinese society have unexpectedly passed the censors—provided the filmmakers made some revisions and added a "brighter tail." Two examples are Li Yang's *Blind Mountain* (*Mang Shan* [2007]) and Cai Shangjun's *People Mountain People Sea* (2012). After returning from studies in Germany, Li Yang devoted himself to the realistic portrayal of the shocking social problems of contemporary China. *Blind Shaft* (*Mang Jing* [2003]), the first in a planned three-film series, tells the story of two criminals' cold-blooded murder of miners in staged mine accidents to obtain financial compensation. Although it won numerous international awards, the film was prohibited in China. The second movie, *Blind Mountain,* fared better and was ultimately allowed to be released in mainland China. A brutally realistic work, *Blind Mountain* touches on the theme of the rampant abduction of women in rural China. It tells the tale of female college student Bai Xuemei, who is abducted and sold to a peasant to be his wife. She attempts to escape and eventually kills her husband. The domestic version of the film went through more than forty revisions before it was allowed to be publicly screened in China. The biggest difference between the international and domestic versions is the ending: In the international version, no one can save Bai Xuemei. Surrounded by the ruthless peasants, a desperate Bai stabs her peasant husband to death as he beats her father, who has come with the police to rescue her. Yet in the domestic version, Bai is saved by the police and returns home. This "happy ending" weakens the film's strong social criticism of human nature, lawlessness, and moral decline.[37]

Based on a true story that took place in remote southwestern China, *People Mountain People Sea* tells of a peasant's journey to avenge the murder of his brother. In the process, the movie uncovers the dark side of contemporary Chinese society: the senseless murder just to steal a motorcycle, the terrible living conditions of migrant workers, enslaved miners forced to labor in illegal coal mines, and the widespread distrust and indifference among people. The film's realistic style impressed the jury at the Sixty-Eighth Venice International Film Festival, where it won the Silver Lion Award for best director. Jury president Darren Aronofsky commented, "The committee was deeply touched by the movie. It reveals a world that we never knew before."[38] In theme and setting, the film resembles Li Yang's *Blind Shaft* and Wang Bin's *Jiabiangou,* both of which were prohibited in China. Cai's strategy was to revise certain aspects of the plot and the ending. In the original version, the peasant Lao Tie blows up the mine and kills everyone, including himself, but the murderer escapes. This is the version that was shown internationally and at the Venice International Film Festival. Although the film was originally labeled a Hong Kong movie, for it to be released in mainland China, it had to satisfy the censors. This meant giving it a "happy ending" in which Lao Tie is saved, the murderer is arrested, and a police officer persuades Lao Tie to place his trust in the local government. Given the unfolding story line, this ending seems bizarre and abrupt, and it confused the audience. But only with such a "happy ending" would the Film Bureau issue a release license.[39]

Because most independent and critical movies are screened at international film festivals, they play a crucial role in supporting these movies and pressuring China to reconsider its ban. The Nantes Three Continents Festival, which is held every November, is the most influential of these festivals. There, the French government awards funds to support film production in developing countries in Asia, Africa, and Latin America. This festival promotes multiculturalism, with special attention paid to Chinese independent movies. Sixth-generation director Zhang Yuan's movies earned a reputation at this festival. Similar to the Nantes Festival is the Youth Forum hosted by the Berlin Film Festival, where two banned films, Zhang Ming's *In Expectation* (*Wushan yunyu* [1995]) and Jia Zhangke's *The Pickpocket* (*Xiao Wu* [1997]), were first shown. The Rotterdam Film Festival, which fosters new talent and encourages innovative works in their early stages, plays a similar role. Shi Runjiu's *All the Way* (*Zoudaodi* [2001]) and Lou Ye's *The Suzhou River* (*Suzhouhe* [1999]) both received financial assistance from the Rotterdam Film Festival. After 1998, the Pusan International Film Festival of Korea became another important source of support. It hosts the Pusan Promotion Project, to which many Chinese independent filmmakers have applied. In addition to these film festivals, France's South Fund fosters film production in developing countries and has financed a number of Chinese films, including Zhang Yuan's *Beijing Bastards* (*Beijing zazhong* [1993]), Ning Ying's *For Fun* (*Zhaole* [1993]), Jia Zhangke's *Platform* (*Zhantai* [2000]), and Liu Bingjian's *Crying Woman* (*Kuqi de nvren* [2002]).[40] The financial assistance available from these foreign funds allows China's independent and critical filmmakers to resist domestic censorship and oppression. When they form alliances with foreign capital, they enhance their ability to negotiate for freedom of expression and basic civil rights with the party-state and create a larger space and better leverage.

Jia Zhangke, China's leading director, has made the most of this local-global alliance. Owing to their social realism and representation of underprivileged, marginalized groups, Jia's films were banned in mainland China between 1999 and January 2004. SARFT even warned the major postproduction companies in mainland China not to cooperate with Jia, so he had no choice but to partner with overseas investors. Traditionally considered an underground filmmaker, Jia claims he often "jumps out of bed to check if the film rolls were hidden" whenever he hears "a police siren."[41] His strategy is to obtain foreign investments to make underground films, without the sanction of the Film Bureau, and then to smuggle the films overseas for screenings at international festivals and art-house theaters. After his movies win awards and are well received at theaters, he is able to recoup the production costs.

Jia started making movies in 1995, and *The Pickpocket* (1997) was his second film. It was financed by Hong Kong's Hu Tong Communications and India's Radiant Advertising Company, and it was distributed by Hu Tong Communications and Spain's Prodimag. The film won awards at the Berlin International Film Festival, the Nantes Three Continents Festival, the Pusan International Film Festival, the San Francisco International Film Festival, and the Vancouver International Film Festival.

After this auspicious international debut, Jia went on to make the 2000 film *Platform*, funded by France's Artcam International, Hong Kong's Hu Tong Communications, and Japan's Bandai Entertainment Inc., Office Kitano, and T-Mark. Jia originally hoped to release *Platform* in mainland China, and he revised the screenplay many times in cooperation with the Shanghai Film Studio until they believed it was "clean enough" to pass the censors. The Shanghai Film Studio submitted the screenplay to the Censorship Committee and called for the lifting of the ban on Jia's films. However, after two years, the committee had not yet made a decision on the film. During that time, the committee asked Jia to write several "self-criticism" essays to ensure he would not violate the censorship rules. Jia finally gave up hope and shot the film on his own with the support of foreign capital.[42] *Platform* was a huge success, winning six awards at five international film festivals, including the Netpac Award at the Venice Film Festival. The film was released in fourteen countries between 2000 and 2005.[43]

The success enjoyed by young film directors like Jia on the international stage, coupled with the state's revised strategy with regard to foreign imports between 2001 and 2003, eventually led the Chinese government to change its attitude toward underground filmmakers. Starting in January 2004, the Film Bureau allowed Jia to direct films, and he is no longer considered an "underground" director. *The World*, his first film to be shown in mainland China, was released in 2004. In 2006 Jia's *Still Life*, about the misery of the people living in the Three Gorges Project area, won the Golden Lion Award at the Venice Film Festival and five other awards at four international film festivals. On March 14, 2008, Jia won an Outstanding Achievement Award at the Tenth French Deauville Asian Film Festival. Bruno Bard, chairman of the festival, said that although Jia had been making films for only a decade and had produced only eight feature-length films, his achievements should be recognized. "Jia's movies have had a great impact on the international cinema," Bard said. "He deserves to get the prize."[44] Jia's 2013 movie *A Touch of Sin* (*Tianzhuding*), based on four real-life stories about the struggles of the underclass, won the award for best screenplay at the Sixty-Sixth Cannes Film Festival. As of February 2014, Jia was still negotiating with the Film Bureau to release the film in China.[45]

Chinese filmmakers have employed various strategies to deal with the censors. For example, Jia Zhangke persuaded the Censorship Committee that *Still Life* is not about opposition to the Three Gorges Project but about environmental protection. The movie, according to Jia, tells people to cherish their motherland. Jia's strategy is to have frank talks with members of the Censorship Committee to obtain their understanding. To negotiate with the Censorship Committee, filmmakers must have patience, wisdom, and a bit of "rogue spirit."[46]

Director Zhang Yuan is another outstanding example. He is perhaps the most decorated Chinese director and is famous for his confrontational stance against the Chinese government. Zhang's 1991 film debut, *Mama*, tells the story of a young mother raising a mentally challenged child on her own. Its artistic style is typical of Zhang's films, which depict a dark, realistic, cruel society without any superficial beauty. *Mama* was banned by the Chinese government but won several awards: the Critics' Award and the Public Award at the Nantes Three Continents Festival, the Best Film Award at the Berlin International Film Festival, and the Critics' Award at the Edinburgh International Film Festival. The film was finally released in the Netherlands in 1994. However, the film that really put Zhang at the top of Chinese film directors was *Beijing Bastards* (1993). It tells the story of a rock musician, played by Chinese rock star Cui Jian, and the search for his pregnant girlfriend, who has left him. The film demonstrates a strong sense of disorientation, loneliness, and sadness amidst drastic social change and reflects young people's crisis of faith in the early 1990s, when China rushed to transform into a market economy. Zhang Yuan received financial support from the Hubert Bals Fund, an initiative of the Rotterdam International Film Festival that provides grants to promising cinema projects at various stages of completion. *Beijing Bastards* was prohibited by the Chinese government but was released in Japan in November 1994. The film won a Special Mention Award at the 1993 Locarno International Film Festival and was nominated for the Golden Leopard Award; it also won the Critics' Award at the Singapore International Film Festival.

Zhang's 1996 film *East Palace West Palace,* also known as *Behind the Forbidden City* (*Dong gong xi gong*), may be the first mainland Chinese movie to touch on the theme of homosexuality. It tells the story of a young gay man who is routinely persecuted by the police. To complete production, Zhang secured foreign funding from Ocean Films, Amazon Entertainment Ltd., and Quelqu'un d'Autre. The film won five international awards, including Best Director, Best Screenplay, and Special Mention Awards at the 1996 Mar del Plata Film Festival and the Best Actor Award at the 1997 Taormina International Film Festival.[47] In 1997 the Chinese government put Zhang Yuan under house arrest and confiscated his passport because of the unsanctioned screening of this movie at international film festivals. His friends had managed to smuggle the movie out of the country, and it was eventually selected for the 1997 Cannes Film Festival.[48]

Zhang Yuan's 1998 film, *Seventeen Years,* describes a family's pain and forgiveness after one daughter accidentally kills her stepsister and spends seventeen years in jail. Like his previous movies, *Seventeen Years* was funded and distributed by foreign companies from various countries. The film won four awards at the 1999 Venice Film Festival, was nominated for the Golden Lion Award, and won five additional awards at other international film festivals. Tired of the years of confrontation with the government, and anguished by the fact that his films were unavailable to domestic audiences, Zhang Yuan negotiated with the Film Bureau, arguing that *Seventeen Years* reflected the progress of China's judicial system. The bureau lifted the ban on the movie in 1999, making *Seventeen Years* Zhang's first movie to be publicly screened in mainland China.[49]

Nevertheless, Zhang Yuan remains pessimistic about the future of China's film industry and criticizes the Chinese government's lack of support for domestic filmmakers. Whereas other countries' governments have taken various measures to foster domestic filmmakers and reward directors whose movies win awards at international film festivals, the Chinese government remains cold and unsupportive, treating many film directors like "bad guys." Because of his achievements, *Time* named Zhang Yuan one of the world's top 100 young leaders in the twenty-first century, and the United Nations gave him a Culture and Peace Award in 2001.[50] Ironically, all these awards and achievements have come without the support of his home country and government.

It has become common for talented young artists to go abroad, bypassing the Chinese censors and creating outstanding work. Then, when they return to their homeland, they have more bargaining power and increased leverage. Foreign capital gives these filmmakers the freedom to express themselves and enhance their careers, which in turn places pressure on the government to lift its bans.

## Artistic and Critical Cinema: A Perplexing Picture

Artistic and critical cinema reveals a Chinese society fraught with the daily struggles of ordinary people during the country's unprecedented transition to a primitive, capitalist-style market economy. This category of cinema foregrounds the plight and misery of underprivileged people and paints a gloomy picture of China that is fundamentally different from that shown in main-melody movies. These films, unsurprisingly, become the targets of the censors; at the same time, they reflect the filmmakers' artistic experiments and their profound thoughts on Chinese reality.

Jia Zhangke is the leading figure in critical cinema. His movies boast a distinctive perspective on Chinese society and emphasize humanistic concerns. Jia grew up in a small town in Shanxi Province and witnessed first-hand the desperate living conditions of the underprivileged. According to Jia, he wants his films to remind people of the huge regional imbalance and the gap between the rich and the poor in contemporary China. He aims to use his camera to arouse the awareness of the entire society and draw attention to the plight of marginalized people.[51] Between 1997 and 2007, Jia produced a number of brilliant, award-winning movies—*The Pickpocket, Platform, Unknown Pleasures,* and *Still Life*—that captured underclass people's struggle, disorientation, and despair during the ten years of profound social change initiated by China's integration into the global capitalist system.

*The Pickpocket* is a candid portrayal of a thief's life and his attempts to break with his criminal past. It is a dismal picture of life in a small inland town: rundown buildings along littered streets, filthy public baths, secret brothels camouflaged as karaoke bars, and a girl who falls in love with the pickpocket but eventually "contracts" herself to a rich man. The film describes the confusion of small-town residents in a rapidly changing era. *Unknown Pleasures* uses cinematic realism to display the bleak existence of two insecure, aimless young people as they strive for unachievable American-style freedom. *Platform* follows a troupe of amateur theater performers whose experience mirrors that of the general population as massive socio-economic changes sweep across mainland China. The film covers a decade of tremendous upheaval, opening in 1979 with the troupe performing songs to celebrate Mao Zedong and ending in the late 1980s with a performance that reflects the influx of Western culture into China. Finally, *Still Life,* which won the 2006 Golden Lion Award at the Venice Film Festival, along with other accolades, uses realistic shooting techniques to record the devastating impact of the Three Gorges Project on area residents: homes flooded, people left homeless, towns torn down, and buildings destroyed. A young boy is killed in a bloody street fight, and migrant workers are forced to labor in the coal mines, where accidents and death are daily routines. Yet officials celebrate their "work performance" by building a shining bridge decorated by neon lights. Employing a strong realistic style without any beautification of the bitter reality, Jia's movies often star amateur actors and actresses and are characterized by long shots, natural lights, and slow pacing. All these techniques convey the banality and the stifling atmosphere of daily life in small towns.

Jia Zhangke's aesthetic pursuits and historical reflections are carried into his 2008 film *The Story of 24 City.* The film follows three generations of characters in Chengdu from the 1950s to the present day—from a once-privileged Mao-era state factory worker who is now aging and ill to a modern young consumer—symbolizing China's dazzling social transformation. Similarly, Factory 420, once a top-secret manufacturer of military aviation, is destined to become 24 City, an upscale high-rise office, residential, and entertainment complex. The film is a blend of fictional and documentary storytelling, featuring five interviews and four fictional scenes delivered by actors but presented in a documentary format. Jia once said, "I have been simultaneously recording the process of domestic transitions. I am living in an era of transformation that requires a film director's sensitive and spontaneous judgment. I believe my works will become landmarks of a changing China."[52] On another occasion he said: "From *The Pickpocket* of 1998 to *Useless* of 2007, my works have accompanied the tremendous change of Chinese society. From a personal point of view, it is perhaps safer to keep silent on the complicated social reality. But whenever I am standing behind the camera to shoot films, it helps me overcome my weakness and maintain the basic love and the sense of justice. I am grateful for films!"[53]

While Jia Zhangke dedicates himself to recording contemporary Chinese society's transition from a socialist to a semicapitalist market economy and its impact on ordinary people's lives, film director Wang Quan'an is more devoted to the misfortunes of the underprivileged. His most famous film is *Tuya's Marriage* (2006), which won the 2007 Golden Berlin Bear Award at the Berlin International Film Festival. Tuya is the wife of Bater, a herdsman who lost his legs while looking for water in the Inner Mongolia grassland, which is quickly vanishing as a result of desertification. She takes on the sole responsibility of supporting her family, but when she suffers a spinal injury from her hard labor, she herself risks paralysis. Faced with this brutal reality, the couple decides to divorce so that Tuya can marry someone else who is able to support her and her children. Imposing her own conditions on this remarriage—her new husband must take care of Bater, their children, and their land—Tuya embarks on an arduous search for a new husband. She meets admirers who are either rich but disingenuous or genuine but shy, and along the way she saves a suicidal Bater, who still longs for her and their children. Tuya possesses all the traditional Chinese virtues—perseverance, hard work, selflessness, and sympathy—but her life is full of hardship. The film depicts the suffering and helplessness of underprivileged Chinese people and their miserable existence to its fullest extent and concludes with a melancholy Mongolian song that offers no sign of hope.

Aesthetically distinct from both Jia Zhangke and Wang Quan'an, cinematographer-turned-director Gu Changwei focuses on the tragic impact of volatile times and the unfairness of ordinary people's lives; in particular, he accentuates people's unfailing pursuit of dreams and love and their unceasing hope for a better life. His early film *Peacock* (*Kongque* [2005]) is a gloomy tale that traces the lives of a family's three children. Set in a small Chinese town in the 1970s, the film tells how these children's dreams are shattered in the unpredictable political climate of the Cultural Revolution. Like the momentary spreading of a peacock's tail feathers, their dreams are crushed just as they blossom. The elder sister aspires to join the army, but that dream is shattered when she is replaced by someone else who has better personal connections. The elder son is obese, mentally challenged, and constantly bullied by others. He ends up married to a handicapped girl, and the two of them run a food booth for their livelihood. The younger boy tries to break away from his family and his banal daily life by leaving town, but he winds up married to a divorced singer on whom he is dependent. Their growing up is a journey of lost dreams. The movie reflects the tragedy of an entire generation and, to some extent, reveals the cruelty of everyday life with profound pessimism. The film is so gloomy that some critics have questioned whether the Chinese people ever had an idealistic spirit in their socialist past, or whether their socialist dream is merely an illusion.[54] The film won the Silver Berlin Bear Award at the 2005 Berlin International Film Festival.

Gu's later movies magnify the persistence of the human spirit even in the most desperate and harshest conditions. *And the Spring Comes* (*Li Chun* [2007]) recounts the story of a gifted music teacher and her fruitless attempts to become a singer. Wang Tsai-ling has a beautiful voice and is a masterful opera singer. She dreams of singing on a national stage, despite her lack of beauty and limited personal connections. Despite years of effort, she is unable to reach her goal and ends up living with her adopted child in her old school. At the end of the movie, Wang Tsai-ling sits on the ground in Tiananmen Square with her lovely daughter, her tired and bewildered eyes gazing at the rostrum, as if reflecting on her lost dreams. At this point, a beautiful voice singing Tosco's "Vissi d'arte, Vissi d'amore" is heard, and the scene switches to the glittering Beijing Opera Hall, where a dressed-up Wang Tsai-ling passionately sings onstage. A subtitle reads, "This scene is dedicated to Wang Tsai-ling," implying that the scene exists only in the imagination of the audience or of Wang Tsai-ling. The movie uses a mostly realistic approach to highlight the conflict and distance between ordinary people's dreams and the unfavorable social conditions, but an idealistic touch marks the entire movie.

Gu Changwei's 2011 film *Love for Life* (*Zui Ai,* also known as *Life Is a Miracle* or *Till Death Do Us Part*) tells the tearful story of two AIDS patients who find true love despite being abandoned by their families and society. The movie celebrates the endurance of the human spirit and true love even in the most unbearable situations, and the glory of human dignity shines through. Unlike Jia Zhangke's documentary style, Gu Changwei's movies blend a realistic approach with stylistic touches and idealistic brightness. They are characterized by carefully designed scenes and sounds, nuanced performances, and symbolic close-ups and songs.

Wang Xiaoshuai is another distinctive Chinese film director. He employs a unique individualistic angle to display the struggles of the underclass and their fate in the urban environment of social transition. For example, his *So Close to Paradise* (*Biandan guniang* [1998]) describes the different experiences of two migrant workers in the city who get involved in gangster brawls and police raids. At the end, one is killed by gang cross-fire, while the other submerges himself in tedious labor. The film has a dark, gloomy style reminiscent of classic Hollywood B movies and film noir. Wang's *Beijing Bicycle* (*Shiqisui danche* [2000]) is about the conflict between two boys. One is a migrant worker who delivers packages and works very hard to purchase the bicycle his company has lent him; the other is a lower-class urban dweller who wants a fancy bicycle and steals the first boy's. The two boys eventually agree to share the bicycle. The movie reflects the gap between urban dwellers and migrant workers, depicting the daily struggles of both social strata.

The movies described above realistically depict the harsh living conditions of the underprivileged and their struggles in a rapidly changing and globalizing society. These films paint a very gloomy picture of Chinese society: the huge gap between the rich and poor, the helpless working class, marginalized social groups. All the fancy things made possible by rapid economic development and the arrival of global capital—modern shopping malls and restaurants, luxurious villas and cars, designer clothing and jewels—seem to be out of reach for these poor people, who struggle just to maintain their basic existence. They face too many difficulties and uncertainties; happiness and a materially sufficient life seem like unattainable dreams. These filmmakers employ realistic shooting techniques and implicit political satire to depict these people's miserable lives and harsh social realities. One recurring scene involves the sharp contrast between the voice-over of a radio or TV broadcast of government policies and the people's indifference and antipathy toward it. In the film *So Close to Paradise,* broadcasts of official speeches are repeatedly contrasted with the helplessness and struggles of migrant workers. In *Still Life,* close-ups of a portrait of Mao Zedong and the image of a worker, a peasant, and a People's Liberation Army soldier printed on the 100-yuan bank note are seen through the eyes of the main actor, in contrast with demolished buildings and homeless people. The voice-over reiterates that construction of the Three Gorges Project is the wish of several generations of Chinese party leaders. A deep sense of cynicism and implicit political satire are revealed through these scenes and cuts, as if asking, "Whose country is this?"

These movies also exhibit a profoundly pessimistic attitude about the future. This shift in filmmakers' perspectives is reflected by two films that document the digging of wells. The 1986 film *Old Well* (*Lao jing*) tells the story of several generations of Shaanxi villagers who battle severe weather conditions and must dig a well to get water. Their struggle to dig the well emphasizes the villagers' perseverance, endurance, and solidarity and demonstrates the power of the human spirit. By contrast, the digging of a well in *Tuya's Marriage* is portrayed as sad and hopeless, an endeavor that ultimately results in no water and an injured herdsman. The difference in these films reflects different times. During the 1980s, the Enlightenment view of modernity was embraced by cultural workers, and the decade was infused with optimism about the future. The post-1990s era, in contrast, has been marked by political disillusionment, a power-money coalition, and an alliance between the government and global capital. Working people have been largely neglected and omitted from the official agenda. Filmmakers capture the mood of the time and profoundly reflect people's grief and confusion.

As such, critical films depict a Chinese society trapped in a handicapped market economy characterized by power-money deals, government corruption, and moral collapse. People are helpless and hopeless, in the sense that they are victims of the corrupt system rather than victims of global capitalism. These films symbolize an entirely different national identity from that in main-melody movies: a corrupt system with imposed capitalism, besieged by social problems, and full of disoriented people. China is a country with fractured national identities, and there are no signs of hope for the future.

## Striving for Market Survival

As mentioned earlier, one of the major conflicts in China's film industry is that between market demands and filmmakers' desire for self-expression. Previously, these filmmakers were concerned primarily with their artistic achievements and whether they could win awards at international film festivals in order to secure financial support. Because of the lack of government support for domestic filmmaking, Chinese filmmakers had to depend on investments obtained through international film festivals sponsored by foreign countries and support from foreign film funds. They therefore had to consider the tastes of foreign critics and make films that would appeal to them. Because most of China's artistic filmmakers were graduates of the Beijing Film Academy, they were deeply influenced by French avant-garde and European artistic styles, and their movies were not well received by domestic audiences. Thus, before 2003, and before the establishment of a unified national film market and film industry, Chinese filmmakers neglected the domestic market to focus on international film festivals and foreign critics. The only movies that were successful in China were Feng

Xiaogang's series of New Year's celebration movies before 2000. As director Zhang Yang said in 2012, "Seven or eight years ago, what concerned us was the artistic reputation of our movies, and if our movies could win any awards at international film festivals. Now we have to take into consideration the market, audience, and box office, and be involved in marketing our movies."[55]

Fifth- and sixth-generation filmmakers have attempted to keep up with market trends and cater to the domestic market. Some have adjusted well and have gotten used to commercial operations; others have found it hard to adjust to market demands; and a few have remain resolute, insisting on following their own artistic tastes and pursuits. Among fifth-generation film directors, Zhang Yimou was the first to be successful in the Chinese market. Encouraged by the global success of Ang Lee's 2000 film *Crouching Tiger, Hidden Dragon,* Zhang produced several ancient-costumed martial arts movies in quick succession between 2002 and 2006, establishing him as a top box office earner in China. *Hero* (2002) set box office records domestically (250 million yuan), and its record of US$177 million in international distribution revenue remains unbroken. *House of Flying Daggers* (2004) and *Curse of the Golden Flower* (2006) also earned large sums at the box office. Zhang's films have helped reestablish martial arts as a distinguished genre and have created new space for domestic filmmakers to maneuver. Martial arts cinema has reemerged as a collective cultural phenomenon that both satisfies state censors and meets market demands (this cultural phenomenon is explored further in the next chapter). Facing some criticism about the vulgarity of his movies, especially his 2009 comedy *A Simple Noodle Story* (*Sanqiang paian jingqi*), Zhang made an artistic movie about pure love in 2010; *Under the Hawthorn Tree* (*Shanzhashu zhilian)* netted 150 million yuan, a total unmatched by any artistic movie from mainland China in the past ten years.[56] Zhang's 2011 movie *The Flowers of War* (*Jinling shisanchai*) is an epic about the Nanjing massacre and the resistance of local residents, including prostitutes. Although it was severely criticized for being tasteless and using the nation's trauma for sensual stimulation, it was the top Chinese-language movie of 2011, making 620 million yuan; however, it fell short of its anticipated earnings of 1 billion yuan.[57]

Another leading fifth-generation film director, Chen Kaige, has been exploring new methods of filmic expression to adapt to the sweeping marketization trend. Well known for his artistic movies that won numerous awards in the 1980s and 1990s—including *Yellow Earth* (*Huangtudi* [1984]), *King of the Children* (*Haiziwang* [1987]), and especially Palme d'Or winner *Farewell My Concubine* (*Bawang bieji* [1992])—Chen has a reputation for loading his films with cultural reflections, historical inquiries, and philosophical depth. Some critics have argued that Chen's elite and intellectual perspective makes his movies less appealing to mass audiences. It appears that Chen is reluctantly turning to more commercial and entertaining movies, while holding on to his cultural ideas and humanistic spirit. His 1999 film *The Emperor and the Assassin* recounts the history of the first Chinese emperor, Qin Shihuang, and his assassin, Jing Ke, exploring the contradiction between human nature and the imperial crown. It was not well received by audiences. His 2005 film *The Promise* (*Wuji*) examines the impact of inescapable destiny on people's lives. Through the format of mythical prophecy, the film explores the perplexing question of whether human beings have free will or are merely the puppets of fate. All the characters in the movie—a pretty prince, a brave slave, an ambitious general, and a treacherous duke—behave in accordance with their desires: greed, ambition, revenge, loyalty. These desires determine their fates. The film's point is that human beings are partners in controlling their own fates, even if their ultimate destinies are predetermined.[58] The film was shot at Yunnan Province's Tianchi Resort, with its stunning natural scenery. The film earned 210 million yuan, largely due to Chen's reputation, high audience expectations, and skillful promotion. But it has been the subject of much criticism, ranging from harsh assessments of its weak and illogical plotting, pretentious settings, and exaggerated performances to condemnation of the film team's destructive impact on the environment at Tianchi Resort.[59]

Chen's 2010 *Sacrifice* (*Zhaoshi guer*) is based on a well-known Yuan Dynasty play, but it completely deconstructs the original theme. The original play tells the true story of a doctor, Cheng Ying, who sacrifices his own son in exchange for the orphan of the prime minister of Jin State, whose entire family has been killed by a rival. The play highlights the loyalty and righteousness of Cheng Ying and praises his self-sacrifice and virtue. Chen Kaige's film, however, foregrounds the elements of ineluctable fate and unpredictable chance. Cheng Ying's self-sacrifice is portrayed not as a noble virtue but as a forced choice and the consequence of uncertain circumstances. Chen Kaige, who wanted to tell a believable story that was close to the heart of modern-day audiences, uses this film to reflect on the ethos of the Chinese people, whose perseverance enables them to survive and prosper even under the most desperate circumstances.[60]

Because of their humanist and philosophical concerns, Chen Kaige's movies seem incompatible with the current trends of marketization and mass-market appeal. Still, Chen has tried to integrate his cultural and philosophical elements with the selling points of modern cinema, and some of his movies have earned impressive receipts at the box office. Critics, however, have argued that Chen Kaige's movies are awkward combinations of commercial elements and cultural, historical, and philosophical components, and they believe Chen Kaige is out of touch with the times. Hong Kong–based Phoenix TV has even called Chen "an orphan" who sings "awkward songs of the time."[61] Chen himself once said: "The present is a time of collapse. Many things that once were pillars of our life all collapse. Everyone is kidnapped by money, and everyone is confused. We have paid a high price for social progress and economic development. Now we should think how to live our lives and how to live a decent life."[62] His 2012 movie *Caught in the Web* (*Sousuo*) represents his most recent effort to blend commercial, entertaining elements with artistic expression and philosophical thinking. The movie describes the impact of the Internet on people's lives and reflects in some depth on the Web's intrusion into people's privacy, the dictatorial nature of the "human flesh search," and hypocritical moral judgment at the expense of individual rights. The movie did well at the box office, garnering 180 million yuan within the first six weeks of its release and leading domestic artistic movies in 2012.[63]

Chen's case demonstrates the conflict between artistic expression and profit-driven market demand. Other fifth-generation directors have had more or less similar experiences. Tian Zhuangzhuang returned to the Beijing Film Academy to teach after his award-winning film *The Blue Kite* (*Lanfengzheng* [1993]) was banned in China. From 1993 to 2006 he produced only two feature films and one documentary. In 2009 Tian directed *The Warrior and the Wolf* (*Langzaiji*), marking his transition from artistic to commercial filmmaking. *The Warrior and the Wolf*, adapted from a novel by the famous Japanese writer Inoue Yasushi, tells the story of a female prisoner and an ancient general who transform into wolves after seven nights of sexual encounters. The film combines a number of subjects that might have been commercial selling points: war, myth, sexual desire. However, Tian's exploration of grand themes, such as human and animal nature, as well as human-animal relationships, overshadows the film's commercial elements, making it difficult for audiences to understand. The film has been criticized for a lack of logical development in both character and plot, which results in considerable confusion. The film suffered a box office Waterloo. In a July 2010 interview, Tian admitted he had been unable to adjust to market demands and would wait for an appropriate opportunity to arrive before trying again.[64] However, in early 2011, reports appeared that Tian was going to direct a film called *Guan Gong* and had submitted a synopsis to SARFT. That film, however, conflicted with four other movies with exactly the same subject matter and was delayed.[65] It seems that Tian has decided to follow the path of other film directors, producing martial arts cinema in an attempt to satisfy the market—or at least what he perceives the market to be.

Promising young directors whose work has appealed to audiences and performed well at the box office include Xu Jinglei, Ning Hao, Lu Chuan, Jin Yimeng, and Li Weiran. One of mainland China's rising female directors is Xu Jinglei. Her commercial movies typically depict elements of contemporary China's cosmopolitan lifestyle, such as fashion, love, and competition between young white-collar workers and the upper middle class. These characters' lives are entirely different from those of the underprivileged characters in the movies of Jia Zhangke, Wang Quan'an, and Cai Shangjun. Xu's movies focus on modern urban interpersonal relations and cosmopolitan values. Her two most successful movies, *Go, Lala, Go* (*Dulala shengzhiji* [2010]) and *Dear Enemy* (*Qinmi diren* [2011]), are love stories set against a backdrop of commercial competition. Their selling points include vibrant cosmopolitan settings, beautiful and smart female characters, handsome and gentle male characters, and a focus on the successful careers and comfortable living conditions of the upper middle class. These elements cater to the young urban generation and exemplify the glamour and bourgeois flavor of an ascendant and increasingly rich and globalized China, representing the ideal lifestyle of many young people. Similarly, young female director Jin Yimeng, who trained in the United States, has emerged as a rising star in China's film industry. Her debut, *Sophie's Revenge* (*Feichang wanmei* [2010]), earned more than 100 million yuan, and the *Hollywood Reporter* selected Jin as one of twenty "Next Generation Asia" awardees in 2010.[66] *Sophie's Revenge* transplants the Hollywood romantic comedy genre into Chinese soil and stars famous actors who add to its charm. Its humorous style provides a fresh type of enjoyment for Chinese audiences.

Blending black comedy with social criticism, Ning Hao's *Crazy Stone* (*Fengkuang de Shitou* [2006]) and *Crazy Racer* (*Fengkuang de saiche* [2009]) both achieved market success. *Crazy Stone* is about three thieves who plan to steal a tightly guarded piece of jade on exhibit at a bankrupt factory. Throughout, the film displays the ugliness of society: previously state-owned factories sold to private owners; corrupt officials joining with businessmen to sell public properties and pocket public funds; unemployed workers plunged into financial difficulties with no way to make a living. *Crazy Racer* satirizes the grotesque social phenomena of contemporary Chinese society. The film charts four parallel story lines involving a bicycle racer, thieves, gangsters, and the police. These characters become entangled with one another through various unexpected encounters and coincidences, creating seemingly inexhaustible fodder for laughs. *Crazy Racer* earned 190 million yuan at the box office, making Ning Hao the fourth director in mainland China who can boast box office receipts exceeding 100 million yuan, along with Zhang Yimou, Feng Xiaogang, and Chen Kaige.[67] Ning Hao's 2012 film *Guns and Roses* (*Huangjin dajie'an*) netted 150 million yuan. After many rounds of revisions, his film *No Man's Land* (*Wu Renqu*) passed the censors and was released in December 2013, garnering box office receipts of 220 million yuan.[68]

Another film director, Guan Hu, has produced black comedies with unique characteristics. His movie *Cow* (*Dou Niu* [2009]) tells the story of a peasant and his cow during the War of Resistance against Japan between 1937 and 1945. The peasant is responsible for taking care of a Dutch cow sent to China by the international community to provide nutrition to injured Chinese soldiers. The Japanese army slaughters all the villagers, leaving the peasant and the cow as the only survivors in the remote mountain terrain. The film demonstrates humankind's perseverance and will to live under the desperate conditions of war, as well as the touching relationship between the man and the animal. The film was highly regarded at the Venice International Film Festival.[69] Guan Hu's other film, *Design of Death* (*Sha Sheng* [2012]), has strong symbolic implications. It is set in a remote village in southwestern China and tells the story of the entire village's complicity in the murder of an erratic and wild young man. The village is a metaphor for societies that suppress creativity and innovation, a theme to which every viewer can relate. The film's settings and the rituals and costumes of the villagers all have strong symbolic meanings. Guan Hu has said he does not want to produce films that appeal to foreigners, nor does he want to reproduce the clichéd commercial movies that are seen everywhere. His way is risky, but it may lead to success.[70] Guan Hu always aims high and pushes his movies to convey something bigger than a simple or funny story. He has explored a fresh blend of black comedy and serious reflections and metaphorical implications, qualities that will establish him as a rising star of the next generation in terms of both market success and artistic expression.

Another rising star is film director Lu Chuan, who has made four movies so far—each of them unique. The three movies he made between 2001 and 2009—*The Missing Gun* (*Xun Qiang* [2002]), *Mountain Patrol* (*Keke xili* [2004]), and *City of Life and Death* (*Nanjing! Nanjing!* [2009])—won a total of thirty-eight awards at various film festivals.[71] The first two were not box office hits, but both boasted high artistic achievements. The third recounts the well-known history of the Japanese army's slaughter of Nanjing residents in 1937 through the unique perspective of a Japanese soldier, employing black-and-white cinematography to achieve an arresting visual effect. The film profoundly reveals the atrocity of war, the distorted humanity of the Japanese soldiers, and the unbearable torture and misery suffered by the Chinese people, especially women. Different from other similarly themed movies, which tend to portray the Japanese soldiers as evil "foreign devils" and Nanjing residents as passive and weak victims, Lu Chuan's version of the Nanjing massacre treats Japanese soldiers as human beings. His movie also highlights the Chinese people's bitter and desperate resistance, mutual assistance, and fortitude during this calamitous period. The filmmaker's use of brutally realistic black-and-white shots, along with angles and close-ups that create an unspeakably shocking impact on the audience, is reminiscent of *Schindler's List* (1993). Although it caused lots of controversy and was especially criticized by audiences in Nanjing, Shanghai, and other areas in close proximity to the actual event, the movie was a huge market success, earning 180 million yuan at the box office.[72] Compared with Zhang Yimou's vulgar *Flowers of War*, Lu Chuan's movie is a sincere and profound reflection on history and human nature.

Others have been trying to find their place in the market. Jia Zhangke, the leading Chinese director of independent artistic films, declared in March 2011 that he too would start making commercial blockbusters. Well known for his artistic and realistic movies based on his experiences in Shanxi Province, Jia confidently claimed, "If I wish to make commercial movies, it will not be difficult for my movies to achieve box office revenue of more than 100 million yuan."[73] His first commercial film (and also his first foray into the martial arts genre), *In the Qing Dynasty* (*Zai Qingchao*), started production at Shanxi in August 2011 with an investment of nearly 100 million yuan; it reflects the social turmoil that followed the abolishment of the imperial examination system. Jia's second commercial movie, *Shuangxionghui*, which documents post-1949 Hong Kong society, is also in preproduction. To ensure decent economic returns, Jia used the method of "product-placement" advertising in his movies *24 City* and the documentary *Yulu*. According to Jia, investors in *The Pickpocket* and *I Wish I Knew* (*Haishangchuanqi*) earned good financial returns from overseas royalties and commercial activities. However, China's theaters have not profited from his movies. By making commercial movies, Jia hopes to extend his commercial success to domestic theaters. Jia argues that "to make a functional film industry, you have to let every sector of the industry make profits." In his opinion, the biggest problem with China's commercial movies is that they lack realism and have no connection to the real lives of ordinary people. He wants to make movies that reflect the true reality of Chinese society.[74]

Similar to Jia, Yang Shupeng has tried to satisfy market demands. Yang's film debut, *The Robbers* (*Wo de tangchao xiongdi* [2009]), vividly tells the story of two bandits in a small village in the ancient past. The film adopts the style of Japanese and Korean samurai films: fast-paced, captivating plots with surprises along the way. Such a film has no precedent in Chinese film history. Its fresh style has earned Yang a good reputation, and the film is considered representative of the work of China's newly emerging filmmakers. However, the film used no professional marketing strategies and was a disappointment at the box office. Taking a lesson from his first movie, Yang endeavored to improve his marketing techniques and tell a better story in his second, *An Inaccurate Memoir* (*Pi Fu*). It was released in April 2012, immediately following the lifting of the quota on Hollywood imports, and struggled in the newly competitive market. Yang has openly declared war on Hollywood and hopes to use his movies to counter its influence.[75]

Zhang Yang and Wang Xiaoshuai are among those who have persisted in their artistic pursuits, regardless of market pressures. Zhang Yang's movies are dedicated to family relationships in general and father-son conflicts in particular. Despite the trend toward more commercial movies, his films always portray genuine interpersonal interactions and family ethics. Human emotion, the generation gap, and the conflict between tradition and modernity are common themes in Chinese society, and these elements in Zhang's films resonate with audiences. His latest movie, *Full Circle* (*Fei yue lao ren yuan* [2012]), assembles a number of older movie stars and tells an inspiring story of individuals who refuse to succumb to age but rather seek to revitalize their lives and search for meaning. The movie caters to an older audience, given that China's populace is aging. This represents Zhang Yang's most recent effort to relate to the market while remaining true to his artistic vision. He hopes to recoup US$1 million to US$2 million in production costs from the overseas market.[76]

Wang Xiaoshuai's movies have a distinct personal style and are imprinted with his own life journey; consequently, they are often rejected by theater managers, who fear market failure. Some considered Wang's *In Love We Trust (Zuoyou* [2007]), which features nudity and explicit sex, to be an attempt to cater to market demands. However, the plot is too unrealistic and too coincidental, making it seem artificial and therefore not pleasing to audiences. Wang's 2012 film *11 Flowers* (*Wo shiyi*) examines a remote community from the perspective of an eleven-year-old boy in the 1970s, exploring Chinese teenagers' oppressed psyche in the Mao era. Critics have commented that this film, a Sino-French coproduction, is Wang's first effort with both commercial and market appeal and artistic value.

At the end of 2012, a dark horse became the first domestic movie to earn more than 1 billion yuan at the box office. The comedy *Lost in Thailand* (*Renzai lvtu zhi Taijiong*), directed by newcomer Xu Zheng, made 1.236 billion yuan.[77] It tells the story of a young manager who travels to Thailand to find his boss, who is meditating in a Thai temple, and get his authorization to sell a newly invented product with huge market potential. However, the young manager is followed by a colleague, a rival at the company, who is seeking the same thing. Their journeys are unexpectedly intertwined with that of a chef who is hoping to plant a "tree of health" in the temple in an attempt to save his mother from Alzheimer's disease. As the story unfolds, the rivals' fierce business competition gradually yields to the chef's unsophisticated charm and genuine human affection. Eventually the young manager withdraws from the competition, reconciles with his wife, and saves his marriage. The numerous encounters and conflicts between the shrewd and ambitious manager and the simple-minded yet pious chef provide the main source of laughter, while the exotic and beautiful Thai landscapes and culture provide visual enjoyment. Although it is a comedy, the film also explores the serious themes of family values and moral and ethical standards. It thus resonates with a Chinese audience that is experiencing fast-paced economic development and is worried about the loss of family values and cultural traditions. The film posits that family and friends are more important than money and business. *Lost in Thailand* may point to the future direction of Chinese movies in their battle with Hollywood: Chinese films should be rooted in Chinese soil and reflect domestic living conditions and interpersonal relationships; they should disclose the contradiction between modernity and tradition during China's profound social transition; and they should have a gentle touch and a warm human spirit.

Some film critics hailed 2013 as the "Year of the Youth Movie." A number of movies dedicated to youth came out and achieved impressive box office records, including *So Young* (*Zhi women zhongjiang shiqu de qingchun*), *Tiny Times 1.0* (*Xiaoshidai*), *Finding Mr. Right* (*Beijing Yushang Xiyatu*), *American Dreams in China* (*Zhongguo hehuoren*), and *Forever Young* (*Nufang zhi qingchun zaijian*). Inspired by Taiwan's box office hit *You Are the Apple of My Eye* (*Naxienian women yiqi zhuiguo de nvhai*) and Thailand's hit *A Little Thing Called Love* (*Chulian zhejian xiaoshi*), mainland Chinese film producers began tapping the rich treasure of youth. This trend speaks to two noticeable phenomena in Chinese society: First, by the end of 2013, the average age of China's 600 million moviegoers was twenty-one. These audiences were served by 3,500 multifunctional theaters with 18,000 screens nationwide. Thus, movie producers who can win the hearts of young people will win the largest market share.[78] Second, sixth-generation film directors are in their fifties, and fifth-generation film directors are in their sixties—ages when they are likely to feel nostalgic about their youth and prone to reflect on the past. In addition, youth is a common theme and a rich resource for any filmmaker to explore, regardless of generation, and the recollection of youth is a universal phenomenon. As such, these youth movies came at the right time. Four of them were among the top ten box office earners between January and November 2013, with *So Young* ranking third (720 million yuan), *American Dreams in China* sixth (540 million yuan), *Finding Mr. Right* seventh (520 million yuan), and *Tiny Times 1.0* ninth (490 million yuan).[79]

## Struggles under the Triple Threat

The dilemmas of state censorship and market pressure are inextricably intertwined and severely impact filmmakers' artistic expression and filmmaking strategies. With the February 2012 increase in the import quota, domestic movies were outpaced by imports for the first time in ten years, earning only 8.273 billion yuan (48 percent) of the gross box office revenue of 17.073 billion yuan in 2012.[80] In addition, only 237 of the 638 movies produced from January to October 2012 were added to the schedules of theater chains, and of the ten movies with more than 100 million yuan in box office receipts, only three were domestic productions.[81] Hollywood has triumphed over the Chinese market once again, and it is easy to blame Hollywood for China's loss.

However, with deeper scrutiny, one can find a number of internal factors that are contributing to the decline of domestic movies. Censorship is one. The state maintains a double standard toward domestic movies and foreign imports: the censorship criteria for imports are much looser. Furthermore, the thirty-four imports are chosen based on their global influence and box office records, giving them a natural advantage over several hundred domestic movies of varying quality. Therefore, the competition between Hollywood imports and Chinese movies is not a fair one. Chinese film professionals liken it to "a confrontation between an egg and a rock."[82]

The most detrimental factor is the overemphasis on box office records and profits. This is the by-product of China's transition to a market economy and the inevitable consequence of the wholesale shift in the cultural sector from public service to profit. Although this transformation has brought greater economic gains, it has also resulted in prioritizing market interests above everything else, leading to society's shortsighted vision and the neglect of artistic values. This overemphasis on market value at the expense of other factors is somewhat conducive to state rule: market and commercial values do not constitute a threat to state legitimacy; rather, they tend to empower the state and reinforce its legitimacy. This causes film producers to push for more commercial movies and theater chains to give in to market demands and audience desires, neglecting artistic and critical cinema and making the situation even worse. The state has not done enough to address these problems.

Under these circumstances, Chinese filmmakers face many challenges and difficulties. Xie Xiaojing, deputy director of the Beijing Film Academy, believes the state policy should create a more favorable environment for young film directors to emerge: "A platform should be created for young film directors, and a competition system should be established for them to stand out." The problem is that China's film industry is currently sustained by only a few hits and a few famous directors, and theater chains are unwilling to give the films of emerging directors a place on the schedule. Consequently, young directors face many difficulties and an unbalanced distribution of resources.[83]

In recent years, a number of efforts to support young filmmakers have emerged, including official programs sponsored by SARFT and China Film Group Corporation as well as by local administrations such as Andy Lau's program in Hong Kong. However, investors lack confidence in young, unknown directors and are reluctant to take the financial risk of investing in them. Another factor is the lack of an effective market mechanism to find good new directors. In 2011, of the top twenty movies with box office receipts exceeding 100 million yuan, only three were directed by individuals younger than fifty. The majority of the top fifty domestic movies in 2011 were made by directors older than forty. As the fifth generation has gotten older and the sixth generation has reached middle age, the new generation has yet to emerge as a collective force in Chinese film production.[84]

The market economy is not omnipotent, however, especially for a cultural product like film, which has both economic and aesthetic value. Neither pure market logic nor pure political censorship is good for its healthy growth. The state should employ various measures—economically, administratively, and culturally—to foster domestic film production. In fact, SARFT and other state agencies began promulgating a series of protective measures to support domestic film production starting at the end of 2012. As noted in chapter 3, these include a new value added tax system that would tax the revenue share of foreign producers directly, instead of taxing gross box office revenue. This new tax system would lead to an 8 percentage point decrease in foreign producers' share of revenue, and it was the cause of the conflict between CFEIC and 20th Century–Fox over the distribution of *Life of Pi*. Furthermore, on May 31, 2014, seven state administrations, including the Ministry of Finance and the State Administration of Press, Publication, Radio, Film, and Television (a new entity that merged SARFT and the State Administration of Press and Publication in March 2013), issued a number of measures to support film development: the annual allocation of 100 million yuan to foster five to ten movies with "significant themes"; the use of a special fund for the development of cultural industries related to film production; the exemption of film producers and distributors from the value-added tax between 2014 and 2018; financial support for the construction of digital theaters in midwestern areas; and various pilot financing methods for the film industry.[85] As such, the Chinese state continues to devise strategies to adapt to changing circumstances and maintain control over its Hollywood competitors. It is likely that the China-Hollywood battle will turn a new page, with unpredictable outcomes.

At the beginning of this chapter I asked: how has state censorship evolved and changed in a market economy? I would argue that the overemphasis on market demands has had a chilling effect on filmmakers, manifested by the exercise of self-censorship and self-discipline, as observed by Wang Xiaoshuai. The market has become the state's partner in exerting control over film producers. To secure a market share, film producers and directors have rushed to make commercial movies, avoiding serious and sensitive topics. This has had a remarkable influence on Chinese film production, which is the focus of the next chapter.

# 5

# Chinese Martial Arts Cinema in the Twenty-First Century

## *Hybridity and Soft Power*

The resurgence of Chinese martial arts cinema in the first decade of the twenty-first century is a remarkable phenomenon. Neither the genre nor its popularity is new, but its latest resurgence reflects social, political, and global forces with significant implications far beyond the genre's entertainment value and its previous range of filmic expression. These forces include the Chinese state's cultural policy, the demands of film marketization, the inflow and legacy of Hong Kong's kung fu movies, and the influence of global Hollywood. Intertwined and entangled, they become driving forces and determining factors in the revitalization of this genre in contemporary China.

Historically, Chinese martial arts cinema enjoyed three periods of popularity in the twentieth century: its original emergence in the 1920s; its relocation and revival in Hong Kong from the 1950s to the 1980s, after the Nationalist government's anti-superstition campaign and ban in 1934; and its resurgence in mainland China in the 1980s as part of the new wave of entertaining cinema. Its resurgence after 2000 in mainland China has been described as moving "closer to its original base in China, signifying a historic closing of the circle."[1] This closing of the circle is the focus of this chapter.

From the Bruce Lee period, when oriental kung fu movies debuted on the international film market, to the global presence of action-packed Hong Kong films featuring Jackie Chan, Chow Yun Fat, and Jet Li in the 1990s, Chinese martial arts cinema exerted an increasing influence. However, not until Ang Lee's *Crouching Tiger, Hidden Dragon* won an Oscar and Zhang Yimou's *Hero* became both a national and an international box office hit did this genre and its global impact begin to attract intense scholarly interest. Within the fields of international communication, international cultural studies, and film studies, Chinese martial arts cinema has become a popular research topic. A number of studies have investigated the resurgence of the genre and its implications in an era of globalization. Some research has mapped the trajectory of the history of Chinese martial arts cinema.[2] Other studies are devoted to the genre's aesthetic connotations and philosophical implications. Chinese martial arts cinema has been posited as a negotiation between science and fate and between nationalism and modernity,[3] as an embrace of cultural nationalism and a mode of transnationalism,[4] and as an expression of antiorder resistance and a representation of identity crises.[5] Researchers have used *Hero* as a case study, discussing its discourses and themes, philosophical essence, and aesthetic significance.[6] Some have taken the perspective of political economy to analyze the "global-local alliance" in the successful production and distribution of a Chinese "global blockbuster."[7] Others have provided pungent criticism of the "spirit" and "structure" of *Hero* and concluded that the film reflects both the fascist spirit and the post-9/11 imperial logic.[8] Researchers thus bring up the issue of global-local dialectic and raise this question: "In various accounts of 'glocalization,' 'hybridization' and 'transculturation,' which side is prevailing?"[9] They have suggested that *Hero* represents a triumph of globalization. Furthermore, they have argued that the boom in new Chinese martial arts films "means surrendering to the Hollywood mode" and "testifies to the triumph of the Hollywood-style commercial mode of film production in China."[10]

In this chapter I weigh in on this discussion and explore global-local dialogue through China's mass production of martial arts cinema. Working from a perspective of cultural globalization, this chapter positions Chinese martial arts cinema between 2000 and 2012 as a collective cultural phenomenon arising in the broader context of mainland China's change in cultural policy and its encounter with global Hollywood. Combining the analysis of both text and context, I explore this cultural phenomenon within the context of the Chinese government's full embrace of the concept of "soft power" as it attempts to battle the global dominance of US popular culture in general and Hollywood films in particular.

I argue that the new Chinese martial arts cinema is, first of all, a direct outcome of China's changing cultural policy and a survival strategy adopted by mainland Chinese and Hong Kong filmmakers to deal with the dual pressures of film marketization and state censorship. Second, this genre has reemerged in a seemingly hybrid mode that both conforms to the aesthetics of the Hollywood spectacle and promotes Chinese history, culture, and philosophy—an element that is especially encouraged by the Chinese state to advance its soft power. Some films reinforce nationalism, patriotism, and orthodox Confucian values that are specifically conducive to state rule; others explore the unique Chinese way of being, theories of heaven and nature, and the philosophy of Chinese martial arts. Therefore, contrary to the rebellious antiorder implications of martial arts cinema during times of social upheaval and identity crises,[11] new Chinese martial arts cinema represents both escape from and conformity to the established social order.

Here I want to clarify the term "Chinese martial arts cinema." First, scholars in the field of Chinese film studies have long raised the question of nation, cultural identity, and transnational cinema. Some researchers have used "Chinese-language cinema" as an all-inclusive term for trans-regional movies made in mainland China, Hong Kong, and Taiwan.[12] In this chapter, the main objects of analysis are those films solely funded and made by mainland Chinese studios and filmmakers, as well as their coproductions with Hong Kong, Taiwan, and foreign partners. Second, in a broader sense, "martial arts cinema" could refer to all types of action movies, including ancient-costumed *wuxia* movies, kung fu movies, or even police-crime movies set in modern times. As Stephen Teo explains, "*wuxia* was swordfighting and kung fu was fist-fighting," and kung fu evolved from *wuxia*.[13] This chapter focuses on ancient-costumed *wuxia* moves and kung fu movies.

## Social and Policy Context

As a collective cultural phenomenon, the resurgence of Chinese martial arts cinema since 2000 is an outcome of the changing historical context both domestically and internationally. Externally, China's reentry into the World Trade Organization (WTO) and the commitments it had to make to achieve that painted a worrisome picture for domestic filmmakers and increased their already high levels of anxiety. China and the United States signed the agreement on China's accession to the WTO in November 1999, and it was formally approved in November 2001. Under the agreement, the Chinese government agreed to double the annual quota of revenue-sharing film imports to twenty, to allow foreign investors up to a 49 percent share in operating theaters, and to permit foreign investment in video distribution joint ventures.[14] Facing the prospect of "dancing with wolves," both the state and domestic filmmakers felt enormous pressure to compete with Hollywood blockbusters. Internally, the redefinition of the film sector as a cultural industry, and the speedy marketization of those industries, pushed domestic filmmakers to prioritize market appeal and to make films that would maximize profits. Under such circumstances, a genre with a well-established tradition and great entertainment value naturally became filmmakers' top choice. The success of Ang Lee's *Crouching Tiger, Hidden Dragon* (2000) and Zhang Yimou's *Hero* (2002) on the international market also stimulated the boom in martial arts cinema.

The two closer economic partnership arrangements (CEPAs) mentioned in chapter 1 were another important policy factor that served as an incentive for the resurgence of martial arts cinema. The CEPAs opened up cooperative opportunities for filmmakers from the Greater China area. Hong Kong directors considered this a good way to save the declining Hong Kong movie industry. But to benefit from the CEPA and tap into the vast mainland market and its bountiful inland resources, Hong Kong movies had to be "pure entertainment" and reflect "ideological noncommitment."[15] Martial arts movies, as one of "the most popular and well-developed genres in the history of Chinese cinema," rely heavily on "body language that breaks national boundaries."[16] They had already established themselves as successful worldwide cinematic spectacles that met the needs of both mainland and Hong Kong filmmakers and could serve as a means to integrate their respective film industries.

As table 5.1 shows, the number of martial arts movies increased markedly after 2003 as a result of the changing policy environment and the closer partnership between mainland China and Hong Kong. After 2004, when the CEPA formally took effect, martial arts movies took the lion's share of box office receipts among the top ten domestically produced movies, peaking in 2007 and 2008. Therefore, the boom in this genre was initiated by policy and driven by various social conditions such as market demand, state intervention, the legacy of the genre, and mainland–Hong Kong collaboration. After 2008, both the number of martial arts movies and their box office receipts began to drop because of market saturation and audience boredom.

**Table 5.1. Martial Arts Cinema in China, 2000–2010**

| Year | Total Film Output | Number of Martial Arts Movies (Percentage of Total) | Number of Martial Arts Movies among Top Ten Box Office Hits |
|---|---|---|---|
| 2000 | 83 | 7 (8.4%) | 0 |
| 2001 | 71 | 3 (4.2%) | 0 |
| 2002 | 100 | 1 (1.0%) | 1 |
| 2003 | 140 | 14 (10.0%) | 4 |
| 2004 | 212 | 13 (6.1%) | 5 |
| 2005 | 260 | 33 (12.7%) | 4 |
| 2006 | 330 | 15 (4.5%) | 5 |
| 2007 | 402 | 36 (9.0%) | 7 |
| 2008 | 406 | 22 (5.4%) | 7 |
| 2009 | 456 | 24 (5.3%) | 3 |
| 2010 | 526 | 12 (2.3%) | 4 |

*Source: China Film Yearbook 2001–2011* (Beijing: Zhongguo dianying chubanshe [China Film Press], 2001–2011).

Most new Chinese martial arts movies are costumed and set in ancient times. This can be attributed to China's strict censorship system, under which any film that touches on contemporary subject matter is too politically sensitive and financially risky. In an interview, an official of SARFT explicitly confirmed that films with ancient themes have an easy time passing censorship.[17]

Dan Glickman, head of the Motion Picture Association of America, admitted in an interview that "U.S. businesses are wary of taking political stands that might offend the Chinese government because the Americans fear they might lose access to the Chinese market." He said, "a market of 1.3 billion people should present a lot of opportunities for the big studios."[18] To avoid political controversy and retain access to the huge mainland market, filmmakers in Hollywood, Hong Kong, and China all turned to ancient China for their artistic inspiration. These ancient themes are politically safe, are less financially risky, and had a proven market. This consensus led to a dominant mode in martial arts cinema: a preindustrial historical setting and classical-costumed characters.

Martial arts cinema has obtained the Chinese government's blessing, as evidenced by the heavy governmental involvement in the processes of production, distribution, and exhibition. Zhang Yimou's films provide a

**Table 5.2. China Film Group Corporation (CFGC)–Funded Martial Arts Movies, 2000–2010**

| Year | Total Number of Martial Arts Movies | Number of Martial Arts Movies Invested in or Cofunded by CFGC (Percentage of Total) |
|---|---|---|
| 2000 | 7 | 3 (43%) |
| 2001 | 3 | 2 (67%) |
| 2002 | 1 | 0 |
| 2003 | 14 | 10 (71%) |
| 2004 | 13 | 5 (38%) |
| 2005 | 33 | 3 (9%) |
| 2006 | 15 | 1 (7%) |
| 2007 | 36 | 12 (33%) |
| 2008 | 22 | 13 (59%) |
| 2009 | 24 | 5 (21%) |
| 2010 | 12 | 2 (17%) |

*Source: China Film Yearbook 2001–2011* (Beijing: Zhongguo dianying chubanshe [China Film Press], 2001–2011).

typical example. Various accounts have detailed how *Hero* (2002), *House of Flying Daggers* (2004), and *Curse of the Golden Flower* (2006) obtained the approval and collaboration of the government at various levels and were premiered at the Great Hall of the People—the symbolic center of the Chinese state—and other important locations. The government mobilized the media, college students, and other resources to assist with the promotion of Zhang's films; it even secretly arranged for a one-month blackout of foreign films to give his films a screen monopoly. Jia Zhangke's award-winning *Still Life* was also blacked out for the benefit of Zhang's *Curse of the Golden Flower.* Given Zhang Yimou's esteemed status in China's film industry, his close relationship with the government, and the nonprovocative themes of his recent films, it is no wonder that his movies enjoy many privileges that other filmmakers could never hope for.[19]

The largest state-owned film company, China Film Group Corporation (CFGC), played a major role in the production of martial arts films. Since 2000, CFGC's investment in this genre has fluctuated (see table 5.2). Before 2004, when the CEPA formally took effect, most domestic martial arts films were funded by CFGC. After the signing of the CEPA and the wholesale entry of Hong Kong filmmakers into the mainland China market, CFGC tried to maintain its grip and enhance its influence on the production of this genre. CFGC president Han Sanping has talked about the company's goal and strategy on a number of occasions. He noted, "China boasts five thousand years of culture. It has so many superior classics, so many epic legends, so many dramas and operas, and so many folk tales and heroes, which provide extremely abundant resources for filmmaking." Therefore, CFGC's strategy is "to appropriately select subject matter out of the ample Chinese cultural repository."[20] He saw this as a way of competing with Hollywood-represented American culture and of enhancing China's soft power. In an interview with *Sanlian Life Weekly,* Han warned that although China's film sector has successfully transitioned from a planned economy to a market-oriented industry, "we must pay careful attention to the questions of national identity and national characteristics." He cautioned that "movies are too universal" and "America's film industry is crossing national borders to obtain material without regard to the source or the culture. If we do not work hard, then everything could be completely appropriated by Hollywood." When the interviewer mentioned Ang Lee's belief that modernization means Westernization, because the language of film was established by Westerners, Han said:

> Ang Lee was talking about form; I am talking about content. I've read a screenplay written by an American about the Generals of the Yang Clan. How would you assess Mu Guiying and Yang Zongbao? That would involve aspects of culture: it has taken shape out of traditional morality. In this American's script, Mu Guiying kills Yang Zongbao for the interests of the country and of the people. This judgment obviously comes as a result of their particular standpoint, but why shouldn't we have them accept our value system instead of us always accepting theirs? Of course, they're the powerful ones now, but our efforts will eventually allow us to reach that point. Differences exist between the values and morals of China and the West. Good and bad, and right and wrong, are hard to distinguish, so we've got to work hard so that they'll have to accept us. Therefore, I believe that this value system should be expressed through film. This is an expression of China's soft power.[21]

In another interview with *Southern Weekly,* Han explicitly stated that Chinese leaders have been involved in the production process and have set aside many resources. CFGC's success, he claimed, "is directly related to these high-level leaders and the [party's] rich resources for this enterprise." When asked how much support CFGC gets from the state, he said, "China Film is definitely the first pick, because it belongs to the State. But at the same time, . . . there are many responsibilities."[22] Clearly, CFGC's investment in martial arts films has been greatly encouraged and supported by the government. And the government's blessing has created greater space for the new martial arts cinema to prosper.

## Cultural Tradition, Confucianism, and Nationalism à la Hollywood

New Chinese martial arts cinema incorporates talent and cultural elements from global Hollywood, Taiwan, Hong Kong, and mainland China to create a seemingly transnational and transregional hybrid genre. Overdone kung fu movies that combine spectacular Hollywood-style special effects and traditional Chinese cultural elements have become the most influential genre of the domestic film industry and a prime market attraction. These films are characterized by big budgets, famous stars (such as Gong Li, Zhang Ziyi, Michelle Yeoh, Chow Yun Fat, Jet Li, and Tony Leung), spectacular cinematography, and sometimes the ubiquitous sex and violence of Hollywood commercial movies. The production and distribution teams include partners from a variety of regions and countries, meaning that China's film industry has been integrated with and become a part of the global cinema production and distribution system.

The Hollywood imprint has been conspicuous in some Chinese kung fu blockbusters, such as Zhang Yimou's *Curse of the Golden Flower* (2006) and Feng Xiaogang's *The Banquet* (2007). *Curse of the Golden Flower* tells the story of a failed court rebellion conspired by the empress and her son during the Tang Dynasty of the tenth century, on the eve of the Chong Yang Festival. It was the most expensive film ever made in China prior to 2007: it cost US$45 million, whereas the typical big-budget film in China cost closer to US$7 million. Zhang created a gargantuan set, including a mesmerizing gold-laced imperial palace that took five months to build, with 1,000 feet of carpet and 600 luxurious lamps. He hired more than 1,000 real soldiers for the battle scenes and 300 female students from various performance schools, clothed in gorgeous costumes. For the festival scene, he brought in 3 million chrysanthemums to create a spectacular sea of golden flowers measuring 130,000 square feet.[23] The film foregrounds conspiracy, rebellion, bloody repression, and killing, as well as two incestuous relationships: between the empress and the crown prince; and between the crown prince and his secret lover, the imperial doctor's daughter, who turns out to be his half-sister. At the end of the film, the empress is forced to drink poisoned herb soup on the order of the emperor; her faithful second son, who helped her with the rebellion, commits suicide; the crown prince and his lover are both killed at the palace; and the imperial doctor and his wife are assassinated. All the soldiers participating in the rebellion are killed, and the pile of bodies reaches the palace wall. Against a moonlit night, thousands of chrysanthemums are trampled as blood spills in the imperial palace. Zhang's talent as a cinematographer is apparent in this film, with its gorgeous costumes, magnificent settings, and colorful scenes resembling impressionist paintings. All the settings, sceneries, costumes, and props are shiny and splendid, adding an authentic touch of the classic Chinese imperial culture and lifestyle. The film was China's entry for the Academy Award for best foreign-language film for 2006, but it was not nominated; it did, however, receive a nomination for best costume design. In 2007 it received fourteen nominations at the Twenty-Sixth Hong Kong Film Awards and won for best actress, best art direction, best costume and makeup design, and best original film song.

Feng Xiaogang's *The Banquet* is a Chinese version of *Hamlet*. In a pre-Tang era, the emperor's brother kills the emperor and takes the throne and the empress for his own. The empress, the crown prince, the emperor, and various ministers all strive for power, and their final battle occurs at a banquet, where almost everyone is killed. Similar to Zhang's film, *The Banquet* is a story of court rebellion, conspiracy, and killing, as well as incestuous relations between the empress and the crown prince. It also features bloody revenge, violent killings, and female nudity.

Another big-budget blockbuster, John Woo's *Red Cliff* (2008–2009), topped *Curse of the Golden Flower* in terms of expense. When shooting started in April 2007, the original budget was US$60 million; that increased to US$75 million but still fell short. Woo contributed more than US$1 million of his own money, and CFGC added another US$2 million.[24] The film displays breathtaking cinematography and special effects, as well as dazzling kung fu fights. In one scene, as Cao Cao's northern army gathers to prepare for the next battle, the audience gets a bird's-eye view of the army taken from a helicopter—a spectacular scene of thousands of soldiers on ships sprawling over the miles of the Yangtze River.

In Zhang Yimou's 2007 movie *House of Flying Daggers,* special effects are used to create fast-paced kung fu fights. The fantastic scene starring Zhang Ziyi as a blind dancer who waves her long sleeves to hit standing drums has become a cinematographic classic.

Although I agree that these movies signal the triumph of the Hollywood model in China, they also draw heavily on the rich repository of Chinese history and culture. I believe it is more accurate to say that the new Chinese martial arts movies are hybrids that incorporate elements of both Hollywood and China. Moreover, in this hybrid model, the Hollywood portion is merely an extravagant shell; the essence remains Chinese. It is fair to say that most Chinese martial arts films use Hollywood techniques to showcase Chinese culture, history, and tradition. As one CFGC official said: "We should use the language of Hollywood to portray our own 'Moments in Peking.'"[25]

These movies draw on the rich collection of Chinese historical and epic legends, as well as martial arts fiction, to propagate Chinese history, culture, and national heroes. The movies are therefore a deliberate (re)construction of Chinese national identity and nationalism. For example, *Seven Swords* (directed by Tsui [2005]) is based on the famous Chinese martial arts novel *Seven Swords from Tianshan* by well-known Chinese writer Liang Yusheng, a legend of rebellion and resistance set around 1660, when the Qing Dynasty tried to repress an uprising of Han warriors. In *The Myth* (Tong [2005]), treasure-seeking adventure is mixed with the Qin Dynasty's historical figures and legends. *Red Cliff I* and *II* (Woo [2008–2009]), *Three Kingdoms: Resurrection of the Dragon* (Lee [2008]), and *The Lost Bladesman* (Mak and Chong [2011]) all dramatize the Warring States period and highlight real-life historical figures. *Battle of Wits* (Cheung [2006]), *Fearless* (Yu [2006]), *Ip Man* (Yip [2008]), *Yuan Chonghuan* (Xiao [2008]), *Mo Zi* (Jia [2010]), *Detective Dee and the Mystery of the Phantom Flame* (Hsui [2010]), and *The Last Supper* (Lu [2012]) are all based on true historical heroes and legends.

A closer examination of these films leads to another discovery: wrapped in the lavish Hollywood style, some of them actually reinforce orthodox Confucianism and the theme of nationalism. Martial arts cinema has always had a double nature and complex connotations. On the one hand, the genre creates an imaginary world outside of social reality and beyond the reach of mundane authority—a world governed by chivalrous ethics and brotherhood, where knights-errant use their swords to fight for justice when the imperial legal system does not function or is unfair. These films fulfill people's desires and dreams for a harmonious world. The genre is, therefore, often used as a weapon for cultural expression and resistance to the current social order. During times of social turmoil, the genre allows people to escape reality and release anxiety, creating an imaginary space to negotiate fierce social conflicts that otherwise might not be resolved. Martial arts cinema, in this sense, has a critical antiorder edge. This tradition was inherited by Hong Kong action movies, which, during the late 1980s and early 1990s, represented a search for national identity and expressed strong feelings of anxiety and powerlessness during the transition to sovereignty. For example, Tsui Hark's *Once upon a Time in China* series (1991–1997) profoundly reflects the contradiction between modernity and tradition in the grand historical context of revolution. Stephen Chow's *mo-lei-tou* films have a strong touch of cynicism and political satire. When they came to mainland China, they became "the best carrier for post–June-Fourth-1989 cynicism and nihilism about reality and history."[26] As such, the genre's distinct features have become an effective weapon for cultural expression and social criticism.

On the other hand, martial arts cinema has deep historical roots in Chinese martial arts fiction and folk culture and is therefore laden with Chinese cultural values and traditions. Orthodox Confucian values such as loyalty, filial relationships, virtue, and brotherhood—which constitute the foundation of traditional Chinese society—are well represented in martial arts cinema and are often used as an extra force to aid imperial rule and reinforce orthodox ideology. This distinctive feature of martial arts cinema is displayed throughout its history, from *Come Drink with Me* (Hu [1966]) to *New Dragon Inn* (Lee, Ching, and Tsui [1992]). Martial arts movies made after 2000, I believe, especially strengthen and highlight traditional Confucian values and nationalism, but the spirit of social criticism has been weakened. For instance, in *Seven Swords,* martial arts warriors become the upholders of the orthodox Ming Dynasty, which is ruled by the Han majority. Loyalty to the emperor is valued as much as chivalry. *Three Kingdoms: Resurrection of the Dragon* and *Red Cliff* both sanction the imperial Han Dynasty and its legitimate successor Liu Bei and the State Shu, applauding their benevolence and righteousness while disparaging General Cao Cao and his State Wei as duplicitous and cruel. According to *Red Cliff* director John Woo, he wanted to show that a small number of people can defeat larger enemies through "teamwork, innovation, intelligence and courage," and he especially wanted to emphasize Chinese values such as "loyalty, patriotism, righteousness, brotherhood and friendship."[27]

Orthodox Confucian values, however, have a more or less feudalistic nature: loyalty to the emperor, submissiveness to paternalism, and obedience to male domination. Righteousness is understood from the perspective of a ruler's benevolence and paternalistic attitude toward the common people, rather than from the perspective of individual rights. Brotherhood and martial chivalry often mean unconditional loyalty to one's comrades to the exclusion of other principles. As for patriotism, the term is often understood in the sense of loyalty to the emperor-represented state, if not in the sense of modern nationalism. Martial arts movies often tap into the conflict between orthodox imperial successors and rebellious ministers, as in *Three Kingdoms* and *Red Cliff*, or into the conflict between the Han-dominated Ming Dynasty and the minority-dominated Qing Dynasty, as in *Seven Swords*. Here, emperors, their successors, and the Han majority are considered the legitimate rulers of China, rather than the rebels or the minorities. In *Red Cliff II*, General Zhou Yu, who allies with monarch Liu Bei, the legitimate imperial successor, to resist General Cao Cao's invasion, says: "We are not against the emperor. We are loyal to the Han Dynasty." In *Three Kingdoms*, warrior Zhao Zilong explains that his purpose in joining the army is "to reestablish the Han Dynasty and reunite China," although the theme of one's uncontrolled destiny also comes through. Likewise, *Hero* justifies the emperor's logic of reuniting China through war and force. As such, these martial arts movies legitimize the ruler and are especially congenial to the ruling government.

Nationalism is another theme strengthened by a number of new martial arts films. Typical examples are *Fearless* and *Ip Man*. The former tells the story of how famous Chinese martial arts master Huo Yuanjia defeats Japanese warriors and safeguards the dignity of the Chinese nation. The latter recounts a similar tale about Chinese martial arts master Ip Man. Both films culminate in a duel with the Japanese, with the Chinese masters triumphing and being hailed as national heroes. Here, Chinese martial arts are used as an effective tool to inspire the nation, uplift the national spirit, and solidify the unity of the Chinese people. As Ip Man approaches his duel with the Japanese, he soliloquizes: "Martial arts involve armed forces, but Chinese martial arts are Confucius in spirit. The virtue of martial arts is benevolence. You Japanese will never understand this principle of treating others as you would yourselves. If you abuse your military power, you turn into oppressors of others. You don't deserve to learn Chinese martial arts." Martial arts, therefore, represent national identity and national heritage; they are an acclaimed practice for national self-redemption and self-improvement and an irreplaceable symbol of national pride and national spirit.

Martial arts are also used to propagate the theme of patriotism, as typified in *Bodyguards and Assassins* (Chen [2009]). In this film, set in 1905, a group of low-class people in Hong Kong serve as bodyguards to protect the founder of the Republic of China, Sun Yat-sen (1866–1925), from assassins sent by the imperial Qing Dynasty. A rickshaw puller, a bagger, a gambler, an opera actress, and a peddler are all portrayed as martial arts practitioners with a political consciousness and patriotic spirit who volunteer to risk their lives to guard Sun Yat-sen. The film thus integrates martial arts with an anti-imperial theme and revolutionary heroism. However, its overemphasis on patriotism and exaggerated claims of the lower class's political consciousness at the expense of realism give the film an obviously propagandistic tone.

Here, I have argued that orthodox Confucian values and themes of nationalism and patriotism are prominent in some new martial arts movies. However, I also acknowledge other remarkable features displayed in this genre in the twenty-first century, reflecting globalization and a postmodern consciousness.

## New Perspectives

Traditional martial arts cinema from the 1920s to the 1980s usually featured two themes: dynastic conflicts between loyal ministers and treacherous officials, and family or clan enmity and revenge. A number of new Chinese martial arts movies, however, demonstrate distinct new traits.

First, the genre has become a comprehensive expression of the underlying tenets of Chinese martial arts, highlighting the goals of peace, harmony, self-perfection, and mutual understanding. The genre thus surpasses the narrow-minded family revenge theme and displays the core values of modern civilization. *Fearless* is a typical example. Starring Jet Li, the film charts the personal journey of Chinese martial arts master and national hero Huo Yuanjia as he transforms from a proud practitioner with a big ego and a strong drive to defeat others to a true master who displays self-control, courtesy to others, and a patriotic spirit. In an interview, Jet Li said *Fearless* "mirrors my personal journey" and represents "all my belief in martial arts."[28] The film is about how to overcome ego and pride and learn to respect others. After inadvertently killing a rival at a young age, a much more mature Huo Yuanjia speaks of "the true meaning of wushu" at the opening ceremony of his martial arts school. He says, "Wushu is not just about killing, revenge, or hatred and anger. The real goal of practicing wushu is strengthening one's body, soul and mind, and is about making peace." The film conveys the principles of martial arts as a distinct Chinese way of being based on Confucian ethics. Huo Yuanjia also expresses the philosophy of martial arts: "We focus on cultivating three things: these are the training of body, mind and the spirit. . . . Wushu trains and disciplines the body. All disciplines are respected equally. The exchange of knowledge and mutual respect is the key. This way, we will no longer be 'sick man of the East' and stand strong as a nation." He goes on to say: "The real goal of practicing wushu is strengthening one's body and soul. . . . You can only beat the body, you never conquer the heart."

In *Ip Man 2* (*Yip* [2010]), Ip Man escapes to Hong Kong after a duel with a Japanese warrior and gets involved in another duel with an arrogant and rude British fighter. After winning the fight, a wounded and bleeding Ip Man stands at the rostrum and says, "I don't want to prove which one is better, Chinese or Western boxing. I just hope from now on, we can respect each other." The film displays what I call "restrained nationalism" and appeals for mutual respect and mutual understanding. Martial arts is therefore not only a symbol of national dignity but also a forum for the possible emergence of national conciliation and mutual understanding, very much in accordance with the trend of globalization.

New martial arts cinema also dedicates itself to the promotion of Chinese philosophy, cosmology, and the Chinese way of being. The film *The Forbidden Kingdom* (Minkoff [2008]) consciously integrates all the relevant Chinese cultural elements: Monkey Sun Wukong's tale, the Golden Swallow legend, the glamour of the traditional musical instrument known as the pipa, Zhuang Zi's philosophy, and so on. The film's voice-over defines martial arts, based on Zhang Zi's philosophy: "Kung fu is like water. Nothing is softer than water, yet it can overcome rock. It does not fight. It flows around the opponent. Homeless, nameless, the true master dwells within. Only you can find him." Martial arts is therefore elevated to a state of philosophy and the Chinese way of being.

Another film, *Battle of Wits* (Cheung [2006]), draws on the philosophy of Mo Zi of the Warring States period to tell a story about the unachievability of "universal love" and the failed ideal of peace. Mo's tenets of universal love, respect for life, and peace were doomed during that tumultuous and violent period. The film is based on a Japanese comic book and combines martial arts, fierce war scenes, and the conflict between Mo Zi's philosophy and the cruelty of warmongering states.

Second, whereas some new martial arts movies reinforce orthodox Confucianism and the theme of nationalism, others demonstrate a trend toward reinterpreting history, reconstructing historical figures, and deconstructing traditional values. This trend is remarkably reflected in movies depicting the Han–Three Kingdoms history, such as *The Lost Swordsman* (Mai and Zhuang [2011]) and *The Assassins* (Zhao [2012]). Both these films reverse the traditional point of view in which General Cao Cao is portrayed as a treacherous minister with the goal of overthrowing the Han Dynasty and establishing his own empire. In *The Lost Swordsman,* Guan Yu, China's symbol of loyalty and righteousness, is described as an awkward hero who is blindly loyal to monarch Liu Bei, who is incapable of saving his people from the violence and atrocity of war. General Cao Cao, in contrast, is portrayed as a wise strategist with great talent and vision who is capable of providing food and shelter, peace, and social order and is loved by the people. Guan Yu is torn between his loyalty to Liu Bei and Cao Cao's vision, and he eventually dies as the "lost swordsman." *The Assassins* portrays Cao Cao through the eyes of his mistress (whose parents he killed) as a caring monarch who is loyal to the Han emperor and can restore peace and order.

In another deconstruction of traditional values, *The Warlords* (Chan and Yip [2007]) tells the story of loyalty and conflict among three brothers who vow to honor their bond and put brotherhood before everything. However, the oldest brother, Pang, takes advantage of the brotherhood to pursue his personal ambition in the court of the Qing Dynasty and kills thousands of war prisoners. At the end of the film, Pang betrays his vow and kills his two brothers to obtain the position of number-one officer in the richest province of Jiangsu. The film puts one of the most highly praised values, brotherhood, to a harsh test and deconstructs it into lost faith and sheer illusion. The fragile brotherhood eventually decomposes into emptiness and is replaced by ugly human nature, thus giving the film a postmodern touch.

In terms of a new perspective, Zhang Yimou's *Curse of the Golden Flower* is worth mentioning again. Both this film and Feng Xiaogang's *The Banquet* were harshly criticized for their bloody violence, nudity, and lack of moral standards. Cui Weiping, a professor at the Beijing Film Academy, said, "Big-budget films can certainly exist, but they don't have to be so ugly."[29] Tao Dongfeng, a well-known film critic, commented, "I have never seen any country's megaproductions that are as overtly violence worshipping as China's megaproductions, without any moral restrictions and moral values." He continued:

> Most domestic megaproductions love to express the so-called theme of revenge, like *Curse of the Golden Flower* and *The Banquet.* However, none of the avengers and those being avenged upon, rulers and rebels, as well as the status quo advocates and challengers, represent justice and conscience. Avengers, when resorting to violence to get revenge, do not have any justified reason except for satisfying their own desire for power. The moral positions and value judgments in these films are completely void: we don't know which character we should sympathize with, and we cannot tell good guys from bad guys. They only have lust, conspiracy, and hatred: the hatred between princes, and the hatred between empresses and crown princes. Because the hatred has nothing to do with value judgment, the massacre that results from the hatred is merely the abuse of violence.[30]

Other critics commented, "Our eyes are dazzled by gorgeous settings but our hearts are left in the dark." Such megaproductions lack "humanistic concern and the height of human thought," and "it seems that we have everything but soul."[31]

However, *Curse of the Golden Flower* touches on one issue that is rarely seen in old martial arts films: the oppression of women, their depressed and distorted nature, and their desperate but failed rebellion. As director Zhang Yimou said: "There is an old Chinese proverb, 'gold and jade on the outside, rot and decay on the inside.' It means beneath a beautiful exterior lies a dark and appalling truth." All the film's delicate and splendid settings merely hide the dark, cold-blooded, repressive side of society. The Empress Phoenix is the central figure in this oppression and rebellion against it. Gong Li's superb performance captures the empress's depression and despair living in this feudalistic, patriarchal dynasty. She is forced to drink poisoned herb soup by the emperor; engages in a secret affair with her stepson, the crown prince, whom she trusts and seeks comfort from; and conspires to lead a court rebellion with her own son, but it fails. Her distorted human nature and desperate defiance speak to the oppressive nature of society; her failed rebellion reveals her desire for control and power. As Zhang Yimou comments: "[The empress] is a tragic figure. In a male-dominated society, she is the central victim. Even though she is the empress, she suffers the most. What I want to portray is, first, a female victim. But at the same time, I also describe her rebellion." According to Zhang, martial arts served this purpose: "The story of a large family is a reflection of feudalism in China. Chinese culture evolved under male domination. The story represents a time when men dominated society. Women were oppressed. It was a repression of humanity."[32]

*Curse of the Golden Flower* depicts the hierarchy and patriarchy of a feudalistic society, and women's hopeless struggle. In this sense, Zhang's film goes beyond the traditional family revenge plot and the loyalty-betrayal conflict. He offers a new perspective and new aesthetic expression for martial arts cinema. Therefore, a purely moral judgment is not sufficient to analyze the significance of this film.

New perspectives are also displayed in the 2010 movie *Detective Dee and the Mystery of the Phantom Flame*—a combination of the Hollywood model and Chinese cultural components. It draws on the legend of Di Renjie, a real-life figure from the Tang Dynasty who is famous for solving crimes. It tells the story of how Di Renjie foils a conspiracy against Wu Zetian, the only female emperor in Chinese history. Similar to *Curse of the Golden Flower,* the movie takes a feminist perspective and demonstrates women's power and wisdom. In addition to this modern perspective, other impressive aspects of the film are its computer-generated visual effects, all-star cast, and spectacular settings, including a sixty-six-foot-tall Buddha tower that overlooks the imperial temple. A fast pace, shifting camera angles, breathtaking fight scenes, suspense, and unexpected twists and turns add to the film's success. By integrating martial arts with components of thrillers and detective stories, a new genre has emerged—one that scriptwriter Chen Guofeng labeled "historical police-crime." The film employs modern cinematographic technology and computer-created 3D special effects, providing visual pleasure and splendid scenes that mirror the heyday of the prosperous Tang Dynasty. It won awards for best art design, best visual effects, best costume design, and best actress at the Hong Kong Film Awards. Both *Time* magazine and the *New York Times* praised the film as "a historical epic" following in the footsteps of Zhang Yimou's *Hero.*[33]

## Overseas Reception

Although the new Chinese martial arts cinema has obtained the government's blessing and the support of state-owned film groups as a showcase for Chinese culture and a strategy for promoting Chinese soft power, serious problems have surfaced. Because of their obvious commercial value, market popularity, and relative ease of passing the censors, both mainland China and Hong Kong film producers have rushed to make martial arts movies. This has led to a number of problems, such as overlapping subject matter, repetitive story lines, and recurring themes and characters, all of which indicate a lack of artistic imagination and creativity. The market is saturated with martial arts movies, and the audience has gradually become fed up.

This overlap reached a peak in 2011 and 2012. Among those movies approved by SARFT, five tapped the historical Three Kingdoms era, with a focus on Guan Yu; four drew on the legendary tale of the Journey to the West and Monkey Sun Wukong; three recounted the legend of Mu Guiying of the Song Dynasty; and three focused on Liu Bang-Xiangyu's battle in the late Han Dynasty.[34] Because of market saturation and audience boredom, box office receipts for these ancient-costumed martial arts movies also fell short of expectations. In 2011 three big-budget martial arts movies failed to earn the target of 200 million yuan. *The Lost Swordsman* and *A Chinese Ghost Story* cost 150 million yuan and 120 million yuan, respectively, yet both netted only about 150 million yuan. With an investment of 150 million yuan, *The Warring State* made only 70 million yuan at the box office. After their release, these three movies followed a similar trajectory: they performed well the first week, thanks to a marketing and promotion strategy that featured their all-star casts and gorgeous settings; the second week witnessed a 50 percent decline in box office receipts; after the third week, box office receipts bottomed out. This pattern is not dissimilar to what happens in the United States, where films are expected to open wide and achieve their best results in the first week. However, films are often removed from theaters earlier in China than in the United States; therefore, box office receipts in a three-week window largely reflect a film's market performance. Meanwhile, the Hollywood blockbusters *Kung Fu Panda 2* and *Pirates of the Caribbean: On Stranger Tides* both earned more than 300 million yuan within ten days of their release in China.[35]

In 2012 *Taichi, The Last Supper*, and *The Assassins* also fell short of expectations. *Taichi* boasted an investment of about 220 million yuan and was expected to net at least 600 million yuan at the box office, but its actual revenue was a mere 260 million yuan. With an investment of 80 million yuan, *The Last Supper* was expected to net 300 million yuan, but it barely recouped its investment.[36] *The Assassins*, which cost 130 million yuan, managed to make only 103 million yuan.[37]

In resonance with their declining domestic box office revenue, new Chinese martial arts films have suffered in the international market as well, contrary to the government's expectation that they would help expand Chinese soft power overseas. According to Stanley Rosen, among the top twenty-five foreign-language box office successes between 1980 and 2008, five Chinese-language films made the list: *Crouching Tiger, Hidden Dragon; Hero; Fearless; Kung Fu Hustle*; and *House of Flying Daggers*.[38] All five are martial arts movies, indicating this genre's international popularity. However, the box office records set by *Crouching Tiger, Hidden Dragon* and *Hero* have never been repeated, and the genre's popularity has declined considerably. In 2011 fifty-two Chinese movies, mainly coproductions, were released overseas and made a total of 2.024 billion yuan—a 42 percent decrease compared with the 3.517 billion yuan made by the forty-seven movies released in 2010. Although martial arts remains the most popular genre overseas, more than one-third of foreign audiences have never watched any Chinese movie, and only 26 percent of foreign audiences consider Chinese movies their main source of learning about Chinese culture.[39]

The situation did not improve much in 2012: of the fifteen Chinese movies released, only eight boasted ticket sales of more than US$100,000. No martial arts movie achieved overwhelming success. Chinese movies were far behind Indian and Korean movies in terms of popularity, and China failed to make the list of top thirty foreign movie producers on the American market.[40]

There are many reasons for the lack of success of Chinese movies, especially martial arts movies, in both domestic and overseas markets. For domestic audiences, the films' disconnection with contemporary daily life is the main reason. After a constant barrage of visual feasts, spectacular scenes, splashy fights, and gorgeous settings, the audience want something that can satisfy their hearts and souls, something that can arouse deep feelings and evoke thoughts about life, love, family, and society. They want something that relates to the contemporary world and reflects their own life journeys. As entertaining as ancient-costumed martial arts films might be, they rarely satisfy such deep desires. The audience's yearning for more contemporary, more relevant entertainment explains the success of low-budget youth movies such as *Love Is Not Blind, You Are the Apple of My Eye,* and *Go, Lala, Go.*

For American audiences, the language barrier and American parochialism are obstacles that make it difficult for foreign-language titles to find more than a niche audience. The lack of internationally recognized stars is another reason. Restrictions on themes, creativity, and artistic expression imposed by China's censorship system is also a major factor. In addition, there are fundamental differences in the narrative and storytelling styles of Chinese versus Western filmmakers. For instance, many martial arts movies use historical reference points and assume the audience is familiar with ancient politics and legends, leaving Western audiences in the dark. According to David Lee, a Chinese movie expert who heads a coproduction company and once ran an Asian film fund for Harvey Weinstein: "Hollywood often doesn't make American movies, it makes globally appealing movies." In contrast, "Chinese filmmakers run on the assumption people already understand the story. It's laziness, and it makes it difficult to tell a story to a global audience." Zhang Yimou commented, "There are not many goods films . . . good stories that people all over the world can understand and be touched by. . . . People won't like the film if the story isn't told in a way to move people, no matter how big the investment and structure."[41]

## Martial Arts Cinema and Chinese Soft Power

Chinese martial arts cinema has reemerged as a transnational and transregional hybrid genre. Using Hollywood language, these films glorify Chinese culture, Confucian ethics, and nationalism. They are, therefore, particularly conducive to the government's strategy of constructing a common Chinese identity to ameliorate contemporary social conflicts. The Chinese government has taken great advantage of this genre and has used it to enhance its soft power. This brings us back to the question: in a global-local dialectic and in the process of cultural hybridization, "which side is prevailing?"[42] Viewing the latest martial arts movies as a collective cultural phenomenon, and taking the Chinese government's goals into consideration, we can see that this genre is actually part of the Chinese government's strategy to battle global Hollywood while maintaining its economic grip on the domestic market and its cultural grip on the film industry. The party-state considers the film industry an indispensable manifestation of China's soft power. Fully embracing Joseph Nye's concept of "soft power" after 2006, the Chinese government believes that culture is a significant source of such power and that cultural industries are crucial mechanisms for materializing it.

As defined by Chinese president Hu Jintao in his October 24, 2007, speech to the Seventeenth National Congress of the Chinese Communist Party, the Chinese version of soft power is composed of four aspects: (1) a "socialist core-values system" that highlights Marxism, "socialism with Chinese characteristics," patriotism, and collectivism; (2) a "harmonious culture" and a morally uplifting society based on honesty and integrity; (3) the exaltation of traditional Chinese culture to foster "a spiritual home commonly identified with by the entire Chinese nation"; and (4) the innovation of culture and the liberalization of the "cultural production force."[43]

While the task of building a "socialist core-values system" has been assumed by the so-called main-melody films, with limited success, the task of fostering "a spiritual home" for "the entire Chinese nation" has been delegated to martial arts cinema and the Confucian ethics this genre conveys. Since the reform era, China has faced a "crisis of faith" and moral degradation. Confucianism seems to be a convenient tool to fill this ideological vacuum and impose a common cultural heritage on the entire Chinese population, both on the mainland and beyond. The Chinese government even erected a giant statue of Confucius in Tiananmen Square, just in front of the National Museum of China—two symbols of Chinese revolutionary triumph. Although the statue was recently moved to behind the National Museum, its symbolic significance lingers. In addition, nearly 300 Confucius Institutes have been established throughout the world, and the film *Confucius* (Hu [2010]) premiered to great fanfare in China and elsewhere in the world. As such, the role of Confucianism in the government's control of ideology is self-evident. Martial arts cinema, which is both commercially successful and ideologically friendly to the government, thus satisfies both the state and the market.

Based on the China case, if what prevails in a global-local dialectic is the government's subtle agenda and its refined ability to govern, then perhaps it is safe to say that the so-called Chinese soft power includes both governmental and cultural power and that the latter is in the service of the former, as demonstrated by martial arts movies. The state's refined power to govern has resulted in two consequences: On one hand, the government's cultural policy has created a relatively open space for film collaboration domestically, regionally, and internationally, and it has enabled martial arts films, drawing on the strength of Hollywood, to become the primary mode of promoting Chinese culture and philosophy. On the other hand, martial arts movies, especially those set in ancient times, reconstruct a traditional and preindustrial China, not a modern China. They represent a form of escapism and a compromise with reality, not a way out or a future direction. If these movies and the traditional values they convey constitute part of Chinese soft power, then that soft power is a double-edged sword with mixed and complicated implications.

On the international market, Chinese martial arts films have lost their appeal among foreign audiences, and the Chinese state is unlikely to advance its soft power through these movies. One reason is the genre's disconnect with contemporary China and its lack of core values that are compatible with modern societies.

Nevertheless, because of their great entertainment and box office value, overdone kung fu movies that combine spectacular Hollywood-style special effects and traditional Chinese cultural elements have become the domestic film industry's most influential genre and its primary market attraction. Other film genres, especially social realism, have been marginalized or even driven out of the market, leading to a more monotonous film industry. Based on the preceding analysis, new Chinese martial arts films have dubious and dual functions.

# *Conclusion*

# The Chinese State, Hollywood, and Postsocialist Modernity

In the preceding chapters I examined mainland China's encounter with global Hollywood from 1994 to 2013. This complicated encounter is manifested in the Chinese state's changing cultural policy and counterhegemonic strategies, in the extensive debate over Hollywood, and in the formation of the Chinese film industry featuring multiple ownerships, a state-sponsored theater chain system, and genres with market appeal. Here, my purpose is to analyze the consequences of this encounter. I aim to answer three questions: First, what is the impact of such an encounter on the Chinese state's role and power? That is, how has the Chinese state evolved, and how will it continue to change? Second, what is the role of Hollywood and transnational capital in China's film modernization project and cultural landscape? Third, how should we evaluate the consequences of this encounter?

## The Chinese State: Both Changing and Unchanging

The Chinese state's multiple roles and evolving cultural policy toward global Hollywood indicate its capacity for accommodation and adaptation. For the Chinese state, what has changed is its specific approach to governing. By selectively opening up opportunities for Hollywood-represented global capital and for domestic private capital, the state has demonstrated its flexibility—unlike the Communist Party's classic approach to ruling. By integrating party ideology and socialist doctrine with market logic and cultural industries, the state has revealed its ability to incorporate and compromise. As such, global Hollywood has facilitated the transformation of the state's role in China. Consequently, the impact of the China-Hollywood encounter on the Chinese state can be analyzed from three perspectives. First, the Chinese state took the initiative, opening up to Hollywood to revitalize its own ailing film industry. However, once the door was open and market forces started to operate according to their own logic, the state had to adjust its role. The presence of global Hollywood in China has forced the Chinese state to face the challenges of the global market. To do so, the state has had to change its mind-set by intervening in and accelerating the market-oriented transformation of the film industry. Second, market and global forces have pushed the state to transform itself from an ossified, omnipresent ruler to a manager, negotiator, and regulator. The state has also introduced market mechanisms into the cultural arena and combined business management methods with mandatory administrative regulations. Third, market and global forces have helped refine the statecraft of the Chinese government, prompting its flexibility and pragmatism. One of the most noticeable functions of Hollywood has been to educate the Chinese state about the persuasive power of cultural industries (including the film industry) based on market preferences. Although there is no convincing evidence of a direct connection between Hollywood's influence and the state's embrace of the thesis of cultural industries, it is evident that China has enhanced its adaptive capability by absorbing all the useful elements of capitalist business models to build Chinese cultural industries with a socialist core value system.

What has not changed is the Chinese state's authoritarian power and its grip on both the film industry and the market. The state selectively applies Hollywood's capitalist model to the Chinese film industry while securing its own policy space, maintaining the supremacy of state-owned film groups, and promoting the socialist culture—all of which are conducive to the consolidation of the party-state's governmental power. Hollywood has helped elevate the Chinese state to a so-called comprehensive national power or soft power. The state strategy of "borrowing a boat to go to sea" has been well played and is at least partially successful. In this sense, both the market and global capital have empowered the state.

## Hollywood and Transnational Capital: A Double-Edged Sword

While global capital empowers the Chinese state, it can have both positive and negative impacts on national modernization projects. On the positive side, Third World countries like China can use transnational capital for their own modernization schemes. They can use foreign investment to update their industrial structures and add technological innovations to theaters; they can use Hollywood's advanced filmmaking techniques to promote their own national cultures and images and employ Hollywood's established distribution networks. Furthermore, independent filmmakers can ally with foreign investors to resist oppressive authoritarian governments and negotiate for more freedom of expression. In this regard, Hollywood serves as a resource for national film development.

In China's case, foreign capital has played a positive role in building the film industry's infrastructure. The total number of movie screens in China had increased to 18,195 by the end of 2013. With 8,500 3D screens and 100 IMAX screens in 2012, China became the number-two film market in the world that year.[1] IMAX also revised its contract with Wanda in July 2013, planning to build 40 to 120 additional IMAX theaters and eventually bring the total number to 420, making IMAX the top contractor with China.[2] These technologically advanced theaters account for up to 70 percent of box office receipts nationwide. In addition, multipurpose theaters have appeared in big shopping malls, greatly enhancing the revenue of theater chains. All these improvements were made possible by the introduction of foreign investment after 2000, and especially after 2003, when the Chinese government allowed foreign investment in theaters. In 2004 alone, nearly 100 multipurpose theaters were established in China through the use of foreign funds. The speed of theater construction and renovation has been skyrocketing. In less than ten years, the major theaters in China's big cities have caught up with most theaters in the United States in terms of technology and service.[3] Although the main purpose of transnational investment is to make a fortune in China, it has brought China's film infrastructure to a new level. As a result, both audiences and domestic businesses are the major beneficiaries.

As reported by the *Wall Street Journal,* financiers and filmmakers from Hong Kong, China, and Hollywood have teamed up and formed alliances: "The new paradigm has allowed the Chinese film industry to duplicate Hollywood's long-successful formula: Earn enough money domestically to cover the costs of making a film and then generate big profits through distribution abroad. . . . In just five years, China has become what Hollywood considers the world's most important producer of foreign-language blockbusters, catapulting beyond France, Spain or India in global box-office receipts."[4] This paradigm has worked well, enabling a number of Chinese films to become international hits: *Crouching Tiger, Hidden Dragon* (2000), *Hero* (2002), *House of Flying Daggers* (2004), *Kung Fu Hustle* (2004), *Red Cliff I* and *II* (2008–2009). Taking advantage of transnational corporations' worldwide distribution networks, Chinese films have made a promising debut on the international stage, and the world has been exposed to traditional Chinese culture and a positive Chinese image.

In promoting commercially successful and entertaining kung fu movies, foreign studios and transnational capital have actually obtained the blessing of the Chinese government, and the two have become allies and partners, sharing the economic profits and each other's resources. Transnational corporations maximize profits by outsourcing film production overseas and by competing for other countries' domestic film markets; the Chinese government benefits from growing revenue and an increasingly positive cultural and national image that helps it maintain its legitimacy. Furthermore, by selling audiovisual pleasure and entertainment to the masses, the government has diverted Chinese people's attention away from their overwhelming social and political problems. In terms of making money and entertaining people, Hollywood transnational capital and the Chinese government are allies rather than enemies.

On the negative side, the Chinese state–global capital alliance has led to hypercommercialism and an overemphasis on market value and box office returns. As a result, the film industry has tilted in favor of purely commercial movies, while social realist movies and artistic movies have been marginalized. Under the triple threat of marketization, Hollywoodization, and state censorship, China's critical and artistic film producers have had to fight for survival and confront unprecedented difficulties. Consequently, the most chilling effect has been filmmakers' exercise of self-censorship and self-discipline. In this sense, both global capital and the market have become the state's accomplice in extending its control over film production. Furthermore, Hollywood's big-budget model and its obsession with sex and violence have been embraced by many Chinese film producers, leading to increasingly monotonous films and the loss of an indigenous cultural tradition that makes more sense to local audiences. The double alliances of state-capital and state-market have remarkably changed the cultural landscape of China, enabling martial arts cinema to become the most popular genre up to 2012.

To conclude, I believe the influence of Hollywood and transnational capital—whether positive or negative—depends on how it is used by both the government and filmmakers. If the state policy is wise, transnational capital can enhance the overall quality of the domestic film industry and fulfill the national agenda. Conversely, transnational capital can also swamp the domestic market, impose a homogeneous cultural format, and pose a threat to domestic film production. Furthermore, if transnational capital is used only to produce commercial movies that please the government and divert people's attention from serious social concerns, it creates a climate conducive to the ruling party. If, however, transnational capital helps independent filmmakers produce serious work that provokes critical thinking about social problems, it can be a tool for social change. The complex and intertwined relationships among the state, local agency, and global capital render any simple theory untenable.

I hold that the conceptualization of the Hollywood and US global influence should transcend the debate between cultural imperialism and cultural globalization. It should focus on how people of other nations make sense of US culture and use it to achieve their own national agendas and their own modernization goals.

## The Status of China's Postsocialist Modernity

The encounter between China and global Hollywood speaks to the central issue of modernity and alternative modernities. The analysis of this issue relies largely on our definition of modernity. In the past, modernity usually meant Western modernity or capitalist modernity that was associated with a particular period and a particular geographic location. According to Anthony Giddens, modernity "refers to modes of social life or organization which emerged in Europe from about the seventeenth century onward and which subsequently became more or less worldwide in their influence."[5] Modernity contains such basic elements as reason and science, industrial capitalism and market economy, secular state administration through the rule of law, citizenship rights, and so forth. However, in the last decade, scholars (especially those from the global South and developing countries) have come to realize that modernity has many meanings, and they have been searching for alternatives to capitalist modernity. While acknowledging the existence of "diverse expressions and practices" of modernity, they have tried to find "an essence," "some commonality," and "some core features" of modernity; at the same time, these scholars recognize the "immense difficulties in trying to offer a concrete definition for a concept as abstract and (seemingly) all encompassing as 'modernity.'"[6] Accordingly, many conceptualizations have been used to describe the paths of various countries, such as Asian modernity and Confucian modernity, hybrid modernity and socialist modernity.[7] Nevertheless, most scholars agree that, in general, modernity is associated with a "good life" and the "methods, techniques and processes that the society sees as appropriate for the betterment of itself and the development of its population." As such, a "good life" also implies a "moral ethos."[8]

Politically, the socialist model of modernity of the former Soviet Union and Mao's China presented an alternative. However, both countries' socialist experiments with modernity had largely failed by the late 1970s. The fall of the Berlin Wall and the collapse of the Soviet Union in 1989 also led to the breakup of the socialist alliance and the termination of socialist modernization projects in those countries. Francis Fukuyama's declaration of "the end of history" and the triumph of Western liberal democracy was a response to the failure of socialist modernity.[9] However, this view has been criticized by those who point out the violence, poverty, and inequality under the capitalist and liberal democratic model. Left-wing scholars refute the universal claim of the metanarrative of the Enlightenment vision and continue to explore alternative modernities. For example, reflecting on the successful industrialization experiences of the four Asian "mini-dragons"—Hong Kong, Taiwan, Singapore, and South Korea—scholars have explored Confucian traditions in East Asian modernity.[10] As Dilip Gaonkar contends, elements of alternative modernities are embedded in every national and cultural site.[11]

Echoing both Takeuchi Yoshimi's and Lawrence Grossberg's argument that modernity happens in East-West encounters, and using the term "postsocialism" as the analytical framework, this book is fundamentally about Chinese postsocialist modernity. Within the context of the transformation of China's film industry, I define this modernity as two-dimensional: a tangible or material dimension consisting of the industrial infrastructure, and an intangible or nonmaterial dimension consisting of film texts in which the elements of a good life and a moral ethos are denoted. Or, put another way, there are both "hardware" and "software" elements in cinema. In terms of industrial infrastructure, there should be a technologically advanced film production, distribution, and exhibition system that serves as a solid foundation for filmmaking. In terms of film texts, in addition to pure entertainment, films should reflect a moral ethos that enhances human and social well-being and progress. I would also argue that good films should reflect the complex social reality and shed some light on its future direction. Judged on these two dimensions, modernity in the Chinese film industry has yet to be achieved.

By the end of 2012, China's gross box office revenue had reached US$2.7 billion, accounting for 8 percent of global ticket sales and making China the world's number-two box office earner.[12] Despite reaching a total of 18,195 movie screens in 2013, China still lagged far behind the United States, with 36,000 screens. Furthermore, all of China's modern theaters are located in big cities like Beijing, Shanghai, Guangzhou, Shenzhen, Nanjing, and Wuhan. In middle-sized cities and towns in the eastern part of the country, many theaters are still in urgent need of renovation. And in China's vast rural territory, the few theaters available are inadequate to meet the needs of rural audiences. In the 1960s China boasted more than 10,000 film exhibition venues. That number fell to 1,527 venues with 3,527 screens in 2007 and 4,097 in 2008, whereas the population doubled during this period.[13] This uneven development indicates that modernity has yet to be achieved.

Most domestic films are not listed on theater schedules, and some fail to recoup their production costs. At the same time, only a few movies have become international hits; most domestically made movies have little impact on the international market. In addition, by-products of films, such as DVDs and royalties from Internet downloading and TV broadcasting, are underdeveloped, leaving ample room for the growth of film-related businesses. Therefore, in terms of the tangible, material dimension, China's film modernity is only partially fulfilled.

In terms of the intangible soft power, China's film industry has a long way to go in that respect as well. Contemporary Chinese movies reflect a fractured national identity and moral collapse, a strong sense of dislocation and disorientation, and a "no way out" perspective. A profoundly pessimistic attitude about the future is especially prominent in artistic movies. Jia Zhangke's *Still Life,* as well as other films such as *Tuya's Marriage* and *Peacock,* have been criticized for overdoing the dark side of Chinese society and twisting past collective memory to conform to the views of Westerners. These movies have no optimism and no idealism; they posit no possible solutions and few prospects for the future. In *Peacock,* the idealism and collective spirit of the Mao era are turned into shattered dreams and family tragedies. Although this may reveal the bitter truth about life, the film's extremely pessimistic outlook runs counter to the collective memory of a self-dependent nation that once cherished the socialist dream and wholeheartedly worked to achieve a better future through collective, concerted effort. In addition, few movies depict any positive social changes, such as a more expansive worldview and better lifestyle, the growth of a middle class and its enhanced material well-being, an awareness of citizens' rights and increased civic participation, the widespread consensus about the importance of environmental protection, and the growing spirit of volunteerism, as shown after the Sichuan earthquake. These films do not draw on the rich Chinese cultural heritage, such as "the Confucian spirit of self-cultivation, family cohesiveness, social solidarity, benevolent governance, and universal peace to practice responsibility."[14]

China's popular martial arts genre portrays a traditional and preindustrial China fraught with traditional values. These films are both a form of escapism and a call for conformity to the established social order. A moral ethos for a modern China is absent in martial arts cinema and lacking in other genres. The so-called main-melody films are especially encouraged by the state and function as purveyors of officially sanctioned ideology. This genre shoulders the burden of reconstructing a national identity and a "spiritual home" featuring "the socialist core value system." However, because of their strong propagandistic flavor and little market attraction, this genre and the value system it conveys are increasingly irrelevant to the Chinese people and increasingly distant from the social reality of contemporary Chinese society. An ideological vacuum remains, and current Chinese movies have yet to fill it. They fail to manifest the inner strength, spiritual power, and social dynamics of a nation struggling for modernization. Although many films boast excellent cinematography and spectacular scenes, they fall short of providing the new trends and new spirit necessary for building a postsocialist modern China.

In both Chinese and Western societies, critical scholars point out the flaws of their own systems and look for better alternatives, often adapting beneficial elements from the opposite camp. Some Asian scholars have argued for transcending the confrontation between socialism and capitalism that has lasted for more than a century and taking a lesson from history.[15] Joining many Asian scholars, I advocate an integrated West-East model of modernity. As Asian studies scholar Tu Wei-ming put it:

> In the eyes of East Asian intellectuals, the strength of the United States as a model of modernity lies in vibrant market economy, functioning democratic polity, dynamic civil society, and culture of freedom. The Enlightenment values, such as liberty, rights consciousness, due process of law, and dignity of the individual, are evident in American economy, polity, society, and culture. Yet, unfortunately, American life is also plagued by inequality, litigiousness, conflict, and violence. The American people could benefit from a spirit of distributive justice in economy, an ethic of responsibility in politics, a sense of trust in society, and, above all, a culture of peace.[16]

To conclude, a complicated relationship exists among the Chinese state, transnational capital, and the domestic film industry. The East-West encounter, as manifested in the China-Hollywood engagement, has created an uneven and struggling modernity in China. This particular postsocialist modernity currently works to bolster the Chinese state's grip on power, but it may possibly nourish new elements and create new space for new alternatives.

# Acknowledgments

This book evolved over nearly ten years and involved not only my own serious commitment and hard work but also the help and guidance of others. I would like to express my deep gratitude to all the people who assisted me on this long journey. This book would not have been possible without their support.

First of all, I would like to thank my professors at the University of Minnesota, where I first envisioned this project. Professors Kathleen Hansen, Mark Pedelty, and Shayla Thiel-Stern of the School of Journalism and Mass Communication all provided valuable advice. I am particularly grateful to Professor Ronald Walter Greene of the Department of Communication Studies and one of the founding organizers and former chair of the Critical and Cultural Studies Division of the National Communication Association. He has been a great mentor to me for many years, introducing me to the field of critical communication studies, familiarizing me with critical theories and theoretical debates, and drawing my attention to cutting-edge scholarship and new trends. His own brilliant scholarship and noble personality set high standards for me. He has always been (and will always be) a role model and a source of support.

Special thanks to Professor Lary May of the American Studies Department. I formulated many of my research ideas in his classes and learned from his scholarship. His genuine interest in China studies and the Chinese Revolution inspired me to think and explore more deeply. I also benefited in many ways from the study group organized by him and his wife, Professor Elaine May. Those meetings at their home, lectures, free and open discussions, and good food left me with many cherished memories.

I would also like to thank Professor Chin-Chuan Lee for his early advice during my graduate studies. He urged me to strengthen my theoretical training in the field of mass communication and introduced me to a wide range of critical theories. His quest to determine whether the logic of modernity is universally applicable became one of my own research interests.

I started writing this book after I became a faculty member at the University of California–Riverside (UCR). My colleagues in the Department of Media and Cultural Studies extended their warm and consistent support, for which I am very grateful. Professor Toby Miller, the department's founding chair, was always supportive and encouraging and provided insightful advice and administrative assistance. His successor, Keith Harris, also provided much administrative support. My colleagues, Freya Schiwy, Lan Duong, and Ruhi Khan, helped me in many ways, from intellectual conversations to friendship. Other colleagues also offered advice and assistance. My book project received financial support from UCR, including travel and research funds and a Regent's Faculty Fellowship. I made multiple trips to China to conduct interviews and collect data. I thank Yu Haibo for sharing his connections with film professionals in China so that I could conduct interviews and obtain firsthand information on China's film industry. Libraries at Peking University and Renming University provided access to their archives. I thank Chiu Kuei and Pam Sun at the UCR library for their assistance in locating and purchasing research materials, especially the valuable *China Film Yearbooks*. Without my home institution's steadfast support and my colleagues' warm encouragement, this project would not have been completed.

Conference presentations and journal publications of earlier versions of individual chapters provided me with invaluable opportunities to get feedback, test my research rigor, and refine my arguments. I am very grateful for the generous suggestions and comments from my colleagues, and for their professionalism. Specifically, I am thankful to Dal Yong Jin, Stanley Rosen, Hyung Gu Lynn, Michael Keane, Anthony Fung, Zhu Ying, Daya Thussu, and Terry Flew, among others. Thanks to the insightful comments and professional assistance of these colleagues, my book eventually took shape.

I thank Steve Wrinn and Allison Webster of the University Press of Kentucky and Professor Shiping Hua, the editor of the Asia in the New Millenium series, for their warm welcome and for their professionalism during the publishing process.

Finally, I would like to thank my family for their love, patience, and support, which have sustained me throughout the years. My aging parents supported my study and research in the United States and helped take care of my baby girl in China. My father, a retired professor and editor in chief at prestigious Peking University, has always encouraged me to aim high and publish more. My mother, very sorrowfully, passed away in 2012. My daughter Susan has grown up learning to tolerate her busy and sometimes neglectful mother. My husband Jerry takes on many family responsibilities, often at the expense of his own teaching and research, and he is always there to back me up. It is to all of them that I am ultimately indebted.

# Notes

## Introduction

1. Xia Chen, "Dapian ruqin banian ji" [An elegy for eight years of the Hollywood invasion], *Nanfang Weekend,* February 28, 2002.

2. John Tomlinson, "Culture Globalization and Cultural Imperialism," in *International Communication and Globalization: A Critical Introduction,* ed. Ali Mohammadi (London: Sage Publications, 1997), 181.

3. "Preface: How to Use This Book," in *Internationalizing Cultural Studies: An Anthology,* ed. Ackbar Abbas and John Nguyet Erni (Malden, MA: Blackwell Publishing, 2005), xxvi.

4. Zhou Tiedong, interview by the author, Beijing, July 7, 2011.

5. Sina Entertainment, "2012 piaofang chao 170 yi; Tai Jiong jin 12 yi po jilu" [2012 box office revenue exceeds 17 billion yuan], January 10, 2013, http://ent.sina.com.cn/m/c/2013-01-10/06283831414.shtml (accessed January 10, 2013).

6. Zhou Tiedong, "Speech at the US-China Film Summit," Los Angeles, November 2, 2010.

7. Feng Xiaoning, "Zhongguo shi weiyi weibei mei dapian yakua de dianying da guo" [China is the only giant film producer not knocked down by American blockbusters], *Chinese Economy Network,* March 5, 2010, http://msn.ent.ynet.com/view.jsp?oid=63808971 (accessed March 5, 2010).

8. Zhang Wei, "Avatar zhongguo piaofang jin liangyi meiyuan, weiju haiwai shichang bangshou" [*Avatar* makes China top overseas box office moneymaker with US$200 million], April 1, 2010, http://www.chinanews.com.cn/yl/yl-dyzx/news/2010/04-02/2204684.shtml (accessed November 11, 2010).

9. Yu Deshu, "Zhongguo jiang qudai riben chengwei haolaiwu diyida haiwai shichang" [China to replace Japan as Hollywood's number-one overseas market], *Fazhi Wanbao,* January 13, 2012, http://news.entgroup.cn/movie/1312625.shtml (accessed January 17, 2012).

10. Yu Deshu, "Zhongguo yingshi fanrong beihou cang weiji jin sancheng guochanpian shangying" [The crisis behind the prosperous Chinese film market with only 30 percent domestic movies in theaters], *Fazhi Wanbao,* March 18, 2013, http://news.entgroup.cn/movie/1816115.shtml (accessed March 22, 2013).

11. Toby Miller, Nitin Govil, John McMurria, and Richard Maxwell, *Global Hollywood* (London: British Film Institute, 2001).

12. Silvio Waisbord and Nancy Morris, "Introduction—Rethinking Media Globalization and State Power," in *Media and Globalization: Why the State Matters,* ed. Nancy Morris and Silvio Waisbord (Lanham, MD: Rowman & Littlefield, 2001), vii–xvi.

13. Marwan Kraidy, *Hybridity or the Cultural Logic of Globalization* (Philadelphia: Temple University Press, 2005), 156.

14. Michael Curtin, *Playing to the World's Biggest Audience: The Globalization of Chinese Film and TV* (Berkeley: University of California Press, 2007), 22.

15. Zhao Yuezhi, *Communication in China: Political Economy, Power, and Conflict* (Lanham, MD: Rowman & Littlefield, 2008), 5, 145, 146.

16. Anthony Fung, *Global Capital, Local Culture: Transnational Media Corporations in China* (New York: Peter Lang, 2008), 29, 30, 35, 79.

17. Eric Kit-wai Ma, "Rethinking Media Studies—The Case of China," in *De-Westernizing Media Studies,* ed. James Curran and Myung-Jin Park (London: Routledge, 2000), 21–34.

18. See Stephanie Hemelryk Donald, Michael Keane, and Yin Hong, eds., *Media in China—Consumption, Content and Crisis* (London: Routledge Curzon, 2002), 5; David Harvey, *A Brief History of Neoliberalism* (New York: Oxford University Press, 2005); Zhao, *Communication in China.*

19. Ma, "Rethinking Media Studies," 27.

20. For a detailed discussion of the China model and its difference from the Western liberal model, see Zhao Suisheng, "The China Model: Can It Replace the Western Model of Modernization?" *Journal of Contemporary China* 19 (2010): 419–36.

21. Takeuchi Yoshimi, *What Is Modernity? Writings of Takeuchi Yoshimi* (New York: Columbia University Press, 2005), 53, 57.

22. Lawrence Grossberg, *Cultural Studies in the Future Tense* (Durham, NC: Duke University Press, 2010), 42, 84, 85.

23. Ibid., 83.

24. Liu Kang, *Globalization and Cultural Trends in China* (Honolulu: University of Hawaii Press, 2004), 11.

25. Arif Dirlik, "Postsocialism? Reflections on Socialism with Chinese Characteristics," in *Marxism and the Chinese Experience* (Armonk, NY: Sharpe, 1989), 364.

26. Sheldon Hsiao-peng Lu, "What Is Chinese Postsocialism?" in *Chinese Modernity and Global Biopolitics: Studies in Literature and Visual Culture* (Honolulu: University of Hawaii Press, 2007), 204–10.

27. Zhang Yingjin, "Rebel without a Cause? China's New Urban Generation and Postsocialist Filmmaking," in *The Urban Generation—Chinese Cinema and Society at the Turn of the Twenty-First Century,* ed. Zhang Zhen (Durham, NC: Duke University Press, 2007), 49–80.

28. Toby Miller, "Introduction," in Abbas and Erni, *Internationalizing Cultural Studies,* 229.

29. "Preface," in Abbas and Erni, *Internationalizing Cultural Studies,* xxvi.

30. J. Lewis and Toby Miller, eds., *Critical Cultural Policy Studies: A Reader* (Malden, MA: Blackwell Publishing, 2003), 8.

31. Stuart Cunningham, "Cultural Studies from the Viewpoint of Cultural Policy," in Lewis and Miller, *Critical Cultural Policy Studies,* 13–22, 14.

32. Wang Jing and David Goodman, "A Matter of Choice: Critical Policy Studies of China," 2003, http://web.mit.edu/chinapolicy/www/documents/founding.pdf (accessed November 14, 2009).

## 1. Cultural Policy as Negotiation of Power

1. Joseph Kahn, "Change in China: Man in the News; Mystery Man at the Helm Hu Jintao," *New York Times,* November 15, 2002, http://query.nytimes.com/gst/fullpage.html?res=950CE4D71430F936A25752C1A9649C8B63 (accessed October 25, 2007).

2. Central Committee of Chinese Communist Party, "The Resolution on Speeding Up the Development of the Tertiary Industry," June 16, 1992, http://news.xinhuanet.com/ziliao/2005-02/17/content_2586400.htm (accessed October 15, 2011).

3. Rao Shuguang, *Zhongguo dianying shichang fazhanshi* [The development of the Chinese film market] (Beijing: Zhongguo dianying chubanshe [China Film Press], 2009).

4. Mao Yu, interview by the author, Beijing, August 15, 2011.

5. Zhao, *Communication in China,* 162.

6. Wang Yongzhi and Ren Yi, "The Embarrassments Caused by Importing Major Films," *Chinese Sociology and Anthropology* 32, no. 1 (1999): 9.

7. Rao Shuguang, *Development of the Chinese Film Market,* 456.

8. Fang Cheng, "Dianying de yongtan" [Film speaks], *China Film Market* 8 (1997).

9. For a more detailed account of the crisis and reform in the Chinese film sector, see Zhu Ying, "Chinese Cinema's Economic Reform from the Mid-1980s to the Mid-1990s," *Journal of Communication* 52 (2002): 905–21; and Zhu Ying, *Chinese Cinema during the Era of Reform—The Ingenuity of the System* (Westport, CT: Praeger, 2003).

10. Wan Ping, "Jinkou Fenzhang yingpian shinian piaofang fenxi" [An analysis of ten years of box office revenue sharing from imports], *Journal of Beijing Film Academy* 6 (2005): 49–60.

11. Wu Mengchen, "Wu Mengchen's Speech on National Conference of General Managers," *China Film Market* 2 (1994): 7.

12. *Xinhua,* July 14, 1994, cited in Stanley Rosen, "The Wolf at the Door: Hollywood and the Film Market in China," in *Southern California and the World,* ed. Eric J. Heikkila and Rafael Pizarro (Westport, CT: Praeger, 2002), 49–77.

13. Yang Lin, "Yinjin shoubu dapian beizhi 'yangmaiban'" [Importer of first

Hollywood blockbuster criticized as "foreign comprador"], *New Beijing Daily,* December 19, 2008, http://news.sina.com.cn/c/2008-12-19/091616880300.shtml (accessed December 21, 2008).

14. Ibid.

15. Zhou Tiedong, "Xinzhongguo dianying duiwai jiaoliu" [Foreign exchange of Chinese cinema in new China], *Dianying yishu* [Film art] 1 (2000): 113–18.

16. Wu Houbin, "How to Deal with Upcoming 20 Imports," *China Consumer News,* February 14, 2000.

17. See, for example, Rosen, "Wolf at the Door," as well as relevant reports from *China Film Weekly, China Film Market,* and *Wenhui Film Times* between November 1994 and March 1995.

18. Lu Zhengming, "Wangming tianya zai jing shangying yinqi fengbo" [The debut of *The Fugitive* in Beijing causes dispute], *Wenhui Film Times,* December 3, 1994.

19. Yang, "Importer of First Hollywood Blockbuster."

20. "News," *Wenhui Film Times,* January 21, 1995.

21. Rao Shuguang, *Development of the Chinese Film Market,* 465.

22. Associated Press, November 19, 1994, cited in Rosen, "Wolf at the Door."

23. Mao Yu interview.

24. Wan Ping, "Analysis of Ten Years of Box Office Revenue Sharing from Imports."

25. Rosen, "Wolf at the Door."

26. Zheng Dongtian, "To Be, or Not to Be?—Jinru WTO yihou de zhongguo Dianying shengcun fenxi" [An analysis of the survival of the Chinese film industry after joining the WTO], *Dianying yishu* [Film art] 2 (2000): 4–8.

27. Rosen, "Wolf at the Door."

28. Liu Jianzhong, "Produce More Excellent Films; Emphasize on Implementation about the Consideration of the Key Points of the Film Work in 1996 [*sic*]," in *China Film Yearbook 1997* (Beijing: Zhongguo dianying chubanshe [China Film Press], 1997), 15–17.

29. State Administration of Radio, Film, and Television (SARFT) and Ministry of Culture, "The Detailed Regulations to Implement Structural Reform of the Mechanism of Film Distribution and Presentation," in *China Film Yearbook 2002* (Beijing: Zhongguo dianying chubanshe [China Film Press], 2002), 15–16.

30. Jiang Zemin, "A Speech on the Sixth National Conference of China Federation of Literary and Art Circles and the Fifth National Conference of Chinese Writers Association," in *China Film Yearbook 1997,* 1–3.

31. Lu Shaoyang, "Zhuxuanlv yingpian de fazhan jiqi shehui jiazhi" [The development of "main melody" films and their social values], *Yishu Pinglun* [Arts criticism] 10 (2007): 36–37.

32. Wang Zhiqiang, "A Summary of 1995 Imports," in *China Film Yearbook 1996* (Beijing: Zhongguo dianying chubanshe [China Film Press], 1996), 203–5.

33. Ding Guangen, "Produce More Outstanding Works; Fund the Chinese Film Industry," in *China Film Yearbook 1997,* 7–10.

34. Liu Jianzhong, "Retrospective of 1996 and Prospects for 1997," in *China Film Yearbook 1997,* 59–64.

35. Wang Gengnian, "Frequent Rain Brings Spring, Warm Breeze Brings Dense Forests—My Impression of China's Film in the 1990s," in *China Film Yearbook 2001* (Beijing: Zhongguo dianying chubanshe [China Film Press], 2001), 21–27.

36. Tong Gang, "Grab the Opportunity; Make Good Plans Together; Promote a Prosperous Film Industry in China," in *China Film Yearbook 1997,* 38–42.

37. Mao Yu, "A Summary of the 2000 Domestic Film Market," in *China Film Yearbook 2002,* 169–72.

38. Lu Shaoyang, "Development of 'Main Melody' Films and Their Social Values."

39. Rosen, "Wolf at the Door."

40. Chen Zewei, "Dianying shichang guochanpian zhan duoda fen'er?" [What is the market share of domestic films?], *Outlook Weekly,* July 28, 2003, 17–18.

41. Li Jingfu, "Daole zui weixian de shihou lema?" [Are domestic films in a critical situation?], *Popular Cinema* 15 (2004): 63.

42. Xia Chen, "Dapian ruqin banian ji" [An elegy for eight years of the Hollywood invasion], *Nanfang Weekend,* February 28, 2002.

43. Quoted in ibid.

44. Liu Jianzhong, "Promote Our Film Industry to a Higher New Stage," in *China Film Yearbook 1998/1999* (Beijing: Zhongguo dianying chubanshe [China Film Press], 1998–1999), 29–34.

45. Fan Jianghua, Mao Yu, and Yang Yuan, "A Summary of the Film Market in 1996," in *China Film Yearbook 1997,* 177–81.

46. Liu Jianzhong, "Dianying de rushi tanpan yu wo'men de chengnuo" [WTO negotiation with regard to film and our commitment], in *WTO yu zhongguo dianying* [WTO and Chinese cinema], ed. Zhang Zhenxin and Yang Yuanying (Beijing: Zhongguo dianying chubanshe [China Film Press], 2002), 3–8. See also Tong Gang, "How Does China's Film Industry Face the Challenge Brought by China's Joining of the WTO?" in *China Film Yearbook 2001,* 17–20.

47. Zhu, "Chinese Cinema's Economic Reform from the Mid-1980s to the Mid-1990s," 902.

48. Cited in Zhao Shi, "The Mission of Chinese Films to Stride into the New Century in 1999," in *China Film Yearbook 2000* (Beijing: Zhongguo dianying chubanshe [China Film Press], 2000), 13.

49. Ibid., 11.

50. Guo Qupo, "Pozai meijie de weiji" [An urgent crisis—a predication of the impact of China's WTO access on Chinese films], in *China Film Yearbook 2000,* 155–58.

51. Xu Guangchun, "To Inspire Enthusiasm, to Reform and Create, and to Flourish and Develop China's Film Industry," in *China Film Yearbook 2001,* 10.

52. Xu Guangchun, "To Promote a More Prosperous New Stage of Chinese Films—A Talk on the National Film-Work Forum," in *China Film Yearbook 2002,* 24.

53. Jiang Zemin, "Speech on the 16th National Congress of the Communist Party of China," November 17, 2002, http://news.xinhuanet.com/ziliao/2002-11/17/content_693542.html (accessed May 13, 2008).

54. Wang Jing, "Culture as Leisure and Culture as Capital," *Positions* 9, no. 1 (2002): 69–70.

55. Xu Guangchun, "With the Guidance of the 16th National Congress of the CPC, Make Great Efforts in Reforming and Developing the Chinese Film Industry," in *China Film Yearbook 2004* (Beijing: Zhongguo dianying chubanshe [China Film Press], 2004), 25.

56. Xu Guangchun, "Promote Chinese Film Industrialization," in *China Film Yearbook 2004,* 38–39.

57. SARFT and Ministry of Culture, "Some Opinions about Carrying Out Further Reform in the Film Industry," in *China Film Yearbook 2001,* 1.

58. SARFT, "Notification about Several Notions on Promoting the Development of the Film Industry," in *China Film Yearbook 2005* (Beijing: Zhongguo dianying chubanshe [China Film Press], 2005), 9–13.

59. State Council, "Film Managerial Regulations," in *China Film Yearbook 2002,* 9–14.

60. SARFT and Ministry of Culture, "Provisional Regulations of the Foreign Investment in Film Theaters," in *China Film Yearbook 2004,* 18–19.

61. SARFT, "Provisional Regulations for Approval of Film Script (Storyboard) and Film Censorship," in *China Film Yearbook 2004,* 13–14.

62. Ministry of Commerce of the People's Republic of China, "Closer Economic Partnership Arrangement (CEPA)," 2003, http://tga.mofcom.gov.cn/subject/cepanew/index.shtml (accessed December 15, 2009).

63. Sina Entertainment, "2012 piaofang chao 170 yi; Tai Jiong jin 12 yi po jilu" [2012 box office revenue exceeds 17 billion yuan], January 20, 2013, http://ent.sina.com.cn/m/c/2013-01-10/06283831414.shtml (accessed January 10, 2013).

64. For annual film output, see Tong Gang, "Fruitful Industrial Policy and New Epoch for Chinese Film—2004 Annual Report on the Chinese Film Industry," in *China Film Yearbook 2005,* 32–36; Tong Gang, "Inherit the Centennial Tradition to Compose a New Chapter on Chinese Film Production," in *China Film Yearbook 2006* (Beijing: Zhongguo dianying chubanshe [China Film Press], 2006), 61–69; Lu Liang, "Report on 2006 Film Production," *Film* 1 (2007): 6–8.

65. Sina Entertainment, "2012 Box Office Revenue Exceeds 17 Billion Yuan."

66. Cui Ding, "Guangdian gongbu 2013 nian piaofang, 217 yi zengzhang 27%" [2013 box office revenue reaches 21.7 billion yuan], January 4, 2014, http://news.entgroup.cn/movie/0419126.shtml (accessed January 19, 2014).

67. Tong Gang, "Fruitful Industrial Policy and New Epoch for Chinese Film," 32–36.

68. Yin Hong and Wang X., "The Industry Year of Chinese Film," *Dangdai dianying* [Contemporary cinema] 2 (2005): 18–26.

69. Yin Hong and Zhan Q., "2007 nian zhongguo dianying chanye beiwang" [Memo on the 2007 film industry], *Dangdai dianying* [Contemporary cinema] 2 (2008): 13–21.

70. Bloomberg, "Time Warner to Quit China Cine Business," November 8, 2006, http://www.financialexpress.com/news/time-warner-to-quit-china-cine-business/183270/ (accessed February 5, 2009).

71. J. Landreth, "Co-prod'n Unit Xinhua Media Bridges China, U.S.," *Hollywood Reporter*, April 15, 2008, http://www.hollywoodreporter.com/hr/esearch/searchResult.jsp?keyword=prod%27n+unit+Xinhua+Media+bridges+China%2C+U.S.&exposeNavigation=true&kw=&configType=&searchType=ARTICLE_SEARCH&an=thr&action=Submit&searchInterface=THRSearch&matchType=mode%2Bmatchallpartial&numOfrecordsPerPage=10&x=21&y=10 (accessed May 4, 2008).

72. Richard Verrier, "A Boost for U.S. Films in China?" *Los Angeles Times*, May 12, 2011, B4.

73. Xiao Yang, "Haolaiwu quanqiu gongchengluedi, zhongguodianying jinru beizhan zhuangtai [China film industry prepares for Hollywood's global expansion], *Beijing Youth Daily*, April 15, 2010, http://ent.ifeng.com/movie/news/mainland/detail_2010_04/15/526755_0.shtml (accessed August 11, 2011).

74. Richard Verrier, "IMAX Plans Expansion in China," *Los Angeles Times*, May 25, 2011, B3.

75. Ben Fritz, "Legendary Pictures Ventures into China," *Los Angeles Times*, June 10, 2011, B3.

76. Emily Rome, "Coming Soon to China: Digital Movie Theaters and Training," *Los Angeles Times*, September 22, 2011, B3.

77. Sohu Finance, "Haolaiwu 'xinjia' luohu shoudu jingjiquan" [Hollywood sets up a "new home" in Beijing], July 4, 2011, http://www.cc2.cn/ShowNews.aspx?id=332&tid=227 (accessed September 21, 2012).

78. Richard Verrier, Dawn C. Chmielewski, and David Pierson, "Hollywood Finds New Venue," *Los Angeles Times*, June 16, 2011, A6–A7.

79. Tong Gang, "Inherit the Centennial Tradition," 61.

80. Yu Deshu, "Jiedu dianying xinzheng: yingzhan haolaihu, guochanpian dei zhangdexing" [Domestic movies should sharpen their competitive edge to compete with Hollywood], February 21, 2012, http://news.entgroup.cn/c/2112925.shtml (accessed March 7, 2012).

## 2. The Debate about Hollywood

1. H. I. Schiller, *Culture Inc.: The Corporate Takeover of Public Expression* (New York: Oxford University Press, 1989).

2. Berndt Ostendorf, "Americanization and Anti-Americanism in the Age of Globalization," 2004, http://scholar.google.comscholar?hl=en&lr=&q=cache:p499a_xy2EkJ:www.uiowa.edu/~ifuss/documents/Ostendorf_article.doc+Berndt+Ostendorf (accessed February 27, 2007).

3. See H. I. Schiller, "Transnational Media and National Development," in *National Sovereignty and International Communication,* ed. K. Nordenstreng and H. I. Schiller (Norwood, NJ: Ablex, 1979), 21–32; H. I. Schiller, "Not Yet the Post-Imperialist Era," in *Communication and Culture in War and Peace,* ed. C. Roach (Newbury Park, CA: Sage, 1993), 97–116; Robert W. McChesney, "The Political Economy of Global Communication," in *Capitalism and the Information Age: The Political Economy of the Global Communication Revolution,* ed. R. W. McChesney, E. M. Wood, and J. B. Foster (New York: Monthly Review Press, 1998), 1–26.

4. Quoted in Richard Maltby, "Introduction: The Americanization of the World," in *Hollywood Abroad—Audiences and Cultural Exchange,* ed. Richard Maltby and Melvyn Stokes (London: British Film Institute, 2004), 1.

5. Toby Miller, Nitin Govil, John McMurria, and Richard Maxwell, *Global Hollywood* (London: British Film Institute, 2001).

6. Quoted in Miller et al., *Global Hollywood,* 77.

7. Berndt Ostendorf, "Why Is American Popular Culture So Popular? A View from Europe," *American Studies in Scandinavia* 34, no. 1 (2003): 1–46.

8. Schiller, "Transnational Media and National Development."

9. I. Ang, *Watching* Dallas (London: Methuen, 1985); T. Liebes and E. Katz, *The Export of Meaning: Cross-Cultural Readings of "Dallas"* (New York: Oxford University Press, 1990).

10. Schiller, "Not Yet the Post-Imperialist Era," 101; H. I. Schiller, "Striving for Communication Dominance," in *Electronic Empires,* ed. D. Thissu (London: Arnold, 1998), 17.

11. Annabelle Sreberny-Mohammadi, "The Many Cultural Faces of Imperialism," in *Beyond Cultural Imperialism,* ed. Peter Golding and Phil Harris (London: Sage Publications, 1997), 51; J. Petras, "Cultural Imperialism in the Late 20th Century," *Journal of Contemporary Asia* 23, no. 2 (1993): 140.

12. R. Garofalo, "Whose World, What Beat: The Transnational Music Industry, Identity and Cultural Imperialism," *World of Music* 35, no. 2 (1993): 16–22.

13. John Tomlinson, *Cultural Imperialism: A Critical Introduction* (Baltimore: Johns Hopkins University Press, 1991).

14. Marwan Kraidy, *Hybridity, or the Cultural Logic of Globalization* (Philadelphia: Temple University Press, 2005), 29.

15. John Tomlinson, *Globalization and Culture* (Chicago: University of Chicago Press, 1999), 6.

16. See A. Giddens, *The Consequences of Modernity* (Stanford, CA: Stanford University Press, 1990); A. Giddens, *Modernity and Self-Identity* (Oxford: Polity, 1991); Roland Robertson, "Globality and Modernity," *Theory, Culture & Society* 9, no. 2 (1992).

17. Mike Featherstone, *Undoing Culture: Globalization, Postmodernism and Identity* (London: Sage Publications, 1995), 73.

18. Dilip Parameshwar Gaonkar, "On Alternative Modernities," in *Alternative Modernities,* ed. Dilip Parameshwar Gaonkar (Durham, NC: Duke University Press, 2001), 1–23.

19. Featherstone, *Undoing Culture,* 87.

20. Mike Featherstone and Scott Lash, "Globalization, Modernity and the Spatialization of Social Theory: An Introduction," in *Global Modernities,* ed. Mike Featherstone, Scott Lash, and Roland Robertson (London: Sage Publications, 1995), 4.

21. Tomlinson, *Globalization and Culture,* 16.

22. Featherstone, *Undoing Culture,* 83; Kraidy, *Hybridity.*

23. See Arjun Appadurai, *Modernity at Large* (Minneapolis: University of Minnesota Press, 1996), 32; Roland Robertson, *Globalization: Social Theory and Global Culture* (London: Sage Publications, 1992); John Tomlinson, "Culture Globalization and Cultural Imperialism," in *International Communication and Globalization: A Critical Introduction,* ed. A. Mohammadi (London: Sage Publications, 1997), 181; Fredric Jameson, "Notes on Globalization as a Philosophical Issue," in *The Cultures of Globalization,* ed. Fredric Jameson and Masao Miyoshi (Durham, NC: Duke University Press, 1998), 75; Fredric Jameson, "Preface," in ibid., xi–xvii.

24. Yu Shaowen, "Longjuanfeng qishixiongxiong, zainanpian yu chuang gaochao" [Twister and disaster films come to town], *Beijing Youth Daily,* August 20, 1996; "Wu Mengchen de shuofa" [What Wu Mengchen says], *Beijing Youth Daily,* July 6, 1995.

25. Shao Mujun, "Guanyu zhongguo dianying qiantu de pifuzhijian" [My personal opinion on the future of Chinese domestic films], *Dazhong Dianying* [Popular cinema] 9 (1995): 8.

26. See Xi Rubing, "Moshi jingzheng ru laohu" [Don't consider competition a scary tiger], *Beijing Youth Daily,* May 7, 1995; Song Chunyi, "Shibu dapian kan silu" [Think about ten blockbusters], *Beijing Youth Daily,* May 7, 1995; Zheng Dongtian, "Shibu jinkou dapian laile yihou . . ." [After ten blockbusters are imported . . . ], *Zhongguo dianying shichang* [Chinese film market] 6 (1994): 8–9.

27. Zheng Dongtian, "After Ten Blockbusters Are Imported," 8.

28. Song Guoqiang, "Yijiujiusi: yingjie zhongshengxiang" [1994: a look at film circle], *Xiju dianying bao* [Theater and film news], February 10, 1995, 5.

29. Zhou Anhua, "Jingshi: Hollywood da qinshi" [Be alert to Hollywood's poisoning], *Cinematic Creation* 4 (1998): 54–55, 71; Zhou Mingrong, "Jinkou yingpian dou haokan?" [Are all imported movies good for watching?], *Popular Cinema* 11 (1996): 22; Yin Hong, "Haolaiwu de quanqiuhua celue yu zhongguo dianying de fazhan" [Hollywood's global strategy and the development of Chinese films], in *Yin Hong zixuanji* [Yin Hong's self-selected anthology] (Shanghai: Fudan University Press, 2004), 121.

30. Zhou Mingrong, "Are All Imported Movies Good?" 22.

31. Song Qiang, Zhang Zangzang, and Qiao Bian, *Zhongguo keyi shuo bu*

[China can say no] (Beijing: Zhonghua gongshang lianhe chubanshe [China Industry and Commerce Joint Press], 1996).

32. Yu Min, "Youguan yingpian shuru de shuosandaosi" [Some comments on importing movies], *Popular Cinema* 7 (1995): 1.

33. Dai Jinhua, "Wo kan haolaiwu" [How I view Hollywood], *Beijing Youth Daily,* October 9, 1995.

34. See Chen Xiaoyun, "Meiguo dianying: huayu baquan yu yishixingtai shenhua" [American films: hegemony of discourse and ideological myth], *Contemporary Cinema* 2 (1998): 39–44; Lan Aiguo, *Haolaiwu zhuyi* [Hollywoodism] (Guangxi, China: Guangxi Normal University Press, 2003).

35. Yin Hong, "Quanqiuhua, haolaiwu yu minzu dianying" [Globalization, Hollywood and national film], *Wenyi yanjiu* [Literature and art studies] 6 (2000): 99.

36. Sun Li, "Huashuo zhengjiu dabing Lei'en" [Talk about *Saving Private Ryan*], *Beijing Youth Daily,* November 28, 1998.

37. He Dong, "Zhengjiu dabing Lei'en huawaiyin" [Comments on *Saving Private Ryan*], *Beijing Youth Daily,* November 28, 1998.

38. Zuo Heng, "Wo kan zhengjiu dabing Lei'en" [How I view *Saving Private Ryan*], *Beijing Youth Daily,* December 12, 1998.

39. Fang Weijin, "Haoran zhengqi changcun—Jianping Yonggan de xin" [A brief review of *Braveheart*], *Popular Cinema* 9 (1996): 45.

40. Bei Ming, "Xinzuo kuaiping" [Prompt comments on new releases], *Beijing Youth Daily,* March 17–24, 1998.

41. Pang Guan, "Zainan jiaru mingtian lailin" [What if disaster comes tomorrow?], *Beijing Youth Daily,* August 18, 1997; Yu Shaowen, "Longjuanfeng qishixiongxiong, zainanpian yu chuang gaochao" [Twister and disaster films come to town], *Beijing Youth Daily,* August 20, 1996.

42. Gong Jicheng, "Qing dianying guanxin ren" [Please care about human beings], *Beijing Youth Daily,* May 5, 1998.

43. Long Yingtai, "Gandong, shuide shangpin?" [For whose commodity are we moved?], *Nanfang Weekend,* December 11, 1998.

44. Dai Jinhua, *Dianying piping* (film critique) (Beijing: Peking University Press, 2004), 199.

45. Xiao Ersi, "*Forrest Gump:* meiguo baoshouzhuyi de fengqiu" [*Forrest Gump:* a signal of American conservatism], *China Youth Daily,* June 9, 1995; Ye Bian, "Meiguo lishi he shehui de jiaxin qiaokeli" [An analysis of *Forrest Gump*], *World Affairs* 15 (1995): 22–23, 16 (1995): 16–17.

46. See Zhang Lan, "Jiedu Argan" [A review of *Forrest Gump*], *Beijing Daily,* June 26, 1995; Shao Mujun, "Forrest Gump and Harry: yingxiong chong'er doushi haolaiwu" [Forrest Gump and Harry: heroes of Hollywood], *China Youth Daily,* December 15, 1995; Luo Jiuxiang, "Yige meili er wunai de shenhua—kan meiguo jupian *Forrest Gump*" [I view *Forrest Gump*], *Film Introduction* 5 (1995): 31; Gao Jun, "Guoji dapian Forrest Gump mianlin Beijing guanzhong de Jianyan" [*Forrest Gump* comes to Beijing], *Beijing Evening News,* June 10, 1995.

47. He Dong, "Jianfa rensheng—dianying *Forrest Gump*'s qishi" [What we could learn from *Forrest Gump*], *Popular Cinema* 9 (1995): 1.

48. Huang Li, "Chuantong dui xiandai de qingsuan" [A modern return to tradition], *Beijing Youth Daily,* June 22, 1995.

49. Charles Taylor, "Two Theories of Modernity," in *Alternative Modernities,* ed. Dilip Parameshwar Gaonkar (Durham, NC: Duke University Press, 2001), 183.

50. "Zongshuji miaoyulianzhu guangdongtuan" [General secretary talks among Guangdong delegates], *Yangcheng Wanbao,* March 10, 1998, A1.

51. Phoenix TV's interview with Han Sanping, November 15, 2012, http://phtv.ifeng.com/program/fhdsy/detail_2012_11/16/19229197_0.shtml (accessed July 9, 2014).

52. Zheng Dongtian, "'To Be, or Not to Be?'—Jinru WTO yihou de zhongguo dianying shengcun fenxi" [An analysis of the survival of the Chinese film industry after joining the WTO], *Dianying Yishu* [Film art] 2 (2000): 4–8.

53. Yin Hong, "Hollywood's Global Strategy and the Development of Chinese Films."

54. Hu Hui, "Hollywood de langxing—Hollywood quanqiuhua celue zhi lunxi" [The wolf nature of Hollywood—on Hollywood's global strategy], *Theory and Creation* 2 (2003): 65–68.

55. Quoted in Stanley Rosen, "The Wolf at the Door: Hollywood and the Film Market in China," in *Southern California and the World,* ed. Eric J. Heikkila and Rafael Pizarro (Westport, CT: Praeger, 2002).

56. Toby Miller, Nitin Govil, John McMurria, Richard Maxwell, and Ting Wang, *Global Hollywood 2* (London: British Film Institute, 2005).

57. Gui Qingshan, "Haolaiwu shifou xuyao diyu?—Cong yixie xuezhe de 'wenhua maqinuo fangxian' tanqi" [Do we need to resist Hollywood?], *Dianying chuangzuo* [Cinematic creation] 1 (2002): 57–62.

58. Ibid.

59. Lan Aiguo, *Hou haolaiwu shidai de zhongguo dianying* [Chinese movies in post-Hollywood ages] (Guangxi, China: Guangxi Normal University Press, 2004), 126.

60. Lan Aiguo, *Hollywoodism,* 111.

61. Yan Chunjun, "Quanqiuhua he zhongguo minzu dianying de wenhua zhanlue" [Globalization and the cultural strategy of China's national film], in *Quanqiuhua yu zhongguo yingshi de mingyun* [Globalization and the fate of China's film and television], ed. Zhang Fengzhu, Huang Shixian, and Hu Zhifeng (Beijing: Beijing Broadcasting Institute Press, 2002), 43.

62. Lan Aiguo, *Chinese Movies in Post-Hollywood Ages,* 175.

63. Jiang Fen, "Ningshi xiandaixing: sansishi niandai Shanghai dianying wenhua yu haolaiwu yinsu" [Gazing at modernity: Hollywood factors and Shanghai's cinematic culture in the 1930s and 1940s], *Shi Lin* 3 (2002): 105.

64. Wang Rui, "Meiguo zaoqi dianying dui zhongguo zaoqi dianying de yingxiang—zhongmei dianying bijiao chutan" [A preliminary exploration of the influ-

ence of early American films on early Chinese films], *Contemporary Cinema* 6 (2001): 88–94.

65. Yin Hong, "Hollywood's Global Strategy and the Development of Chinese Films," 341.

66. Li Yizhong, "Jingzhengxing hezuo: rushi hou zhongmei dianyingye de jiaohu taishi" [Copetition: the intertwined situation of the Sino-American film industry after China reenters the WTO], *Modern Communication* 1 (2006): 14–19.

67. Yin Hong and Tang Jianying, "Zoude chuqu caineng zhande qilai—quanqiuhua Beijing xia de zhongguo dianying ruan shili" [The soft power of Chinese film in the global background], *Contemporary Cinema* 2 (2008): 10–14.

68. Wang Qu, "Yinjin dapian shisi nian: ronghe yu fazhan" [Fourteen years after Hollywood blockbuster imports: integration and development], in *Gaige kaifang yu zhongguo dianying sanshinian* [Chinese cinema in the thirty-year reform era] (Beijing: Zhongguo dianying chubanshe [China Film Press], 2008), 439–54.

69. "Xiongmao 2 zao dizhi, haolaiwu zhuanqian hai xienao" [*Kung Fu Panda 2* encounters resistance], *Yangzi Wanbao,* May 20, 2011, http://www.wenxuecity.com/news/2011/05/30/1376622/print (accessed November 9, 2011).

70. Valens, "*Kung Fu Panda* zao dizhi" [*Kung Fu Panda* encounters resistance], June 21, 2011, http://bbs.17173.com/toics/691/200806/21/1941577,1.html (accessed November 7, 2011).

71. Lu Chuan's blog, June 20, 2008, http://blog.sina.com.cn/s/blog_539a023201009e00.html (accessed November 7, 2011).

72. "Kung Fu Panda zaodizhi, sichuansheng beipo tingzhi fangying" [*Kung Fu Panda* encounters resistance, Sichuan Province forced to terminate screening], 2008, http://v.cnmo.com/firm/5/4932.html (accessed October 28, 2011).

73. "Dizhi *Kung Fu Panda 2* qianmudi hezai?" [What is the hidden motive behind the resistance to *Kung Fu Panda 2*?], *Movie Maniacs*, May 31, 2011, http://i.mtime.com/olympia/blog/6054186 (accessed October 28, 2011).

74. "Dizhi *Kung Fu Panda 2* shi sajiao yaochong" [Resistance to *Kung Fu Panda 2* is coquetry and favor-currying], *China Youth Daily,* June 7, 2011, http://www.cq.xinhuanet.com/news/2011-06/07/content_22949485.htm (accessed October 28, 2011).

75. Cheng Manli, "Weishenme zhongguo wenhua chanpin chukounan—you dianying *Kung Fu Panda 2* shangying xiangdao de" [Thoughts on the difficulty of exporting Chinese cultural products—in view of *Kung Fu Panda 2*], *News and Writing* 7 (2011): 66.

76. "Meimei: *Kung Fu Panda 2* yinfa 'wenhua qinlue' zhenglun" [American press debates "cultural invasion" by *Kung Fu Panda 2*], June 21, 2011, http://intl.ce.cn/zgysj/201106/21/t20110621_22491152.shtml (accessed November 2, 2011).

77. Ma Yu, "Kungfu meng haiwai zaopi; cheng long erdu beizhi 'ruhua' cheng kexiao" [Jack Chen accused of "disgracing Chinese" in *The Karate Kid* by overseas Chinese], June 23, 2010, http://news.xinhuanet.com/ent/2010-06/23/c_12250647.htm (accessed November 2, 2011).

78. Zhao Yuezhi, *Communication in China: Political Economy, Power, and Conflict* (Lanham, MD: Rowman & Littlefield, 2008), 138–48.
79. Liu Kang, *Globalization and Cultural Trends in China* (Honolulu: University of Hawaii Press, 2004).
80. Zhang Xudong, ed., *Whither China: Intellectual Politics in Contemporary China* (Durham, NC: Duke University Press, 2001), 325.

## 3. The Film Industry as Negotiation of Space

1. "Wuyuan piaojia chongji longduan liyi; dianying faxing gaige yao maidabu" [Thoughts on film distribution reform], *Caijing Journal*, in *China Film Yearbook 2001*, 182–84.
2. Mao Yu, interview by the author, Beijing, August 15, 2011.
3. Douglas Gomery, *The Hollywood Studio System* (London: British Film Institute, 2005), 4.
4. Jin da, "Shanghai Yongle gufen youxiangongsi de chuangli ji 1993 nian gongzuoqingkuang" [The establishment of Shanghai Yongle Shareholding Company Ltd. and its status in 1993], in *China Film Yearbook 1994* (Beijing: Zhongguo dianying chubanshe [China Film Press], 1994), 200–201.
5. Wang Hongyou, "95 Shanghai shichang mianmianguan" [Shanghai film market in 1995], in *China Film Yearbook 1996*, 212–14.
6. "Thoughts on Film Distribution Reform."
7. Rao Shuguang, *Zhongguo dianying shichang fazhanshi* [The development of the Chinese film market] (Beijing: Zhongguo dianying chubanshe [China Film Press], 2009), 477.
8. Zhao Shi, "Accelerate the Promotion of the Reform and Development of the Film Industry," in *China Film Yearbook 2003* (Beijing: Zhongguo dianying chubanshe [China Film Press], 2003), 25–32.
9. Guo Chang and Gu Qin, "96 zhongguo dianying shichang sikou" [Pondering China's film market in 1996], in *China Film Yearbook 1997*, 185–86.
10. Mao Yu, "Wufa huibi de xuanze—2000 zhi 2002 nian zhongguo dianying faxing fangying gaige zhengce miaoshu" [A choice hard to evade—a description of the reform policy of film distribution and exhibition in China from 2000 to 2002], in *China Film Yearbook 2003*, 227–32.
11. Zhao Shi, "Accelerate the Promotion of the Reform and Development of the Film Industry."
12. "Heshi caiyou zhongguodianying de hangkongmujian?" [Impressions of managers of China's urban theaters on visiting the United States], in *China Film Yearbook 1998/1999*, 435–36.
13. Yang Ji, "Zhongguo dianying faxing fangying xiehui\zhongguo chengshi yingyuan fazhan xiehui lianhe juban dianying yuanxian zuotanhui" [A seminar on the theater chain system], in *China Film Yearbook 2003*, 254.

14. SARFT and Ministry of Culture, "Some Opinions about Carrying out Further Reform in the Film Industry," in *China Film Yearbook 2001,* 1–3.

15. SARFT and Ministry of Culture, "The Detailed Regulations to Implement Structural Reform of the Mechanism of Film Distribution and Exhibition," in *China Film Yearbook 2002,* 15–16.

16. Zhao Shi, "Creatively Fulfill the Target and Task of the New Era—A Talk on the National Film Work Forum," in *China Film Yearbook 2002,* 27.

17. Mao Yu interview.

18. Yu Li, "Zhongguo dianying zhuanyeshi yanjiu—dianying zhipian, faxing, fangying juan" [A study of the history of film production, distribution, and exhibition in China], Beijing, China: China Film Press 2006, 186–89.

19. Rao Shuguang, *Development of the Chinese Film Market,* 521.

20. SARFT, "Notification about Several Notions on Promoting the Development of the Film Industry," in *China Film Yearbook 2005,* 9–12.

21. Ding Yilan, "The Changes in the Market Situation of the Cinema Chain System for Four Years," in *China Film Yearbook 2007* (Beijing: Zhongguo dianying chubanshe [China Film Press], 2007), 273–76.

22. Rao Shuguang, *Development of the Chinese Film Market,* 523.

23. Ding Yilan, "Changes in the Market Situation of the Cinema Chain System," 275.

24. Liu Jia, "2010 zhongguo yuanxian fazhan jinxingshi, qinian shibeisu zengzhang" [Theater chain system enables China's box office revenue to increase by ten times within seven years], http://news.entgroup.cn/movie/249364.shtml (accessed January 26, 2011).

25. Fan Lizhen, "Yuanxianzhi gaige jiunian huimou" [A review of nine years of theater chain system reform], *Zhongguo Dianyingbao,* May 26, 2011.

26. Yu Deshu, "Zhongguo yingshi fanrong beihou cangweiji jin sancheng guochanpian shangying" [Crisis behind the prosperity of the Chinese film industry: only 30 percent of domestic movies screened], *Fazhi Wanbao,* March 18, 2013, http://news.entgroup.cn/movie/1816115.shtml (accessed March 22, 2013).

27. Jing Yu, "2013 Yuanxian diaocha: ersanxian chengshi qiangshi jueqi cheng piaofang xinzhizhu" [A survey of box office revenue in 2013: middle and small cities become backbone box office revenue contributors], January 24, 2014, http://www.1905.com/news/20140124/727328.shtml (accessed July 10, 2014).

28. Huaren Wenzhai, "2013 nian zhongguo shida yuanxian piaofang paihangbang" [The ranking of China's top ten theater chains in 2013], January 8, 2014, http://blog.sina.com.cn/s/blog_45c54c9e0101q1ka.html (accessed December 16, 2014).

29. Michael Curtin, *Playing to the World's Biggest Audience: The Globalization of Chinese Film and TV* (Berkeley: University of California Press, 2007), 22.

30. Qihai, "Guoyou gushipianchang bixu huazhengweiling" [Thoughts on the reform of state-owned film studios], *Zhongguo dianying shichang* [China film market] 2 (1995).

31. Ni Zhen, ed., *Gaige yu zhongguo dianying* [Reform and Chinese cinema] (Beijing: Zhongguo dianying chubanshe [China Film Press], 1994), 91.

32. Rao Shuguang, *Development of the Chinese Film Market,* 431.

33. Ibid., 434–35.

34. Wang Dan et al., "Dang fenghuang niepan shi—dui wujia guoyou dianyingqiye chanye fazhan de diaoyan baogao" [Research report on five state-owned film studios], in *2007 dianying chanye yanjiu zhi guoyou yingshi qiyejuan* [2007 report on the film industry—special issue on state-owned film and television studios] (Beijing: Zhongguo dianying chubanshe [China Film Press], 2008), 3–35.

35. SARFT and Ministry of Culture, "Some Opinions about Carrying Out Further Reform of the Film Industry," 1–3.

36. Li Daoxin, "Zhanlue lianmeng, chanye jiqun yu jiazhichuangxin" [The current status and development of large-scale state-owned film enterprises' structural reform], in *2007 Report on the Film Industry,* 36–56.

37. Tang Rong, "Sanshinian zhongguo dianyingtizhi gaige licheng huigu" [A review of thirty years of reform in China's film system], in *China Film Yearbook 2009* (Beijing: Zhongguo dianying chubanshe [China Film Press], 2009), 29–35.

38. Wang Dan et al., "Research Report on Five State-Owned Film Studios."

39. *Wujia guoyou dianying qiye fazhan baogao* [A report on five state-owned film groups] (Beijing: Zhongguo dianying chubanshe [China Film Press], 2008), 197–225.

40. Yuan Lei, "Han Sanping: shuo zhongying yizhiduda geng zhunque" [Han Sanping believes China Film Group is outstanding], *Southern Weekly,* September 10, 2009, http://www.infzm.com/content/34410 (accessed October 4, 2010).

41. "Zhuanfang Han Sanping: quanmian jiexi zhongying jituan chanquan he jizhi gaige" [Interview with Han Saping], December 11, 2008, http://indus.chinafilm.com/200812/1153882.html (accessed October 4, 2010).

42. Song Weicai, "Dangqian zhongguo dianying guojia zizhujizhi de xianzhuang, wenti ji gaijin shexiang" [The current state and future direction of China's state funding system for film production], in *Gaige kaifang yu zhongguo dianying sanshinian* [Thirty years of reform and China film] (Beijing: Zhongguo dianying chubanshe [China Film Press], 2008), 508–15.

43. Tong Gang, "Annual Report on the Work of the Chinese Film Industry in 2007," in *China Film Yearbook 2008* (Beijing: Zhongguo dianying chubanshe [China Film Press], 2008), 28–36.

44. Liu Jianzhong, "Summarize Experiences, Open Up a New Prospect of Our Film Works," in *China Film Yearbook 2003,* 32–38.

45. Lin Lisheng, "The Economic Changes and Artistic Dividing Line of Films Produced in China in the 1990s," in *China Film Yearbook 1997,* 201–5.

46. Liu Fan, "Systematic Innovation and the Development of a Privately Owned Film Economy," in *China Film Yearbook 2006,* 481–84.

47. Ni Zhen, *Reform and Chinese Cinema,* 104.

48. Wang Zhongjun, "'Huayi xiongdi' zhi jingyantan" [On Huayi Brothers'

business strategies], in *2006 dianyingchanye yanjiu zhi wenhuaxiaofei yu dianyingjuan* [2006 research report on the Chinese film industry—special issue on cultural and film consumption] (Beijing: Zhongguo dianying chubanshe [China Film Press], 2007), 370.

49. Yang Binbin, "Unique Business: Survival Recipe of the 6 Privately Owned Film Companies," in *China Film Yearbook 2006*, 478–81.

50. Xu Jinmin, "Huayi xiongdi zengzi 6000 wan meiyuan tuozhan haiwaishichang" [Huayi Brothers adds US$60 million to explore overseas market], *Daily Economic News*, May 19, 2011, http://news.entgroup.cn/movie/1910193.shtml (accessed May 25, 2011).

51. Wu Ke, "Huayixiongdi jinjun haolaiwu xieshou meiguo chuangqiyule" (Huayi Brothers marches into Hollywood and cooperates with Legendary Pictures), *Tecent*, June 10, 2011, http://news.entgroup.cn/movie/1010380.shtml (accessed June 16, 2011).

52. The Industrial Study Center of the Association of Chinese Film Producers, *The Research Report on Chinese Film Industry 2010* (Beijing: Zhongguo dianying chubanshe [China Film Press], 2010), 51–53.

53. Ibid.

54. Zhao Yifang, speech at US-China film summit, Los Angeles, October 30, 2012; Zhao Yifang, interview by the author, Riverside, CA, October 31, 2012.

55. Tian Zhuangzhuang, interview by the author, Beijing, July 2, 2010; Zhou Tiedong, interview by the author, Beijing, July 7, 2011.

56. Zhang Mengyi, "Jiedu zhongguodianying piaofang de 'baifenzhiwu'· zenmeyong?" [An explanation of the State Special Fund for film production], *Zhongguo guangbodianshi*, November 19, 2012, http://news.entgroup.cn/c/1915207.shtml (accessed November 21, 2012).

57. Ibid.

58. Ibid.

59. Wu Xiaodong, "26 bu yingpian juanzou liucheng zongpiaofang zhongguo dianying quexian tuxian" [26 films take away 60 percent of gross box office revenue of China], *China Youth Daily*, January 25, 2011, http://news.entgroup.cn/movie/259368.shtml (accessed January 26, 2011).

60. Dushi Kuaibao, "Yingping: guochandianying chuxian beilun liuge yihuo nanxun daan" [Six concerns about domestic movies], January 29, 2012, http://news.entgroup.cn/movie/2912692.shtml (accessed January 31, 2012).

61. Yu Deshu, "Zhongguo yingshi fanrong beihou cangweiji jin sancheng guochanpian shangying" [Crisis behind the prosperity of the Chinese film industry: only 30 percent of domestic movies screened], *Fazhi Wanbao*, March 18, 2013, http://news.entgroup.cn/movie/1816115.shtml (accessed March 22, 2013).

62. Wu Xiaodong, "26 Films Take Away 60 Percent of Gross Box Office Revenue."

63. Xie Xiaojing, interview by the author, Beijing, July 1, 2010.

64. Lu Shisan, "Quanmian jiedu faxingfang yuanxian zhizheng yenei: dashi

suoqu" [An analysis of the conflict with theater chains], *Sohu Entertainment,* November 16, 2012, http://news.entgroup.cn/movie/1615189.shtml (accessed November 21, 2012).

65. Zeng Minghui, "Jiexi: dianyingju jiezhe Zhang Yimou xiale yipan henda de qi" [The Film Bureau plays well through Zhang Yimou's film], *Nandu Yule zhoukan,* December 9, 2011, http://news.entgroup.cn/movie/0912340.shtml (accessed December 16, 2011).

66. Lu Shisan, "Analysis of the Conflict with Theater Chains."

67. Zeng Minghui, "Film Bureau Plays Well through Zhang Yimou's Film."

68. Jingbao, "Dianyingpiao 25 nian zhang 800 bei, zhongguo dianying shuizai tangzhe zhuanqian?" [Movie ticket price increases by 800 percent in 25 years], December 13, 2011, http://news.entgroup.cn/movie/1312358.shtml (accessed December 16, 2011).

69. Jessis, "2013 nian dianying zhengnengliang pian" [Film phenomenon in 2013], December 20, 2013, http://www.entgroup.cn/views/a/19083.shtml (accessed January 19, 2014).

70. Lu Shisan, "Analysis of the Conflict with Theater Chains."

71. "Zhuanziwei banbu sixiang tongzhi zhipianfang yingyuan jieshouyi" [Four measures benefit both film producers and theaters], *Beijing Shangbao,* November 23, 2012, http://news.entgroup.cn/c/2315246.shtml (accessed December 5, 2012).

72. Qianjiang Wanbao, "Kuajie zheshang dezhi tonghang sixun tanxi: yingshi zhehang shui taishen" [Zhejiang businessmen lament the death of their counterpart], March 24, 2012, http://ent.sina.com.cn/v/m/2012-03-24/10063589128.shtml (accessed March 24, 2012).

73. Zhang Yi, "Guochanpian piaofang luohou 23 yi hesuidang nengfou wanhui zhanju" [Box office sales of domestic movies overtaken by 2.3 billion yuan, New Year celebration movies expected to save the market], *Xinmin Wanbao,* November 5, 2012, http://news.entgroup.cn/movie/0515099.shtml (accessed November 7, 2012).

74. Liu Yang, "Dianying touzi zauyu bingheqi dianyingju yuchu baohu cuoshi" [The Film Bureau to issue protective measures to encourage film investment], *People's Daily,* July 14, 2012, http://news.entgroup.cn/b/1414182.shtml (accessed July 22, 2012).

75. Zhang Yi, "Piaofang he koubei dachaju zhongguo dianying shichang fayu buchengshu" [Immature Chinese film market], *Xinmin Wanbao,* July 31, 2012, http://news.entgroup.cn/movie/3114327.shtml (accessed August 2, 2012).

76. *Wall Street Journal,* April 28, 2013, http://news.entgroup.cn/c/2816476.shtml (accessed April 28, 2013).

77. Cui Ding, "Guangdian gongbu 2013 nian piaofang, 217 yi zengzhang 27%" [The 2013 box office revenue reaches 21.7 billion yuan], January 4, 2014, http://news.entgroup.cn/movie/0419126.shtml (accessed January 19, 2014).

78. Zhou Ning, Jiang Fang, and Zhang Zhanpeng, "Guochan dapian jueqi beihou zhongguo dianying rengcui sida yinyou" [Four hidden problems behind the

prosperous Chinese film industry], *Xinhua News,* October 13, 2010, http://news.entgroup.cn/movie/138185_2.shtml (accessed October 27, 2010).

## 4. Artistic and Critical Cinema under a Triple Threat

1. "Lu Chuan gengyan tan chuangzuo huanjing: xiwang gei women pingdeng kong jian" [Lu Chuan hopes to be granted equal creative space], June 19, 2012, http://news.entgroup.cn/c/1913984.shtml (accessed June 29, 2012); "Wangdeshengyan zhong guoshen zhengshi sharu hesuidang" [*The Last Supper* eventually passes censorship], November 2, 2012, http://www.chuanfilm.cn/focus/1261.htm (accessed February 28, 2013).

2. Xin Jia, "Lou Ye weibo toulu xinpian 'fucheng mishi' shangying shouzu" [Lou Ye discloses the censorship of *Mystery*], September 7, 2012, http://ent.sina.com.cn/m/c/2012-09-07/21553735322.shtml (accessed September 7, 2012).

3. Xie Fei's blog, December 15, 2012, http://huati.weibo.com/25976#!/25976?order=time (accessed January 20, 2013).

4. "Yangshi shoubo V zi choushadui, yidou weijian wangyou shengzan" [*V for Vendetta* is shown on CCTV uncensored], December 25, 2012, http://book.sina.com.cn/2012-12-25/1149389774.shtml (accessed February 28, 2014).

5. "Daoyan Xie Fei gongkaixin huyu yi fenjizhidu daiti dianying shencha" [Xie Fei's open letter calls for substituting a film rating system for film censorship], *Free Movie News,* December 18, 2012, http://cn.fmnnow.com/2012/12/18/12532/ (accessed February 28, 2014).

6. Jia Zhangke's blog, December 26, 2012, http://ent.sina.com.cn/m/c/2012-12-26/02593820692.shtml (accessed December 26, 2012).

7. Qin Qin, "Wang Xiaoshuai wo shiyi fushan shouying, cheng shencha yifei guochanpian nanti" [Wang Xiaoshuai believes censorship is no longer a problem], October 8, 2011, http://ent.sina.com.cn/m/c/2011-10-08/14133435128.shtml (accessed September 14, 2012).

8. "Siyue yingshi guochanpian kanyou meiguo dapian bazhan 80% shichang [American blockbusters take 80% of the domestic market], *Fazhi Wanbo,* April 20, 2012, http://news.entgroup.cn/movie/2013460.shtml (accessed April 25, 2012).

9. Li X., "2012 quanguo dianying piaofang chao 170 yi cheng quanqiu dierda shichang" [China becomes the second largest film market in 2012 with box office sales of 17 billion yuan], January 10, 2013, http://news.entgroup.cn/movie/1015618.shtml (accessed January 17, 2013).

10. Shanghai Film Festival Industrial Colloquium, "Shanghai dianyingjie chanye luntan: huayupian de jiushu" [How to save Chinese-language films], June 18, 2012, http://ent.sina.com.cn/c/2012-06-18/22413661720.shtml (accessed June 19, 2012).

11. Cited in Pang Laikwan, "The State against Ghosts: A Genealogy of China's Film Censorship Policy," *Screen* 52, no. 4 (Winter 2011): 461–76.

12. Gu Yanmei, "Zhongguo dalu dianying fenji zhidu tantao: yi zhongguo

dalu dianying fenji zhidu yanjiuzhuangkuang weiyin" [A discussion of mainland China's film rating system], December 30, 2010, http://www.sinoss.net/qikan/uploadfile/2010/1230/20101230032337128.pdf (accessed August 30, 2012).

13. Ministry of Broadcasting, Film, and Television, "The Circular on Implementing the Censorship and Rating System for Some Movies," in *China Film Yearbook 1990* (Beijing: Zhongguo dianying chubanshe [China Film Press], 1990), 45.

14. Tang Feng, "Duibi zhongguo yu meiguo de dianying shencha zhidu" [A comparison of the film censorship systems in China and the United States], *Dianying Wenxue* [Movie literature] 2 (2010): 15–17.

15. State Council, "Film Administrative Regulations," in *China Film Yearbook 1997,* 43–46.

16. Ministry of Broadcasting, Film, and Television, "Film Examination Regulations," in *China Film Yearbook 1998/1999,* 7–9.

17. State Council, "Film Managerial Regulations," in *China Film Yearbook 2002,* 9–14.

18. State Council, "Dianyingchanye cujinfa (zhengqiu yijiangao) fabu" [The China film industry promotion law (discussion draft) promulgated], December 15, 2011, http://www.chinanews.com/yl/2011/12-15/3533111.shtml (accessed August 31, 2012).

19. SARFT website, July 25, 2007, http://www.sarft.gov.cn/articles/2007/07/25/20070914165147430381.html (accessed September 4, 2012).

20. SARFT, "Provisional Regulations for Approval of Film Script (Storyboard) and Film Censorship," in *China Film Yearbook 2004,* 13–14.

21. "Zhongguo dianying qiyueqi quanmian shishi 'yibeiershen' zhi" [China to implement a double censorship system], July 1, 2011, http://news.entgroup.cn/c/0110596.shtml (accessed September 7, 2011).

22. Dao He, Jiang Bojing, and Shi Jie, "Zhongguo dianying shencha zhidu daodishi taikuan haishi taiyan" [China's film censorship: too loose or too strict?], September 2, 2011, http://news.entgroup.cn/movie/0211341.shtml (accessed September 7, 2011).

23. B. Weinrabu, "At the Movies; Disney Hires Kissinger," Academic Search Premier Database, October 10, 1997, https://www.lib.umn.edu/indexes/a (accessed November 22, 2008).

24. David Barboza, "Citing Public Sentiment, China Cancels Release of 'Geisha,'" *New York Times,* February 1, 2006, https://www.lib.umn.edu/indexes/a (accessed November 20, 2008).

25. "China Vetoes Film," *New York Times,* February 14, 2008, https://www.lib.umn.edu/indexes/a (accessed November 19, 2008).

26. "Jet Li Attacks Censors," *New York Times,* August 21, 2007, https://www.lib.umn.edu/indexes/a (accessed November 20, 2008).

27. Clarissa Sebag-Montefiore, "Chinese Film Festival Forced Underground," October 21, 2011, http://ipsnews.net/news.asp?idnews=105553 (accessed October 31, 2011).

28. Pan Qi, "Chanye cujinfa libi bingcun buru tuixing fenjizhi?" [How about a film rating system?], January 28, 2012, http://news.entgroup.cn/movie/2812686.shtml (accessed January 31, 2012).

29. Dao He, Jiang Bojing, and Shi Jie, "China's Film Censorship: Too Loose or Too Strict?"

30. Xia Ke, "Guochanpian shencha zuai fazhan zhipiangongsi fengxian guogao" [Censorship obstructs domestic film development and poses high risk for film producers], March 24, 2011, http://news.entgroup.cn/movie/249780.shtml (accessed April 6, 2011).

31. "Quick Bits," *dGenerate Films Newsletter,* June 2012, http://hosted.verticalresponse.com/923225/1c1cd7449b/1549514285/5cce76238a/ (accessed September 11, 2012).

32. Zhang Xianmin, "Zhongguo dalu 1990 hou jinpianshi" [A history of banned films in mainland China after the 1990s], http://www.zmw.cn/bbs/dispbbs.asp?boardID=11&ID=52770 (accessed March 5, 2006).

33. Ibid.

34. For a complete and detailed account of China's underground films, see Paul G. Pickowicz and Zhang Yingjin, eds., *From Underground to Independent—Alternative Film Culture in Contemporary China* (Lanham, MD: Rowman & Littlefield, 2006).

35. Mao Yu, interview by the author, August 15, 2011.

36. Kevin B. Lee, "Interview with Head of Beijing Independent Film Festival Li Xianting," August 24, 2012, http://www.indiewire.com/article/big-trouble-in-china-festival-director-li-speaks-out-about-beijing-independent-film-fest-shutdown (accessed September 11, 2012).

37. Zi Zhu, "Li Yang de dianying xinzuo *Mang Shang*" [Li Yang's new film *Blind Mountain*], *Radio Free Asia,* April 4, 2008, http://www.rfa.org/cantonese/features/art/movie_liyang-20080404.html-04122008223621.html (accessed July 15, 2014).

38. Zhu Xiaojia, "Renshanrenhai: meiqu meihua, yemeiqu chouhua" [*People Mountain People Sea:* no beautification, no uglification], September 16, 2011, http://www.infzm.com/content/63153 (accessed September 11, 2012).

39. Wang Yunian, "Cai Shangjun toulu renshanrenhai wei guoshen yuanyin" [Director discloses the reason *People Mountain People Sea* did not pass censorship], September 8, 2011, http://ent.sina.com.cn/m/c/2011-09-08/16183411505.shtml (accessed September 1, 2012).

40. Zhang Xianmin, "History of Banned Films in Mainland China after the 1990s."

41. Paul G. Pickowicz, "Social and Political Dynamics of Underground Filmmaking in China," in Pickowicz and Zhang, *From Underground to Independent,* 2.

42. Zhang Xianmin, "History of Banned Films in Mainland China after the 1990s."

43. Internet Movie Database, http://www.imdb.com/ (accessed September 4, 2008).

44. "The 10th Deauville Asian Film Festival," March 18, 2008, http://www.chinaculture.org/exchange/2008-03/18/content_129244.htm (accessed May 4, 2009).

45. "Tianzhuding daoban xiazai yiyechuanhong, Jia Zhangke yuan peichang touzisunshi" [Jia Zhangke to compensate investors' financial loss for *A Touch of Sin* due to piracy], March 1, 2014, http://ent.ifeng.com/a/20140301/40006223_0.shtml (accessed July 14, 2014).

46. Yu Wenge, "Jia Zhangke tan dianyingshencha: wei nianqing daoyan quxiao jishu shencha" [Jia Zhangke on film censorship], March 22, 2011, http://news.entgroup.cn/movie/229755.shtml (accessed March 23, 2011).

47. "Ziliao: Daoyan Zhang Yuan geren jianjie" [Biographical information on Zhang Yuan], October 21, 2002, http://ent.sina.com.cn/m/2002-10-21/1724107831.html (accessed September 6, 2012).

48. Internet Movie Database.

49. "Woshi yiba daozi: zhuming daoyan Zhuang Yuan fangtan" [I am a knife: an interview with Zhang Yuan], January 28, 2010, http://cul.sohu.com/20100128/n269884891.shtml (accessed September 6, 2012).

50. Ibid.

51. ChenYiyi, "Jiazhangke: dianying nengzuode jiushi gaosu dajia butong de xianshi" [Jia Zhangke says his films aim to tell a different reality], *Nanfang Dushi Bao* [Southern China metropolitan daily], January 31, 2007, http://www.mtime.com/group/jiazhangke/discussion/41700/ (accessed March 27, 2008).

52. Cinemedia, http://www.cinewiki.cn/w/%E8%B4%BE%E6%A8%9F%E6%9F%AF (accessed March 27, 2008).

53. Ibid.

54. See Xu Jing, "Kongque wei shui kaiping?" [For whom does the peacock spread its tail feathers?], *Art Criticism* 3 (2005): 18–20; Zhang Xiangyang, "Gu Changwei de kongque congwei kaiping" [Gu Changwei's peacock never spread its tail feathers], *Beijing Jishi* 4 (2005): 71–72.

55. Li Xuan, "'Qingnianbang' qiangshi huigui shichang beihou de zhutuili" [The younger generation returns to market], *Zongyibao,* April 12, 2012, http://news.entgroup.cn/movie/1213389.shtml (accessed April 24, 2012).

56. Yang Linran, "Fubusi zhongwenban: Zhang Weiping 'daoyan' Zhang Yimou dianying" [Forbes Chinese: Zhang Weiping and Zhang Yimou], November 1, 2010, http://ent.gd.sina.com.cn/news/2010/11/01/645789.html (accessed February 19, 2013).

57. "Jinling shisancha" [Information on *The Flowers of War*], http://baike.baidu.com/view/1857725.htm (accessed October 10, 2012).

58. Shenyang Jinbao, "Tan paishe wuji xinlu licheng Chen Kaige: mingyun de fansi" [Chen Kaige on *The Promise*], December 8, 2010, http://ent.ifeng.com/movie/special/chenkaige/detail_2010_12/08/3400830_0.shtml (accessed February 20, 2013).

59. "Wuji piaofang po eryi, Chen Kaige paohong Hu Ge diepo daodedixian" [*The Promise*'s box office record is over 200 million, Chen Kaige attacks

Hu Ge], *Shenyang Jinbao*, June 7, 2006, http://www.cnwnews.com/html/ent/ent_ylyw/2006-6/7/1648376895.html (accessed February 19, 2013).

60. Sun Linlin, "Zhaoshiguer laoxigu biaoxi dui yuanzhu jinxing dianfuxing gaibian" [*Sacrifice* overthrows the original screeplay], *Xin Jingbao*, November 27, 2010, http://ent.sina.com.cn/m/c/2010-11-27/01413160171.shtml (accessed February 19, 2013).

61. See http://ent.ifeng.com/movie/special/chenkaige (accessed February 20, 2013).

62. Ibid.

63. "Sousuo 1.8 yi piaofang shouguan, jiuyue ruwei duolunduo dianyingjie" [*Caught in the Web* makes 1.8 million yuan], August 18, 2012, http://ent.ifeng.com/movie/special/tiff37/content-3/detail_2012_08/14/16782742_0.shtml (accessed July 15, 2014).

64. Tian Zhuangzhuang, interview by the author, July 2, 2010.

65. Wang Qiong, "2011nian dianying ticai dazhuangche: wuge guangong sige wukong sange muguiying" [Overlapping film themes in 2011], *Chongqing Wanbao*, February 24, 2011, http://news.xinhuanet.com/society/2011-02/24/c_121117160_3.htm (accessed September 14, 2012).

66. "Jin Yimeng" [Biographical information on Jin Yimeng], http://baike.baidu.com/view/2374071.htm (accessed September 3, 2012).

67. Yu Deshu, "Fengkuangde saiche qing piaofang guoyi, Ning Hao huo wushiwan jiangli" [Ning Hao's *Crazy Racer* earns more than 100 million yuan in box office receipts], *Fazhi Wanbao*, February 24, 2009, http://www.chinanews.com/yl/yrfc/news/2009/02-24/1576798.shtml (accessed July 28, 2014).

68. China News Service, "Wurenqu yi 2.2 yiyuan jiamian piaofang guanjun" [*No Man's Land* obtains 220 million yuan in box office receipts], December 18, 2013, http://cul.sohu.com/20131218/n391960639.shtml (accessed July 28, 2014).

69. Xia Ke, "Douniu liangxiang weinisi pingjiagao liangjing gei Guan Hu dangzhuli [*Cow* highly praised at the Venice International Film Festival], September 11, 2009, http://yule.sohu.com/20090911/n266642495.shtml (accessed February 22, 2013).

70. Ibid.

71. "Lu Chuan" [Biographical information on Lu Chuan], http://baike.baidu.com/view/7465.htm (accessed February 28, 2013).

72. Wang Xiaofeng, "Sanlian zhoukan Wang Xiaofeng duihua Lu Chuan—Dianying Nanjing Nanjing licheng dajiemi" [A dialogue with Lu Chuan on *Nanjing! Nanjing!*], *Sanlian Life Weekly*, April 25, 2009, http://www.360doc.com/content/09/0425/10/109143_3261239.shtml (accessed February 28, 2013).

73. Ni Zifang, "Jia Zhangke: zhiyao woyuanyi dianying piaofang guoyi bushi nanti" [Jia Zhangke says it is not a problem for his movie to reach a box office record of more than 100 million yuan], *Qilu Wanbao*, March 24, 2011, http://news.entgroup.cn/movie/249783.shtml (accessed April 6, 2011).

74. Ibid.

75. Li Xuan "'Qingnianbang' qiangshi huigui shichang beihou de zhutuili" [The younger generation returns to the market], *Zongyibao,* April 12, 2012.

76. Ibid.

77. An Li, "Taijiong piaofang jin shisanyi xuezhe cheng chenggong zaiyu 'jiediqi'" [*Lost in Thailand* earns box office revenue of 1.3 billion yuan], January 19, 2013, http://news.youth.cn/yl/201302/t20130221_2896633.htm (accessed February 23, 2013).

78. Zhu Yuqing, "Dianying qingchunnian: dianying chanye 2013 niandu qida xianxiang" [A year of youth: seven phenomena in the film industry in 2013], *Zongyibao,* January 3, 2014, http://news.entgroup.cn/movie/0319113.shtml (accessed January 19, 2014).

79. Ibid.

80. Li Xiaodao, "2012 piaofang chao 170 yi; cheng quanqiu dierda shichang" [2012 box office revenue exceeds 17 billion yuan], *Mytime,* January 10, 2013, http://news.entgroup.cn/movie/1015618.shtml (accessed January 17, 2013).

81. Li Yunling, "2012 neidi piaofang po 160 yi piaofang qianshi jin sanbu guochanpian" [Mainland China box office revenue reaches 16 billion yuan with only three domestic movies among the top ten], *Dongfang Zaobao,* December 28, 2012, http://news.entgroup.cn/movie/2815523.shtml (accessed January 3, 2013).

82. Liu Yang,"Dianying touzi zouyu bingheqi dianyingju yuchu baohu cuoshi" [Film Bureau to issue new protection measures to break through icy investment climate], *People's Daily,* July 14, 2012, http://news.entgroup.cn/b/1414182.shtml (accessed July 22, 2012).

83. Xie Xiaojing, interview by the author, July 1, 2010.

84. Wang Zhenguo, "Guoyi daoyan 80hou jueji nianqing daoyan zuopin weihe bumaiqian" [Why don't younger directors' films sell well?], *Guangzhou Daily,* March 16, 2012, http://news.entgroup.cn/movie/1613159.shtml (accessed March 20, 2012).

85. Ministry of Finance, "Guangdianzongju deng qibuwei fabu duoxiang zhengce zhichi dianyingfazhan" [Seven administrations issue a number of measures to support film development], June 19, 2014, http://news.entgroup.cn/c/1920869.shtml (accessed June 29, 2014).

## 5. Chinese Martial Arts Cinema in the Twenty-First Century

1. Stephen Teo, *Chinese Martial Arts Cinema: The Wuxia Tradition* (Edinburgh: Edinburgh University Press, 2009), 180.

2. Ibid. See also Stephen Teo, *Hong Kong Cinema: The Extra Dimensions* (London: British Film Institute, 1997).

3. Zhang Zhen, "Bodies in the Air: The Magic of Science and the Fate of the Early 'Martial Arts' Film in China," in *Chinese-Language Film: Historiography, Poetics, Politics,* ed. Sheldon H. Lu and Emilie Yueh-Yu Yeh (Honolulu: University of Hawaii Press, 2005), 52–75; Li Siu Leung, "Kung Fu: Negotiating Nationalism

and Modernity," in *Asian Cinemas: A Reader and Guide,* ed. Dimitris Eleftheriotis and Gary Needham (Honolulu: University of Hawaii Press, 2006).

4. Chris Berry and Mary Farquhar, *China on Screen: Cinema and Nation* (New York: Columbia University Press, 2006); Stephen Teo, "Wuxia Redux: *Crouching Tiger, Hidden Dragon* as a Model of Late Transnational Production," in *Hong Kong Connections: Transnational Imagination in Action Cinema,* ed. Meaghan Morris, Siu Leung Li, and Stephen Chan Ching-kiu (Durham, NC: Duke University Press; Hong Kong: Hong Kong University Press, 2005).

5. Dai Jinhua, "Order/Anti-Order: Representation of Identity in Hong Kong Action Movies," in Morris et al., *Hong Kong Connections.*

6. Gary D. Rawnsley, "The Political Narrative(s) of *Hero,*" in *Global Chinese Cinema—The Culture and Politics of* Hero, ed. G. D. Rawnsley and Ming-Yeh T. Rawnsley (London: Routledge, 2010), 13–26.

7. Anthony Fung and J. M. Chan, "Towards a Global Blockbuster: The Political Economy of *Hero*'s Nationalism," in Rawnsley and Rawnsley, *Global Chinese Cinema,* 198–211.

8. Zhao Yuezhi, "Whose *Hero?* The 'Spirit' and 'Structure' of a Made-in-China Global Blockbuster," in *Reorienting Global Communication—Indian and Chinese Media beyond Borders,* ed. Michael Curtin and H. Shah (Urbana: University of Illinois Press, 2010), 161–82; Cui Weiping, "A Movie Dedicated to Saddam and Kim Jung-Il," *Kaifang* [Open], February 2003, 30.

9. Fung and Chan, "Towards a Global Blockbuster," 200.

10. Chris Berry, "Foreword," in Rawnsley and Rawnsley, *Global Chinese Cinema,* xxiv; Zhao Yuezhi, "Whose *Hero*?" 176.

11. See Dai Jinhua, "Order/Anti-Order."

12. See, for example, Lu and Yeh, *Chinese-Language Film.*

13. Teo, *Hong Kong Cinema,* 98.

14. Liu Jianzhong, "Dianying de rushi tanpan yu wo'men de chengnuo" [WTO negotiation with regard to film and our commitment], in *WTO yu zhongguo dianying* [WTO and Chinese cinema], ed. Zhenxin Zhang and Yuanying Yang (Beijing: Zhongguo dianying chubanshe [China Film Press], 2002), 3–8; Tong Gang, "How Does China's Film Industry Face the Challenge Brought by China's Joining the WTO?" *China Film Yearbook 2001,* 17–20.

15. Dai Jinhua, "Order/Anti-Order," 85.

16. H. Wang and Ming-Yeh T. Rawnsley, "*Hero:* Rewriting the Chinese Martial Arts Film Genre," in Rawnsley and Rawnsley, *Global Chinese Cinema,* 93.

17. SARFT official, interview by the author, Beijing, June 28, 2008.

18. "Taking on Hollywood's China Challenge," *Business Week Online,* February 26, 2008, Academic Search Premier database (accessed November 19, 2008).

19. For detailed accounts, see Wang Ting, "Understanding Local Reception of Globalized Cultural Products in the Context of the International Cultural Economy—A Case Study on the Reception of *Hero* and *Daggers* in China," *International Journal of Cultural Studies* 12 (2009): 299; Fung and Chan, "Towards a Global

Blockbuster"; E. Yueh-yu Yeh, "The Deferral of Pan-Asian: A Critical Appraisal of Film Marketization in China," in Curtin and Shah, *Reorienting Global Communication,* 183–200.

20. "Zhuanfang Han Sanping: quanmian jiexi zhongying jituan chanquan he jizhi gaige" [Interview with Han Sanping], December 11, 2008, http://indus.chinafilm.com/200812/1153882.html (accessed October 4, 2010).

21. J. Martinsen, "Boom Times for Chinese Film, but What Comes Next?" *Sanlian Life Weekly,* February 27, 2008, http://www.danwei.org/magazines/state_of_the_film_industry.php (accessed October 4, 2010).

22. Liu A. X., "What Makes the Most Profit? Risk Does. China Film Group CEO Interview with *Southern Weekly,*" September 28, 2009, http://www.danwei.org/film/what_makes_the_most_profit_ris.php (accessed October 4, 2010).

23. "Huangjinjia zhongjin siqian wubaiwan meijin yusuan gaixie yingshi jilu" [*Curse of the Golden Flower*'s budget of US$45 million breaks the record in film history], October 14, 2006, http://zhidao.baidu.com/question/13833521.html (accessed April 19, 2008).

24. Cici, "Huoshao chibi yisi qishang, yusuan zijin yanzhong touzhi" [One death and seven injuries in *Red Cliff* shooting location; budget overdrawn], July 16, 2010, http://www.rxyj.org/html/2010/0716/2591244.php (accessed October 6, 2010).

25. China Film Group Corporation official, interview by the author, Beijing, July 7, 2011.

26. Dai Jinhua, "Order/Anti-Order," 92.

27. John Woo, special features, *Red Cliff II* (DVD, 2009).

28. Jet Li, postproduction interview, YouTube video, 7:42, posted by Focus Features, September 27, 2006, https://www.youtube.com/watch?v=YeWckl9CN1k (accessed April 8, 2013).

29. Cited in David Barboza, "A Leap Forward, or a Great Sellout?" *New York Times,* July 1, 2007, Academic Search Premier database (accessed November 20, 2008).

30. Tao Dongfeng, "Zhongguo dapian daole shixueruming de shidai" [Chinese megaproductions have entered a bloodthirsty stage], *Art Criticism* 2 (2007): 36–38.

31. Liu Simin, "Zhang Yimou de bingmayong moshi nengfou zhongjie" [Can Zhang Yimou's terra-cotta warrior model be brought to an end?], August 21, 2007, http://news.sina.com.cn/pl/2007-08-21/152413711950.shtml (accessed August 21, 2007); Jin Yan, "Women de dapian meiyou linghun" [Our megaproductions have no soul], *Beijing Jishi* 12 (2007): 12–13.

32. "The Making of *Curse of the Golden Flower,*" special features (DVD, 2006).

33. "Di Renjie zhi tongtian diguo" [Information on *Detective Dee and the Mystery of the Phantom Flame*], http://baike.baidu.com/view/2426824.htm (accessed April 11, 2013).

34. "Ershiyubu dianying leitong: daoyan ai zhuangche, guanzhong zhineng zhuangqiang" [More than twenty movies overlap], *Liaoning Daily,* March 22, 2011, http://news.entgroup.cn/movie/229757.shtml (accessed March 23, 2011).

35. “Guochan dapian zaoyu piaofang pingjin wuxiapian buzai chimian tianxia” [Domestic megaproductions suffer from box office Waterloo; martial arts movies no longer popular], June 15, 2011, http://news.entgroup.cn/movie/1510435.shtml (accessed June 16, 2011).

36. Ar Hua, “Buzhuanye de 2012 dianyingjie: zuiburu yuqide liubu dapian” [Six megaproductions fall short of expectations in 2012], *Wangyi Yule,* January 7, 2013, http://news.entgroup.cn/movie/0715587.shtml (accessed January 10, 2013).

37. Dada Xiansheng and Li Xiaodao, “Shiyi 2012 hesuidang huayu guzhuang dapian luzai hefang?” [In which direction should Chinese ancient-costume megaproductions go?], *Mtime,* January 6, 2013, http://news.entgroup.cn/movie/0615576.shtml (accessed January 10, 2013).

38. For a detailed account, see Stanley Rosen, “Chinese Cinema’s International Market,” in *Art, Politics, and Commerce in Chinese Cinema,* ed. Zhu Ying and Stanley Rosen (Hong Kong: Hong Kong University Press, 2010), 35–54.

39. Li Xiaodao, “Zhongguo dianying guoji chuanbo yanjiu baogao chulu, laowai zhiren gongfupian” [Report on international response to Chinese cinema indicates kung fu movies are the most popular genre among foreign audiences], *Mtime,* May 30, 2012, http://news.mtime.com/2012/05/30/1489488.html (accessed April 11, 2013).

40. Xu Sijian, “Zhongguo dianying beimei biaofang chulu, Love yiwai duoguan” [Love unexpectedly champions North American box office revenue of Chinese movies], *Fazhi Wanbao,* January 4, 2013, http://news.entgroup.cn/movie/0415560.shtml (accessed January 10, 2013).

41. Cited in “History of Chinese Films in the West, http://factsanddetails.com/china.php?itemid=241catid=7subcatid=42#150 (accessed April 14, 2013).

42. Fung and Chan, “Towards a Global Blockbuster,” 200.

43. Hu Jintao, “Hu Jintao’s Speech on CCP 17th National Congress,” October 24, 2007, http://news.sina.com.cn/c/2007-10-24/205814157378.shtml (accessed December 2, 2009).

## Conclusion

1. Peng Kan, “Huiwang 2012: zhongguo dianying de yiyuyou” [A review of Chinese cinema in 2012], December 26, 2012, http://column.entgroup.cn/15504.shtml (accessed January 10, 2013).

2. Global Enterprises, “Zhongguo dianying shichang jingpen, jumu zhizhan yufa jilie” [Fierce competition for booming Chinese film market], May 18, 2014, http://news.entgroup.cn/movie/1820498.shtml (accessed July 18, 2014).

3. Wang Xiaofeng, “3527 kuai yinmu yu 51 yiyuan chanzhi: zhongguo dianying shoufu shidi” [3,527 screens and 5.1 billion output: Chinese film recovers lost territory], *Lifeweek,* February 21, 2008, http://news.sina.com.cn/c/2008-02-21/111114987055.shtml (accessed May 13, 2008).

4. G. Fowler, K. Mazurkewich, and I. Zhang, “How Mr. Kong Helped Turn

China into a Film Power," *Wall Street Journal*, Eastern edition, September 14, 2005, A1–A8, Academic Search Premier database (accessed November 20, 2008).

5. A. Giddens, *The Consequences of Modernity* (Stanford, CA: Stanford University Press, 1990), 1.

6. For a detailed account of modernity, see Raka Shome, "Asian Modernities: Culture, Politics and Media," *Global Media and Communication* 8, no. 3 (2012): 199–214.

7. See Tu Wei-ming, ed., *Confucian Traditions in East Asian Modernity: Moral Education and Economic Culture in Japan and the Four Mini-Dragons* (Cambridge, MA: Harvard University Press, 1996); Anne Raffin, "Postcolonial Vietnam: Hybrid Modernity," *Postcolonial Studies* 11, no. 3 (2008): 329–44; Gaonkar, "On Alternative Modernities."

8. Shome, "Asian Modernities," 202–3.

9. Francis Fukuyama, *The End of History and the Last Man* (New York: Free Press, 1992).

10. Tu Wei-ming, *Confucian Traditions in East Asian Modernity.*

11. Gaonkar, "On Alternative Modernities."

12. Ha Mai, "2012 quanqiu geguo piaofang gongbu, zhongguo cheng dierda piaocang" [China becomes the second largest box office revenue earner in 2012], *Mytime,* March 22, 2013, http://news.entgroup.cn/movie/2216172.shtml (accessed March 22, 2013).

13. Wang Xiaofeng, "3,527 Screens and 5.1 Billion Output."

14. Tu Wei-ming, "Mutual Learning as an Agenda for Social Development," in *The Global Intercultural Communication Reader,* ed. Molefi Kete Asante, Yoshitaka Miike, and Jing Yin (New York: Routledge, 2008), 329–33.

15. Jin Guantao and Qingfeng Liu, "Xunzhao lishi zhi lu" [To seek a historical path], http://www.xschina.org/show.php?id=1658 (accessed January 26, 2009).

16. Tu Wei-ming, "Mutual Learning as an Agenda for Social Development," 333.

# Selected Bibliography

Abbas, Ackbar, and John Nguyet Erni, eds. *Internationalizing Cultural Studies: An Anthology.* Malden, MA: Blackwell Publishing, 2005.

Ang, I. *Watching* Dallas. London: Methuen, 1985.

Appadurai, Arjun *Modernity at Large.* Minneapolis: University of Minnesota Press, 1996.

Berry, Chris, and Mary Farquhar. *China on Screen: Cinema and Nation.* New York: Columbia University Press, 2006.

Chan, Joseph. "Disneyfying and Globalizing the Chinese Legend Mulan: A Study of Transculturation." In *In Search of Boundaries: Communication, Nation-States and Cultural Identities,* ed. Joseph Chan and Bryce McIntyre, 225–48. Westport, CT: Ablex, 2002.

Chen Xiaoyun. "Meiguodianying: huayubaquan yu yishixingtai shenhua" [American films: hegemony of discourse and ideological myth]. *Contemporary Cinema* 2 (1998): 39–44.

*China Film Yearbook* [annual]. Beijing: Zhongguo dianying chubanshe [China Film Press], 1994–2011.

Cui Weiping. "A Movie Dedicated to Saddam and Kim Jung-II." *Kaifang* [Open], February 2003, 30.

Cunningham, Stuart. "Cultural Studies from the Viewpoint of Cultural Policy." In *Critical Cultural Policy Studies: A Reader,* ed. J. Lewis & Toby Miller, 13–22. Malden, MA: Blackwell Publishing, 2003.

Curtin, Michael. *Playing to the World's Biggest Audience: The Globalization of Chinese Film and TV.* Berkeley: University of California Press, 2007.

Curtin, Michael, and H. Shah, eds. *Reorienting Global Communication—Indian and Chinese Media beyond Borders.* Urbana: University of Illinois Press, 2010.

Dai Jinhua. "Order/Anti-Order: Representation of Identity in Hong Kong Action Movies." In *Hong Kong Connections: Transnational Imagination in Action Cinema,* ed. Meaghan Morris, Siu Leung Li, and Stephen Chan Ching-kiu, 81–94. Durham, NC: Duke University Press; Hong Kong: Hong Kong University Press, 2005.

Donald, Stephanie Hemelryk, Michael Keane, and Yin Hong, eds. *Media in China—Consumption, Content and Crisis.* London: Routledge Curzon, 2002.

Fan Jianghua, Mao Yu, and Yang Yuan. "A Summary of the Film Market in 1996."

In *China Film Yearbook 1997,* 177–81. Beijing: Zhongguo dianying chubanshe [China Film Press], 1997.

Featherstone, Mike. *Undoing Culture: Globalization, Postmodernism and Identity.* London: Sage Publications, 1995.

Featherstone, Mike, and Scott Lash. "Globalization, Modernity and the Spatialization of Social Theory: An Introduction." In *Global Modernities,* ed. Mike Featherstone, Scott Lash, and Roland Robertson, 1–24. London: Sage Publications, 1995.

Fukuyama, Francis. *The End of History and the Last Man.* New York: Free Press, 1992.

Fung, Anthony. *Global Capital, Local Culture: Transnational Media Corporations in China.* New York: Peter Lang, 2008.

Fung, Anthony, and J. M. Chan. "Towards a Global Blockbuster: The Political Economy of *Hero*'s Nationalism." In *Global Chinese Cinema—The Culture and Politics of Hero,* ed. G. D. Rawnsley and Ming-Yeh T. Rawnsley, 198–211. London: Routledge, 2010.

Gaonkar, Dilip Parameshwar. "On Alternative Modernities." In *Alternative Modernities,* ed. Dilip Parameshwar Gaonkar, 1–23. Durham, NC: Duke University Press, 2001.

Garofalo, R. "Whose World, What Beat: The Transnational Music Industry, Identity and Cultural Imperialism." *World of Music* 35, no. 2 (1993): 16–22.

Giddens, A. *The Consequences of Modernity.* Stanford, CA: Stanford University Press, 1990.

———. *Modernity and Self-Identity.* Oxford: Polity, 1991.

Gomery, Douglas. *The Hollywood Studio System.* London: British Film Institute, 2005.

Grossberg, Lawrence. *Cultural Studies in the Future Tense.* Durham, NC: Duke University Press, 2010.

Gu Yanmei. "Zhongguo dalu dianying fenji zhidu tantao: yi zhongguo dalu dianying fenji zhidu yanjiuzhuangkuang weiyin" [A discussion of mainland China's film rating system]. December 30, 2010. http://www.sinoss.net/qikan/uploadfile/2010/1230/20101230032337128.pdf (accessed August 30, 2012).

Gui Qingshan. "Haolaiwu shifou xuyao diyu" [Do we need to resist Hollywood?]. *Cinematic Creation* 1 (2002): 57–62.

Guo Qupo. "Pozaimeijie de weiji" [An urgent crisis—a predication of the impact of China's WTO access on Chinese films]. In *China Film Yearbook 2000,* 155–58. Beijing: Zhongguo dianying chubanshe [China Film Press], 2000.

Harvey, David. *A Brief History of Neoliberalism.* New York: Oxford University Press, 2005.

Hu Hui. "Hollywood de langxing—Hollywood quanqiuhua celue zhi lunxi" [The wolf nature of Hollywood—on Hollywood's global strategy]. *Theory and Creation* 2(2003): 65–68.

Jameson, Fredric. "Notes on Globalization as a Philosophical Issue." In *The Cultures of Globalization,* ed. Fredric Jameson and Masao Miyoshi, 54–77. Durham, NC: Duke University Press, 1998.

Jiang Fen. "Ningshi xiandaixing: sansishiniandai Shanghai dianyingwenhua yu haolaiwu yinsu" [Gazing at modernity: Hollywood factors and Shanghai's cinematic culture in the 1930s and 1940s]. *Shi Lin* 3 (2002): 98–105.

Keane, Michael, Anthony Fung, and Albert Moran. *New Television, Globalization and the East Asian Cultural Imagination.* Hong Kong: Hong Kong University Press, 2007.

Klein, Christina. "Hollywood Film? Foreign Film? Globalization and the Erosion of National Boundaries in Contemporary Cinema." Presented at the annual meeting of the American Studies Association, Albuquerque, NM, October 16–19, 2008.

Kraidy, Marwan. *Hybridity, or the Cultural Logic of Globalization.* Philadelphia: Temple University Press, 2005.

Lan Aiguo. *Haolaiwuzhuyi* [Hollywoodism]. Guangxi, China: Guangxi Normal University Press, 2003.

———. *Houhaolaiwu shidai de zhongguo dianying* [Chinese movies in post-Hollywood ages]. Guangxi, China: Guangxi Normal University Press, 2004.

Lewis, J., and Toby Miller, eds. *Critical Cultural Policy Studies: A Reader.* Malden, MA: Blackwell Publishing, 2003.

Li Daoxin. "Zhanlue lianmeng, chanye jiqun yu jiazhi chuangxin" [The current status and development of large-scale state-owned film enterprises' structural reform]. In *2007 Dianying chanye yanjiu zhi guoyou yingshi qiyejuan* [2007 report on the film industry: special issue on state-owned film and television studios], 36–56. Beijing: Zhongguo dianying chubanshe [China Film Press], 2008.

Li Siu Leung. "Kung Fu: Negotiating Nationalism and Modernity." In *Asian Cinemas: A Reader and Guide,* ed. Dimitris Eleftheriotis and Gary Needham, 100–125. Honolulu: University of Hawaii Press, 2006.

Li Yizhong. "Jingzhengxing hezuo: rushihou zhongmei dianyingye de jiaohu taishi" [Copetition: the intertwined situation of the Chinese and American film industries after China reenters the WTO]. *Modern Communication* 1 (2006): 14–19.

Liebes, T., and E. Katz. *The Export of Meaning: Cross-Cultural Readings of "Dallas."* New York: Oxford University Press, 1990.

Liu Jianzhong. "Dianying de rushi tanpan yu wo'men de chengnuo" [WTO negotiation with regard to film and our commitment]. In *WTO yu zhongguo dianying* [WTO and Chinese cinema], ed. Zhang Zhenxin and Yang Yuanying, 3–8. Beijing: Zhongguo dianying chubanshe [China Film Press], 2002.

Liu Kang. *Globalization and Cultural Trends in China.* Honolulu: University of Hawaii Press, 2004.

Lu Shaoyang. "Zhuxuanlv yingpian de fazhan jiqi shehui jiazhi" [The development of "main melody" films and their social values]. *Yishu Pinglun* [Arts criticism] 10 (2007): 36–37.

Lu, Sheldon Hsiao-peng. *China, Transnational Visuality, Global Postmodernity.* Stanford, CA: Stanford University Press, 2001.

———. *Chinese Modernity and Global Biopolitics: Studies in Literature and Visual Culture.* Honolulu: University of Hawaii Press, 2007.

Lu, Sheldon H., and Emilie Yueh-yu Yeh, eds. *Chinese-Language Film: Historiography, Poetics, Politics.* Honolulu: University of Hawaii Press, 2005.

Ma, Eric Kit-wai. "Rethinking Media Studies—The Case of China." In *De-Westernizing Media Studies,* ed. James Curran and Myung-Jin Park, 21–34. London: Routledge, 2000.

Maltby, Richard. "Introduction: The Americanization of the World." In *Hollywood Abroad—Audiences and Cultural Exchange,* ed. Richard Maltby and Melvyn Stokes, 1–20. London: British Film Institute, 2004.

McChesney, Robert W. "The Political Economy of Global Communication." In *Capitalism and the Information Age: The Political Economy of the Global Communication Revolution,* ed. R. W. McChesney, E. M. Wood, and J. B. Foster, 1–26. New York: Monthly Review Press, 1998.

Miller, Toby, Nitin Govil, John McMurria, and Richard Maxwell. *Global Hollywood.* London: British Film Institute, 2001.

Miller, Toby, Nitin Govil, John McMurria, Richard Maxwell, and Ting Wang. *Global Hollywood 2.* London: British Film Institute, 2005.

Morris, Nancy, and Silvio Waisbord, eds. *Media and Globalization: Why the State Matters.* Lanham, MD: Rowman & Littlefield, 2001.

Ni Zhen, ed. *Gaige yu zhongguo dianying* [Reform and Chinese cinema]. Beijing: Zhongguo dianying chubanshe [China Film Press], 1994.

Ostendorf, Berndt. "Why Is American Popular Culture So Popular? A View from Europe." *American Studies in Scandinavia* 34, no. 1 (2003): 1–46.

Pang Laikwan. "The State against Ghosts: A Genealogy of China's Film Censorship Policy." *Screen* 52, no. 4 (Winter 2011): 461–76.

Petras, J. "Cultural Imperialism in the Late 20th Century." *Journal of Contemporary Asia* 23, no. 2 (1993): 139–48.

Pickowicz, Paul G., and Zhang Yingjin, eds. *From Underground to Independent—Alternative Film Culture in Contemporary China.* Lanham, MD: Rowman & Littlefield, 2006.

Pieterse, Jan. Globalization as Hybridisation." In *Global Modernities,* ed. Mike Featherstone, Scott Lash, and Roland Robertson, 45–68. London: Sage Publications, 1995.

Raffin, Anne. "Postcolonial Vietnam: Hybrid Modernity." *Postcolonial Studies* 11, no. 3 (2008): 329–44.

Rao Shuguang. *Zhongguo dianying shichang fazhanshi* [The development of the Chinese film market]. Beijing: Zhongguo dianying chubanshe [China Film Press], 2009.

Rawnsley, Gary D. "The Political Narrative(s) of *Hero.*" In *Global Chinese Cinema—The Culture and Politics of* Hero, ed. G. D. Rawnsley and Ming-Yeh T. Rawnsley, 13–26. London: Routledge, 2010.

Robertson, Roland. *Globalization: Social Theory and Global Culture.* London: Sage Publications, 1992.

———. "Glocalization: Time-Space and Homogeneity-Heterogeneity." In *Global Modernities*, ed. Mike Featherstone, Scott Lash, and Roland Robertson, 25–44. London: Sage Publications, 1995.

Rosen, Stanley. "Chinese Cinema's International Market." In *Art, Politics, and Commerce in Chinese Cinema*, ed. Zhu Ying and Stanley Rosen, 35–54. Hong Kong: Hong Kong University Press, 2010.

———. "The Wolf at the Door: Hollywood and the Film Market in China." In *Southern California and the World*, ed. Eric J. Heikkila and Rafael Pizarro, 49–77. Westport, CT: Praeger, 2002.

Schiller, H. I. *Culture Inc.: The Corporate Takeover of Public Expression*. New York: Oxford University Press, 1989.

———. "Not Yet the Post-Imperialist Era." In *Communication and Culture in War and Peace*, ed. C. Roach, 97–116. Newbury Park, CA: Sage, 1993.

———. "Striving for Communication Dominance." In *Electronic Empires*, ed. D. Thissu, 17–26. London: Arnold, 1998.

———. " Transnational Media and National Development." In *National Sovereignty and International Communication*, ed. K. Nordenstreng and H. I. Schiller, 21–32. Norwood, NJ: Ablex, 1979.

Shome, Raka. "Asian Modernities: Culture, Politics and Media." *Global Media and Communication* 8, no. 3 (2012): 199–214.

Song Qiang, Zhang Zangzang, and Qiao Bian. *Zhongguo keyi shuo bu* [China can say no]. Beijing: Zhonghua gongshang lianhe chubanshe [China Industry and Commerce Joint Press], 1996.

Song Weicai. "Dangqian zhongguo dianying guojia zizhu jizhi de xianzhuang, wenti ji gaijin shexiang" [The current state and future direction of China's state funding system for film production]. In *Gaige kaifang yu zhongguo dianying sanshinian* [Chinese cinema in the thirty-year reform era], 508–15. Beijing: Zhongguo dianying chubanshe [China Film Press], 2008.

Sreberny-Mohammadi, Annabelle. "The Many Cultural Faces of Imperialism." In *Beyond Cultural Imperialism*, ed. Peter Golding and Phil Harris, 49–68. London: Sage Publications, 1997.

Stam, Robert, and Ella Shohat. "De-Eurocentricizing Cultural Studies: Some Proposals." In *Internationalizing Cultural Studies: An Anthology*, ed. Ackbar Abbas and John Nguyet Erni, 481–98. Malden, MA: Blackwell Publishing, 2005.

Tang Feng. "Duibi zhongguo yu meiguo de dianying shencha zhidu" [A comparison of the film censorship systems in China and the United States]. *Dianying Wenxue* [Movie literature] 2 (2010): 15–17.

Tao Dongfeng. "Zhongguo dapian daole shixueruming de shidai" [Chinese megaproductions have entered a bloodthirsty stage]. *Art Criticism* 2 (2007): 36–38.

Taylor, Charles. "Two Theories of Modernity." In *Alternative Modernities*, ed. Dilip Parameshwar Gaonkar, 172–96. Durham, NC: Duke University Press, 2001.

Teo, Stephen. *Chinese Martial Arts Cinema: The Wuxia Tradition*. Edinburgh: Edinburgh University Press, 2009.

———. *Hong Kong Cinema: The Extra Dimensions.* London: British Film Institute, 1997.

———. "Wuxia Redux: *Crouching Tiger, Hidden Dragon* as a Model of Late Transnational Production." In *Hong Kong Connections: Transnational Imagination in Action Cinema,* ed. Meaghan Morris, Siu Leung Li, and Stephen Chan Ching-kiu, 191–204. Durham, NC: Duke University Press; Hong Kong: Hong Kong University Press, 2005.

Tomlinson, John. "Culture Globalization and Cultural Imperialism." In *International Communication and Globalization: A Critical Introduction,* ed. Ali Mohammadi, 170–90. London: Sage Publications, 1997.

———. *Globalization and Culture.* Chicago: University of Chicago Press, 1999.

Tu Wei-ming, ed. *Confucian Traditions in East Asian Modernity: Moral Education and Economic Culture in Japan and the Four Mini-Dragons.* Cambridge, MA: Harvard University Press, 1996.

———. "Mutual Learning as an Agenda for Social Development." In *The Global Intercultural Communication Reader,* ed. Molefi Kete Asante, Yoshitaka Miike, and Jing Yin, 329–33. New York: Routledge, 2008.

Wang Dan et al. "Dang fenghuang niepan shi—dui wujia guoyou dianyingqiye chanye fazhan de diaoyan baogao" [Research report on five state-owned film studios]. In *2007 dianying chanye yanjiu zhi guoyou yingshi qiyejuan* [2007 report on the film industry—special issue on state-owned film and television studios], 3–35. Beijing: Zhongguo dianying chubanshe [China Film Press], 2008.

Wang, H., and Ming-Yeh T. Rawnsley. "*Hero:* Rewriting the Chinese Martial Arts Film Genre." In *Global Chinese Cinema—The Culture and Politics of Hero,* ed. G. D. Rawnsley and Ming-Yeh T. Rawnsley, 90–105. London: Routledge, 2010.

Wang Jing. "Culture as Leisure and Culture as Capital." *Positions* 9, no. 1 (2002): 69–70.

Wang Jing and David Goodman. "A Matter of Choice: Critical Policy Studies of China." 2003. http://web.mit.edu/chinapolicy/www/documents/founding.pdf (accessed November 14, 2009).

Wang Qu. "Yinjin dapian shisinian: ronghe yu fazhan" [Fourteen years after Hollywood blockbuster imports: integration and development]. In *Gaige kaifang yu zhongguo dianying sanshinian* [Chinese cinema in the thirty-year reform era], 439–54. Beijing: Zhongguo dianying chubanshe [China Film Press], 2008.

Wang Rui. "Meiguo zaoqi dianying dui zhongguo zaoqi dianying de yingxiang—zhongmei dianying bijiao chutan" [A preliminary exploration of the influence of early American films on early Chinese films]. *Contemporary Cinema* 6 (2001): 88–94.

Wang Ting. "Understanding Local Reception of Globalized Cultural Products in the Context of the International Cultural Economy—A Case Study on the Reception of *Hero* and *Daggers* in China." *International Journal of Cultural Studies* 12 (2009): 299.

Wang Yongzhi and Ren Yi. "The Embarrassments Caused by Importing Major Films." *Chinese Sociology and Anthropology* 32, no. 1 (1999): 8–11.

Wang Zhongjun. "'Huayi xiongdi' zhi jingyantan" [On Huayi brothers' business strategies]. In *2006 dianying chanye yanjiu zhi wenhua xiaofei yu dianying juan* [2006 research report on the Chinese film industry—special issue on cultural and film consumption], 370. Beijing: Zhongguo dianying chubanshe [China Film Press], 2007.

Xu Jing. "Kongque wei shui kaiping?" [For whom does the peacock spreads its tail feathers?]. *Art Criticism* 3 (2005): 18–20.

Yan Chunjun. "Quanqiuhua he zhongguo minzu dianying de wenhua zhanlue" [Globalization and the cultural strategy of China's national film]. In *Quanqiuhua yu zhongguo yingshi de mingyun* [Globalization and the fate of China's film and television], ed. Zhang Fengzhu, Huang Shixian, and Hu Zhifeng, 34–55. Beijing: Beijing Broadcasting Institute Press, 2002.

Yeh, E. Yueh-yu. "The Deferral of Pan-Asian: A Critical Appraisal of Film Marketization in China." In *Reorienting Global Communication—Indian and Chinese Media beyond Borders,* ed. Michael Curtin and H. Shah, 183–200. Urbana: University of Illinois Press, 2010.

Yin Hong. "Da Wan: kuaguo zhizuo, shangye dianying yu xiaofei wenhua" [Big shot's funeral: transnational production, commercial films, and commercial culture]. In *Yin Hong zixuanji* [Yin Hong's self-selected anthology], 338–49. Shanghai: Fudan University Press, 2004.

———. "Hollywood de quanqiuhua celue yu zhongguo dianying de fazhan" [Hollywood's global strategy and the development of Chinese film]. In *Yin Hong zixuanji* [Yin Hong's self-selected anthology], 73–212. Shanghai: Fudan University Press, 2004.

———. "Quanqiuhua, Hollywood yu minzu dianying" [Globalization, Hollywood, and national film]. *Literature and Art Studies* 6 (2000): 98–107.

———. "Shiji zhijiao: jiushi niandai zhongguo dianying geju" [Cross-century: Chinese films in the 1990s]. In *Yin Hong zixuanji* [Yin Hong's self-selected anthology], 104–21. Shanghai: Fudan University Press, 2004.

Yin Hong and Wang X. "The Industry Year of Chinese Film." *Dangdai dianying* [Contemporary cinema] 2 (2005): 18–26.

Yin Hong and Zhan Q. "2007 nian zhongguo dianying chanye beiwang" [Memo on the 2007 film industry]. *Dangdai dianying* [Contemporary cinema] 2 (2008): 13–21.

Yoshimi, Takeuchi. *What Is Modernity? Writings of Takeuchi Yoshimi.* New York: Columbia University Press, 2005.

Yu Li. *Zhongguo dianying zhuanyeshi yanjiu—dianying zhipian, faxing, fangying juan* [A study of the history of film production, distribution, and exhibition in China]. Beijing: Zhongguo dianying chubanshe [China Film Press], 2006.

Zhang Dong, and Ma Hua, eds. *Haolaiwu pipan* [Hollywood criticism]. Beijing: Zhongyang bianyi chubanshe [Central Compilation and Translation Press], 2001.

Zhang Xianmin. "Zhongguo dalu 1990 hou jinpianshi" [A history of banned films in mainland China after the 1990s]. http://www.zmw.cn/bbs/dispbbs.asp?boardID=11&ID=52770 (accessed March 5, 2006).

Zhang Xudong. *Chinese Modernism in the Era of Reforms: Cultural Fever, Avant-Garde Fiction, and the New Chinese Cinema.* Durham, NC: Duke University Press, 1997.

———, ed. *Whither China: Intellectual Politics in Contemporary China.* Durham, NC: Duke University Press, 2001.

Zhang Yingjin. "Rebel without a Cause? China's New Urban Generation and Post-socialist Filmmaking." In *The Urban Generation—Chinese Cinema and Society at the Turn of the Twenty-First Century,* ed. Zhang Zhen, 49–80. Durham, NC: Duke University Press, 2007.

Zhang Zhen. "Bodies in the Air: The Magic of Science and the Fate of the Early 'Martial Arts' Film in China." In *Chinese-Language Film: Historiography, Poetics, Politics,* ed. Sheldon H. Lu and Emilie Yueh-Yu Yeh, 52–75. Honolulu: University of Hawaii Press, 2005.

Zhao Suisheng. "The China Model: Can It Replace the Western Model of Modernization?" *Journal of Contemporary China* 19 (2010): 419–36.

Zhao Yuezhi. *Communication in China: Political Economy, Power, and Conflict.* Lanham, MD: Rowman & Littlefield, 2008.

———. "Whose *Hero?* The 'Spirit' and 'Structure' of a Made-in-China Global Blockbuster." In *Reorienting Global Communication—Indian and Chinese Media beyond Borders,* ed. M. Curtin and H. Shah, 161–82. Urbana: University of Illinois Press, 2010.

Zheng Dongtian. "To Be, or Not to Be?—Jinru WTO yihou de zhongguo dianying shengcun fenxi" [An analysis of the survival of the Chinese film industry after joining the WTO]. *Dianying yishu* [Film art] 2 (2000): 4–8.

Zhou Tiedong. "Xinzhongguo dianying duiwai jiaoliu" [Foreign exchanges of Chinese cinema in new China]. *Dianying yishu* [Film art] 1 (2000): 113–18.

Zhu Ying. *Chinese Cinema during the Era of Reform—The Ingenuity of the System.* Westport, CT: Praeger, 2003.

———. "Chinese Cinema's Economic Reform from the Mid-1980s to the Mid-1990s." *Journal of Communication* 52 (2002): 905–92.

# Index

## Asia in the New Millennium

Series Editor: Shiping Hua, University of Louisville

Asia in the New Millennium is a series of books offering new interpretations of an important geopolitical region. The series examines the challenges and opportunities of Asia from the perspectives of politics, economics, and cultural-historical traditions, highlighting the impact of Asian developments on the world. Of particular interest are books on the history and prospect of the democratization process in Asia. The series also includes policy-oriented works that can be used as teaching materials at the undergraduate and graduate levels. Innovative manuscript proposals at any stage are welcome.



### Books in the Series

*The Future of China-Russia Relations*
Edited by James Bellacqua

*North Korea and the World: Human Rights, Arms Control, and Strategies for Negotiation*
Walter C. Clemens Jr.

*Contemporary Chinese Political Thought: Debates and Perspectives*
Edited by Fred Dallmayr and Zhao Tingyang

*China Looks at the West: Identity, Global Ambitions, and the Future of Sino-American Relations*
Christopher A. Ford

*The Mind of Empire: China's History and Modern Foreign Relations*
Christopher A. Ford

*State Violence in East Asia*
Edited by N. Ganesan and Sung Chull Kim

*Challenges to Chinese Foreign Policy: Diplomacy, Globalization, and the Next World Power*
Edited by Yufan Hao, C. X. George Wei, and Lowell Dittmer

*The Price of China's Economic Development: Power, Capital, and the Poverty of Rights*
Zhaohui Hong

*Japan after 3/11: Global Perspectives on the Earthquake, Tsunami, and Fukushima Meltdown*
Edited by Pradyumna P. Karan and Unryu Suganuma

*Korean Democracy in Transition: A Rational Blueprint for Developing Societies*
Hee Min Kim

*Modern Chinese Legal Reform: New Perspectives*
Edited by Xiaobing Li and Qiang Fang

*Democracy in Central Asia: Competing Perspectives and Alternative Strategies*
Mariya Y. Omelicheva

*China's Encounter with Global Hollywood: Cultural Policy and the Film Industry, 1994–2013*
Wendy Su

*Growing Democracy in Japan: The Parliamentary Cabinet System since 1868*
Brian Woodall

*Inside China's Grand Strategy: The Perspective from the People's Republic*
Ye Zicheng, Edited and Translated by Steven I. Levine and Guoli Liu

*Civil Society and Politics in Central Asia*
Edited by Charles E. Ziegler

www.ingramcontent.com/pod-product-compliance
Lightning Source LLC
LaVergne TN
LVHW050151080826
844660LV00002B/165

*9780813167060*